Arnold Schoenberg

Arnold Schoenberg

The Composer as Jew

ALEXANDER L. RINGER

CLARENDON PRESS · OXFORD

1990

Oxford University Press, Walton Street, Oxford OX2 6DP

Oxford New York Toronto
Delhi Bombay Calcutta Madras Karachi
Petaling Jaya Singapore Hong Kong Tokyo
Nairobi Dar es Salaam Cape Town
Melbourne Auckland

and associated companies in
Berlin Ibadan

Oxford is a trade mark of Oxford University Press

Published in the United States
by Oxford University Press, New York

British Library Cataloguing in Publication Data
Ringer, Alexander L.
Arnold Schoenberg: the composer as Jew
1. Austrian music. Schoenberg, Arnold 1874–1951
I. Title
780'.92'4
ISBN 0–19–315466–8

Library of Congress Cataloging in Publication Data
Ringer, Alexander L.
Arnold Schoenberg—the composer as Jew/Alexander L. Ringer.
Includes bibliographical references.
ISBN 0–19–315466–8
1. Schoenberg, Arnold, 1874–1951. 2. Judaism–Influence.
I. Title.
ML410.S283R55 1990   780'.92—dc20
89–23030

Typeset by Latimer Trend & Company Ltd, Plymouth
Printed in Great Britain by
Biddles Ltd., Guildford and King's Lynn

In faithful memory of Lion Nordheim,
incomparable mentor, devoted friend,
who lost his life because he was a Jew.

PRO DOMO

THE essays on which this volume is based were written on a number of different occasions over a period of nearly fifteen years. All, however, were motivated by the same basic urge to shed light on the work and personality of Arnold Schoenberg from a perspective which, though no longer entirely ignored in the steadily growing body of Schoenberg literature, has been taken into consideration primarily in connection with the composer's ostensibly biblical, if not always outright Jewish, preoccupations.[1] Very little attention has been paid to the broader ramifications of the socio-political context and, for that matter, the specific cultural background, outlook, and commitment of one whose monumental artistic achievement remains obscured to this day by serious misapprehensions even on the part of well-informed commentators, let alone the ignorant and those who continue to regard him as the source of every evil they perceive in the music of our time. Yet any objective, comprehensive appraisal of the Schoenbergian bequest, which so drastically changed the musical physiognomy of the Western world, must proceed from the fundamental premiss that this composer was not only a profoundly religious artist but also a product of that emancipated Central European Jewry which, after decades of overt popular and governmental oppression, suffered virtually complete physical extinction.

That there are other equally legitimate and necessary avenues of approach to the Schoenbergian aesthetic and its historical context and significance goes without saying. Far from making exclusive claims, these essays merely address some serious lacunae caused as much by the positivistic orientation of a good deal of recent, especially American, musical scholarship as by the traditional alliance of incomprehension and vilification that pursued Schoenberg, the composer and the Jew, throughout his long creative career. Ironically, 'note-counting' of the sort that Schoenberg so heartily despised has intermittently poured fresh oil

---

[1] Aside from a number of smaller pertinent studies published over the years, especially in the *Journal of the Arnold Schoenberg Institute*, two recent publications deserve mention in this context: Michael Mäckelmann, *Arnold Schönberg und das Judentum* (Hamburger Beiträge zur Musikwissenschaft, 28; Hamburg, 1984), and Pamela C. White, *Schoenberg and the God-Idea* (Ann Arbor, 1985).

on the smouldering fires lit and relit throughout the composer's lifetime by reactionary, often undisguisedly anti-Semitic, opponents who saw in him a typical representative of 'Jewish cerebralism' in art and, as such, a dangerous agent of the Jewish conspiracy against Western civilization in general and German music in particular.

The historical roots of this familiar refrain go back to Richard Wagner's mid-nineteenth-century tirade against 'Judaism in Music'.[2] Wagner's true target was the aesthetician and critic Eduard Hanslick, who could claim a single Jewish ancestor at best. But that did not prevent Wagner's venom from inspiring countless subsequent denunciations of the 'Jewish musical establishment'. Actually, it was Hanslick who first raised the issue of 'cerebration'. Greatly impressed with Wagner's *Tannhäuser*, he had written an enthusiastic review, merely noting that the Second Act finale, though 'imaginatively conceived and artfully contrived', seemed rather 'the product of artistic cerebration than of spontaneous inspiration'.[3] Whereupon Wagner, in a long letter dated 1 January 1847, and overflowing with gratitude for that 'extensive discussion of my *Tannhäuser*', sprang to the defence of cerebration: 'don't underestimate the power of reflection', he wrote, 'the unconsciously produced work of art belongs to periods far remote from ours: the art-work of the most civilized of eras can never be a product of anything but consciousness.'[4] What was perfectly in keeping with the spirit of the Middle Ages, he averred, could hardly remain valid for a Goethe who so miraculously wedded 'the power of the reflecting mind to the fullness of creative immediacy'.

Schoenberg could not have described his own conception of the work of art more poignantly. Yet his enemies pursued him mercilessly as the alleged exemplification of the very attitude their hero Wagner had been at pains to uphold against a proponent of creative spontaneity whom he suspected of 'Jewish blood'. Purveyors of myth, needless to say, place little stock in demonstrable fact, let alone truth. In the event, the myth of 'purity' in art unsoiled by 'alien' particles, a myth with deep roots in early German Romanticism, caused Hans Pfitzner, the conservative

---

[2] Nearly 20 years after Richard Wagner first published *Das Judentum in Musik* under a pseudonym in the *Neue Zeitschrift für Musik* he offered additional 'clarifications' in the form of an extensive letter entitled 'Aufklärungen über das Judentum in der Musik'.

[3] Eduard Hanslick, *Vienna's Golden Years of Music 1850–1900*, trans. and ed. Henry Pleasants III (New York, 1950), 31.

[4] Wagner, *Sämtliche Briefe*, ii, ed. Gertrud Strobel and Werner Wolf (Leipzig, 1980), 535.

composer of *Palestrina* as well as a cantata entitled *Von deutscher Seele* ('Of the German Soul'), to state unequivocally that 'in the light of high art music, the world of jazz implies only vulgarity, aharmonicism sheer madness'.[5] Yet jazz, that irrepressible creative response to man's inhumanity to man, generated some of the finest musicianship of the age and, in the process, admittedly gained even Schoenberg's respect, if not his outright devotion, the same Schoenberg whose atonality—Pfitzner's 'aharmonicism'—represented the ultimate 'cry of despair' of a humanity alienated from itself no less than from its Maker.[6] Rather, 'madness' took hold of the darker recesses of the German soul so dear to Pfitzner. Schoenberg with prophetic vision foresaw the ensuing nightmare in all its unprecedented horror well before the Nazi seizure of power. But his desperate appeals to his fellow man, Jew and non-Jew alike, for immediate, effective responses fell on deaf ears until it was too late. To the memory of the millions slaughtered in the name of purity, and the immeasurable creative potential that perished with them, this modest volume is humbly dedicated.

[5] Hans Pfitzner, *Gesammelte Schriften*, i (Augsburg, 1926), 119.

[6] 'Art is the cry of despair of those who experience in themselves the fate of all mankind', reads one of Arnold Schoenberg's 'Aphorismen' in *Die Musik*, 9 (Aug. 1910), 121. See also Schönberg, *Schöpferische Konfessionen*, ed. Willi Reich (Zurich, 1964), 12.

ACKNOWLEDGEMENTS

This book might well have remained unwritten, were it not for that splendid, congenial research venue, the Arnold Schoenberg Institute of Los Angeles, where the entire *Nachlass* of the composer has been deposited thanks to the generosity of his heirs and a host of former students, friends and admirers. Leonard Stein, the Institute's devoted director and editor of its distinguished *Journal*, the late Clara Steuermann, its pioneering archivist, and the current incumbent, R. Wayne Shoaf, responded quickly and warmly to every request, whether on the spot or by correspondence. Director Stein, moreover, kindly authorized the inclusion of pieces, in part or in their entirety, previously published under his editorship. Chapter 1 is in fact based on a paper first read in connection with the Institute's groundbreaking ceremonies and subsequently printed in the initial issue of the *Journal*. Sizeable portions of chapters 5, 7 and 10, as well as the appended *Four-Point Program*, appeared in later issues. The translation of an extended passage from Arnold Schoenberg's drama *Der biblische Weg* (Appendix B), for its part, has the gracious consent of Mr Lawrence Schoenberg, President of Belmont Publishers, who also authorized the reproduction of extracts from copyright material.

For permission to make use of additional earlier writings I am indebted to my colleague Herbert Knust, editor of the September 1975 issue of *Comparative Literature Studies*, to my revered teacher Paul Henry Lang and G. Schirmer Inc., editor and publishers of the January 1973 isue of *The Musical Quarterly*, to Judith Cohen who edited the *Proceedings of the World Congress on Jewish Music, Jerusalem 1978*, to Rudolph Stephan and Elisabeth Lafite, editor and publisher respectively of *Bericht über den 1. Kongress der Internationalen Schönberg-Gesellschaft*, and to Shai Burstyn, editor of *Israel Studies in Musicology III*. Particular thanks are due to Rabbi Clifford Kulwin of Rio de Janeiro who drew my attention to the unique letter addressed to Rabbi Stephen S. Wise, which forms the centre-piece of Chapter 8.

The University of Illinois Research Board supported my work over a period of many years, and a recent appointment to the University's Center for Advanced Study enabled me to complete the manuscript in relative quiet. My colleague Maurice Friedberg gave the draft of the *Introduction* a much appreciated critical reading. And I could hardly say enough in praise of the editorial staff at Oxford University Press, who kept such a watchful professional eye on a volume that was not easily put together. While my warm thanks go out to each and everyone willing to bear with this hard pressed writer, it is my long suffering wife Claude who deserves the fullest measure of my genuine gratitude together with my humble apologies. My only excuse, for whatever it may be worth, is that much in these pages came straight from the heart. I can but hope that it will touch some hearts in turn.

A.L.R.

Urbana–Champaign
September 1989

CONTENTS

LIST OF PLATES

Between pages 112 and 113

LIST OF FIGURES

LIST OF ABBREVIATIONS

JASI *Journal of the Arnold Schoenberg Institute*
ÖMZ *Österreichische Musikzeitschrift*

And I heard the voice of the Lord,
saying:
   Whom shall I send,
   And who will go for us?
Then I said: 'Here am I; send me.'

Isa. 6:8

The voice of God, if it speaks in the twentieth century, does not do so in familiar phrases from the records of the past, but in mysteries from the creative depths of life. Experimental art is one of those mysterious writings on the wall which are in some sense divine revelations because they truly represent the destiny of society.

Walter Abell, The Collective Dream in Art, 359.

Introduction: Composer and Jew

THE seeds of the tragedy that befell European Jewry shortly before and during the Second World War were planted long before the advent of Adolf Hitler. 'Scientific' racism was, after all, a product of the same liberal era which in its unconditional devotion to the cause of progress had done so much to further the cause of Jewish emancipation. By the mid-nineteenth century evolutionist theories of one kind or another had begun to leave their mark not only on science but on human affairs in general. Thus a discourse on the inequality of the races could lay claims to scientific credibility virtually on a par with one detailing the imminent dangers of capitalism and the inevitability of class struggle, albeit that the former invoked biological findings, the latter those of 'social science'. Perhaps inevitably, once traditional faiths no longer sufficed to establish a shared sense of inner security, and rapid material change interfered with hallowed ways respected by previous generations, the promise of universal science as the seemingly infallible guarantor of a better future affected all aspects of human thought and action. Still, of war and sundry conflagrations there came no end. Quite to the contrary, with the rise of nationalism—itself largely a function of the pervasive belief in the blessings of competition at every level of human existence—competition increasingly determined not only personal and commercial but also large-scale collective behaviour, culminating in the ultimate 'war to end all wars'. That bloodiest of confrontations, needless to say, accomplished no such thing—except that it did, for all practical intents and purposes, mark the apocalyptic ending of the nineteenth century.

In 1914, however, there were men and women of considerable intelligence on both sides who actually welcomed a general blood-letting as a much-needed, historically mandated cure for all sorts of ills, real and imaginary, gnawing at European culture. Thus the co-founder of the blaue Reiter group, Franz Marc, was confident that 'with this great war much that managed unpardonably to sneak into the twentieth century, including the pseudo-art with which the German good-naturedly contented himself, will finally come to an end'.[1] Two years later that 'great

---

[1] Franz Marc, *Schriften*, ed. Klaus Lankheit (Cologne, 1978), 159.

war' brought his own life to a premature end. When, after two further years of mutual attrition and exhaustion, the incredible mass-slaughter exhausted itself, even some who had gone to war like eager athletes to a sporting event had every reason to reassess their basic values, whether socio-political or purely spiritual.

Arnold Schoenberg, far from questioning the old order of things, was still doing his first stint in a reserve officers' school when Martin Buber, a fellow Viennese four years his junior, published his first major contribution to the philosophy of Judaism. Appalled by the horrendous spectacle of men killing each other by the hundreds of thousands with the open encouragement of clergy from every religious creed, Buber called for a clear distinction between religiosity and religion. Religiosity, he explained, 'eternally renews itself, eternally finds new expression and manifestation', whereas 'religion is the sum total of the customs and teachings in which the religiosity of a particular epoch and a given people expresses and manifests itself through decrees and articles of faith transmitted to all future generations without regard to any newly generated religiosity yearning for new forms of its own'. Religiosity, Buber insisted (less than a year before Schoenberg completed the text of his oratorio *Die Jakobsleiter*), 'is the creative, religion the organizing principle ... religiosity implies activity—finding an elemental relationship of the self to the absolute; religion implies passivity—acceptance of the burden of the transmitted law'.[2]

The Buberian dichotomy certainly had broad ramifications especially for artists of Schoenberg's generation, who, like his pre-war friend and associate Wassily Kandinsky, identified the 'spiritual in art' with man's last creative opportunity to transcend material reality and thus recover the absolute. In the case of artists and intellectuals of Jewish descent, however, religious attitudes were forcibly affected by socio-political realities which, though governed in some measure by strictly material considerations, reflected both persistent myths of the older Christian variety and the new racial 'myth of the twentieth century'. As the industrialist Walter Rathenau put it in a letter to the wife of General von Hindenburg in December 1917: 'Although my ancestors served our country to the very best of their abilities, I, as a Jew, remain, as you are undoubtedly quite aware, a second class citizen.'[3] Less than five years later Rathenau, the only Jew ever to serve as Germany's Foreign Minister, was struck down by the bullets of political assassins. Nor did

---

[2] Martin Buber, *Vom Geist des Judentums* (Munich, 1916), 51–2.
[3] Cf. Guido Kisch, *Judentaufen* (Berlin, 1913), 118.

conversion to Christianity manage to avert the evil decree. Maximilian Harden, baptized and a conservative journalist, was beaten to a pulp that same year by political thugs for whom the issue was race rather than religion; once a Jew, always a Jew. In 1933, with racism now official policy, the German Nobel Prize winner Fritz Haber, a Protestant since 1893, was to acknowledge ruefully: 'Never before have I felt more like a Jew than now.'[4]

In the summer of 1921 Schoenberg and his family were forced to leave Mattsee, an Austrian lake-area restricted to bona fide Aryans only. As a result, he later claimed, somewhat tongue-in-cheek, he had been among the century's first Jewish expellees.[5] Actually, that experience typified the anomalous position of the Central European Jew born into a society which, all official safeguards to the contrary notwithstanding, rejected him out of hand in ways seemingly devoid of all logic, let alone compassion, and hence quite beyond his control. The novelist Jakob Wassermann, painfully aware of this uniquely Jewish dilemma and the psychological conflicts it produced, wrote that very same year:

No non-Jew could possibly imagine the heart-rending position in which the German Jew finds himself. With his twin loves and his struggle on two fronts he has been pushed to the very abyss of despair. The German and the Jew: I once had a metaphorical dream, but I am not sure that it is easily understood. I placed two mirrors so that they faced each other, and I had the feeling that the two human images contained and preserved in those two mirrors were about to tear each other up.[6]

Wassermann had left his native Fürth shortly before the turn of the century and settled in Vienna about the time his contemporary Schoenberg was beginning to gain the attention of a small but determined circle of fellow idealists. Having spent his early years in close contact with the local Christian population of a small South German town, Wassermann was surprised to find so many Jewish journalists, artists, and musicians at the centre of Viennese cultural life, and he asked himself what was likely to happen once the ageing Emperor Franz Joseph was no longer there to protect the rapidly expanding Jewish community from increasingly well-organized extremists who, in mapping out their political future, banked heavily on the traditional anti-Semitism of the urban petty bourgeoisie

---

[4] Ibid. 49.

[5] See the long letter Schoenberg addressed to Stephen S. Wise, following his arrival in the United States, reproduced in ch. 10.

[6] Jakob Wassermann, *Mein Weg als Deutscher und Jude* (Berlin, 1921), 119.

no less than of a rural population easily seduced by local demagogues, not the least of whom was apt to be the village priest.

History was soon to confirm his worst fears. For, once the presumably invincible Central powers had suffered defeat on the battlefield, potential scapegoats had to be identified, and none seemed more convenient than the Jewish minorities of Germany and Austria. But if in the past it had been customary to accuse the Jew of poisoning an isolated well or killing an occasional Christian baby at Passover, now the responsibility for the misfortunes of entire nations, including the most modern industrial state and the largest continental empire, was thrown at the feet of their Jewish communities. That a far higher percentage of Jewish volunteers had served in the armed forces of these very nations than their populations at large could boast, that many a Jewish scientist like Fritz Haber or industrialist like Walter Rathenau had made major contributions to the German war effort, seemed of little consequence. As Wassermann put it in his unsparing account: 'In vain the attempt to neutralize their poison. They will brew it afresh. In vain living for them and dying for them. All they say is: "He is a Jew." '[7]

Wassermann's forthright appraisal of the much heralded German-Jewish symbiosis had barely appeared, when the court which had convened to judge Maximilian Harden's attackers exonerated the Fascist hoodlums and thus cynically gave aid and comfort to the hate-mongering mob who extolled them as national heroes. Several months thereafter, Schoenberg, still haunted by the traumatic experience of his 'expulsion' from Mattsee, declared in a dramatic exchange of letters with his long-time friend Wassily Kandinsky that he had finally learnt his lesson and would 'never again forget ... that I am a Jew'.[8] Ostensibly, it was the unjustified rumour spread by Gustav Mahler's widow, Alma Werfel, to the effect that Kandinsky too was not free of anti-Semitic tendencies, which caused the composer to reach this fateful conclusion. In reality it proved but the final link in a long chain of painful reminders that he, no more than that much earlier Christian convert, Heinrich Heine, could ever hope to 'wash off' his Jewish identity.

It was precisely this inescapable conclusion which led a number of Jewish intellectuals, among them Franz Kafka's close friend Max Brod, to assert the special relevance of traditional Jewish values and attitudes for an era marked by well-nigh universal frustration and uncertainty.

---

[7] Wassermann, *Mein Weg als Deutscher und Jude*, 122-3.

[8] Schoenberg, *Briefe*, ed. Erwin Stein, (Mainz, 1958), 90. In the English edn. of the letters (London, 1964), 88, the implication of 'never again' is largely lost.

Following Martin Buber's lead, Brod went to great pains to counteract the prevailing liberal tendency to gloss over any substantive differences between 'paganism, Christianity, and Judaism'. In two volumes published in 1921 and distinguished as much by their scholarship as by the author's poetic German usage, Brod laid out precisely what, in his eyes, separated and united the three principal religious conceptions at the very root of Western civilization.[9] Significantly, the work is dedicated to the memory of a young musician of great promise, Adolf Schreiber, who chose to commit suicide rather than face the insoluble problems of one feeling and thinking like a genuine Jew in a modern world of pervasive hypocrisy and rampant materialism. Brod, a pupil of Leoš Janáček, was still a young man working as a music critic in Prague when Schoenberg delivered his famous Mahler lecture there in 1912 on the first anniversary of the death of their common idol. Gustav Mahler, needless to say, had exemplified the very conflict to which Schreiber later succumbed. But Mahler was endowed with the enormous creative strength of one who 'feels himself merely the slave of a higher ordinance under whose compulsion he ceaselessly does his work'.[10] Brod, always on the look-out for new talent, had promoted Schreiber as something of a Mahler redivivus and recognized his tragic mistake too late.

In *Heidentum, Christentum, Judentum* Brod pleads at length for a reconciliation of the Jewish notion of freedom with the seemingly incompatible Christian concept of grace, which, as he correctly stressed, is no less deeply rooted in the Hebrew Bible. Brod's obvious purpose was to establish the relevance of Jewish ethics for a world in crisis, where everything seemed subject to transvaluation—for a blessing and a curse. Five years later his friend Heinrich Berl broached the same general subject in similar but purely musical terms. Employing the very title under which Richard Wagner had denied the Jews any creative contribution to music, Berl pointed to what he called the 'Asiatic crisis in European music' as clear evidence that Jewish musicians could and would leave their historical mark, provided they did so consciously as Jews, i.e. as Europeans of non-European extraction. Schreiber, he felt, had tragically foundered on his inability to bridge the gap between an endemically monophonic Jewish heritage and the structural demand of a Western tradition firmly anchored in centuries of functional harmony. Mahler and Schoenberg, on the other hand, had shown what composers

---

[9] Max Brod, *Heidentum, Christentum, Judentum* (2 vols.; Munich, 1921).

[10] Schoenberg, 'Gustav Mahler: In Memoriam', in *Style and Idea*, ed. Leonard Stein (New York, 1975), 447.

of Jewish descent were truly capable of, once they decided to give their innate musical tendencies full, unrestricted play. As Berl saw it, the West with its fundamentally spatial orientation was by definition at odds with Jewish modes of behaviour, since Jews, in the manner of Orientals, believed in time as the primary condition of existence. By supplanting traditional harmony, the exemplification of the spatial dimension in music, with pure melodic-rhythmic substance, Schoenberg had opened up entirely new vistas in the still underdeveloped realm of musical time, inevitably in violation of conventions that corresponded to intrinsically spatial conceptions.[11] Tonality may represent gravity in Western music, Berl seemed to imply; the Oriental—read Jew—recognizes no such 'natural' laws in art. In short, if Brod argued that the modern world was sorely in need of men and women rooted in the Jewish historical experience, given a Christianity that had spawned theologies closer in many respects to pagan than to Judaic antecedents, Berl saw in Schoenberg's emancipation of dissonance at the behest of the unbridled unfolding of musical time the quintessentially Jewish musical deed of the century.

During those crucial postwar years Schoenberg maintained particularly close contacts with Prague, not only because his brother-in-law, Alexander von Zemlinsky, had become a major force in the city's postwar musical life but also, indeed primarily, in connection with the final arrangements for a local counterpart of the Viennese Association for Private Musical Performances.[12] Whether he saw a copy of *Heidentum, Christentum, Judentum* already then or heard of it subsequently—both its highly personal language and the rather unorthodox ideas it conveyed continued to be widely debated in Jewish as well as non-Jewish circles— the author's conception of creative freedom as a function of divine grace predicated on the freely entered Covenant that transformed what was little more than a loose confederation of desert tribes into God's chosen people surely struck a sympathetic vein in the conservative champion of change, recovering in his maturity what as a young man he had so readily abandoned. Brod wrote:

The realm of freedom is governed by gradual advance, amelioration, eternal progress toward an infinite goal,—in the realm of grace leaps tend to prevail, the return taking possession of the absolute, immediately and outside the dimension

---

[11] Heinrich Berl, *Das Judentum in der Musik* (Stuttgart, Berlin and Leipzig, 1926), 228–9. The book is dedicated to Paul Bekker, 'dauntless fighter for the new music'.

[12] See ch. 11.

of time ... there, the incomplete God in need of help—here, the Infinite, Almighty before whom we are as nothing. There, becoming and a thousand possibilities, human responsibility for ubiquitous yet remediable misery,—here, being and security, unfathomable perfection since time immemorial.[13]

Paradoxically, Schoenberg had forsaken Judaism as a formal religion not, like many others, under secularizing or assimilationist influences, but rather because, virtually untutored in Jewish values, he looked for other vessels to quench his spiritual thirst. If he absorbed but little Jewish knowledge in his youth, the generally unsatisfactory state of religious instruction in Central Europe communities may well have been a contributory factor. In Jakob Wassermann's experience, the lessons were uninspiring and quite out of touch with the religious needs and concerns of modern Jewish youngsters.[14] And Arthur Schnitzler's recollections suggest that in this respect Vienna differed little from Wassermann's provincial Fürth.[15] A genuinely searching youth like Arnold Schoenberg, whose parents could not or would not afford first-rate private instruction, was thus bound sooner or later to seek alternative sources of religious inspiration. As long as Samuel Schoenberg was alive, it appears, the family did observe at least a modicum of Jewish customs.[16] But Arnold, the nominal head of the household following his father's untimely death, was in no way equipped to carry on the tradition.

Whether or not it was his Lutheran friend Walter Pieau who in the end persuaded him to become a Protestant, the fact is that the Bible in Martin Luther's German translation had been his steady companion even in his teens. And it was rarely out of his reach later in the course of a lifetime that embraced two world wars, various revolutions, and long years of exile in Europe and the United States. One of his earliest preserved letters refers to the Bible as the ultimate source of all wisdom and

[13] Brod, *Heidentum, Christentum, Judentum*, i, 171.

[14] 'Religion was a discipline and not an enjoyable one. It was soullessly taught by men without a soul': Wassermann, *Mein Weg als Deutscher und Jude*, 13.

[15] Arthur Schnitzler, *My Youth in Vienna* (New York, 1970), 66. Schnitzler received no religious instruction at all during his early years in the Gymnasium. 'Later, however, study of the Bible and religion became part of the school curriculum.' Since his thirteenth birthday 'was celebrated without any elaborate ritual' (ibid. 48), he apparently never became a bar mitzvah, i.e. a properly instructed, religiously initiated member of the Jewish community with all the duties attached thereto. The same no doubt goes for young Schoenberg, except that he, a poor boy, probably also missed out on the 'exceptionally numerous and handsome presents from parents, grandparents and other relatives', which Schnitzler so fondly recalled.

[16] Cf. Lucy Davidowicz, *The Jewish Presence* (New York, 1978), 38.

morality.[17] In the story of Genesis it was the characteristically Jewish concept of divine creation as the model for all human creativity that impressed him most. 'God's greatest creation', he wrote in 1910, is 'the work of art produced by man.'[18] A year later, while putting the finishing touches to *Gurrelieder*, he responded to a request for comment on the significance of Franz Liszt by praising him both as a prime mover in the field of harmony and above all, as the composer whose oratorio *Christus* retains such special relevance for 'our time', which 'is seeking once again its God; this search characterizes it better than do the most outstanding technical achievements'.[19]

Whatever young Schoenberg, the 'unbeliever' as he called himself in that youthful letter to his cousin Malvina, may have expected of the Jewish establishment during the closing years of the last century, that very establishment had sufficient reason to look with some pride upon its short but, by the same token, remarkable history, if only because in the face of virtually continuous ideological and economic challenges, it had by and large succeeded in meeting both the strictly religious and the material needs of a rapidly expanding community. In the process, it has successfully marshalled and stimulated its cultural resources to the point where, by mid-century, Vienna's reputation as the world's leading centre for Jewish liturgical music was attracting Jewish and non-Jewish visitors from far and wide to its principal synagogue in the Seitenstettengasse (Pl. 1). There, in a uniquely designed place of worship, securely hidden behind the façade of an ordinary apartment house lest it offend a Christian passer-by, Chief Cantor Salomon Sulzer, soon widely admired as Vienna's foremost singer and choir conductor, humbly upheld the musical honour of a city whose once incomparable Imperial Chapel had suffered seemingly irreparable damage during the Metternich era. Indeed, Sulzer's a cappella choir quickly inspired emulation not only in Jewish synagogues all over Europe but also in Roman Catholic churches.[20] Franz Liszt, for one, never forgot 'the awesome experience' that Sulzer and his choir had afforded him 'of seeing and hearing what can happen in Jewish art when in new art forms created by their oriental

[17] H. H. Stuckenschmidt, *Schoenberg: His Life, World and Work* (London, 1977), 25–6.

[18] Schoenberg, *Die Musik*, 9 (Aug. 1910), 160.

[19] Schoenberg, *Style and Idea*, 445.

[20] Cf. Alexander L. Ringer, 'Salomon Sulzer, Joseph Mainzer and the Romantic a capella Movement', *Studia Musicologica*, 11 (1969), 368–70.

genius, the Israelites pour out the full splendor of their fantasies and dreams, the full intensity of their feelings and stifled passions . . .'[21]

In 1900, ten years after Sulzer's long active life had come to an end, friends and colleagues organized a solemn memorial concert in the Kleine Musikvereins-Saal. The Emperor lent his personal patronage, and some of Vienna's leading musicians volunteered their services, among them Heinrich Schenker, who acted as accompanist. A few years later Ferruccio Busoni corresponded with Schenker about the orchestral version of the latter's *Syrische Tänze* for piano duet, suggesting Arnold Schoenberg as the ideal person for the job. But, he asked at the end of his letter of 3 September 1903, 'don't you want to call the child by its correct name and refer to your series of dances simply as "Jewish Dance Tunes"?'[22] Schenker did not accept the suggestion, nor did Busoni insist. For all we know he had fallen prey to the common misconception of the augmented second, beloved of East European cantors and folk-singers, as the identifying interval of everything 'Jewish' in music, although one as familiar as Busoni was with parts of Eastern Europe where Turkish musical influences still persisted must have known better. Salomon Sulzer, for his part, eschewed the augmented second, except where the appropriate prayer-mode called for it. For his principal aim was the reconciliation of the monophonic Jewish tradition with the harmonic tendencies of Central European music. His East European emulators, on the other hand, lacking as a rule his solid musical background and, in many instances, his creative integrity and imagination, tended to treat Western harmony primarily as a sonorous substructure for elaborate vocal displays motivated at times less by intense religious devotion than by the musical expectations of a synagogue 'public' yearning for the forbidden delights of Italian opera. It was this sentimentalized exoticism which evoked such negative associations in progressive musical circles, conditioned to thinking of Max Bruch's romantically effusive *Kol Nidre* for cello and orchestra as the 'Jewish' concert work *par excellence*.

At a time when chromatic harmony was about to reach the point of no return, previously untapped melodic resources nevertheless held considerable stylistic appeal, especially in France and, of course, in Russia,

---

[21] As translated from Franz Liszt, *Les Bohémiens et leur musique*, in Sam Morgenstern, *Composers on Music* (New York, 1956), 163.

[22] See Hellmut Federhofer, *Heinrich Schenker* (Hildesheim, Zürich, New York, 1985), 83. Charlotte E. Erwin and Bryan R. Simms, 'Schoenberg's Correspondence with Heinrich Schenker', *JASI* 5/1 (June 1981), 26, offers a slightly different translation.

where the St Petersburg school under Rimsky-Korsakov's tutelage engaged in serious folk-music research, while the more mystically inclined turned to the music of the Orthodox Church. French musical exoticism antedated even the authentic Arab chants in Félicien David's choral 'ode' *Le Désert*, not to speak of Saint-Saëns's Turkish and North African predilections or the Persian and Indian ruminations of Bizet and Delibes. From there it was but a short step to the genuinely non-European ensembles that so excited Claude Debussy at the Parisian World Exhibition of 1889. By then, however, Debussy had already been to Russia and become well acquainted with orientalizing composers like Balakirev, Borodin, and Mussorgsky, in whose work the melodic fourth, so characteristic of both Russian peasant and Orthodox Church music, often assumes generative functions long reserved for the harmonic third, the *fons et origo* of Western music from late medieval days on. Rhythmically, on the other hand, he could draw on neighbouring Spain and its Caribbean extensions, as in the music of the American Louis Moreau Gottschalk.[23] In short, Debussy and like-minded French contemporaries had benefited from outside melodic-rhythmic infusions well before the turn of the century, many years ahead of the later Franco-Russian symbiosis exemplified by Igor Stravinsky.

Central Europe, by contrast, had the institutionalization of the Classical–Romantic tradition to contend with and, at the other extreme, the nationalistic clamourings of the Wagnerian *Neutöner*. Moreover, Germany's musical affinities and predilections historically militated against foreign, in particular non-European, influence. No German musician, not even Max Reger, ever dared leave the harmonic path, however tortured its layout as a result of nineteenth-century theory and practice. The well-publicized stylistic quarrels among the nineteenth-century musicians and critics, far from questioning the continued validity of that tradition, pertained mostly to proper methods of ensuring its lasting survival against suspected 'alien' attempts to undermine it.

One such pernicious force had been identified as early as the 1850s, when both Wagner and Liszt issued their urgent warnings to the effect that international Jewry was about to destroy European music. Half a century later Gustav Mahler appeared to prove the point. That he was an ardent admirer of Wagner and derived much of his early inspiration from

[23] During the closing decades of the 19th cent., Paris harboured a sizeable colony of Spanish musicians. Gottschalk, the expatriate pianist-composer of Jewish and Creole descent, was well known to every piano student at the Conservatoire, since two of his most famous pieces were on the list of obligatory works for the final examination.

Liszt was of no consequence. What did matter was his cavalier treatment of harmony at the behest of melodic-rhythmic 'banalities' that sorely offended the stolid ears and minds of self-appointed guardians of 'purity in music', who saw in the virtuoso composer-conductor from Moravia the very incarnation of the Jewish seducer of German musical innocence. Mahler, to be sure, never hesitated to mix seemingly incompatible musical elements or to overstep the conventional boundaries of the symphonic genre, if need be, to tell his musical story in the literary manner of a Dostoevsky or a Tolstoy. Indeed, where Wagner had offered romantic retreats into a world of illusion populated by artificial heroes and lifeless gods, Mahler forced an understandably recalcitrant public to come face to face with its own social and psychological dilemmas, its inhumanity to man and the contingent refusal to acknowledge its awesome burden of guilt. Mahler projected the uncomfortable image of the Hebrew prophet condemning priest and king alike as obfuscators of truth and morality. Had he not urged a group of startled choral singers to think of the final movement of his Second Symphony in terms of a Jacob struggling with the Angel of the Lord, rather than of humble worshippers prostrated in church?[24] Surely that 'great summons' called upon man to examine himself without mercy so that his immortal soul might emerge cleansed and healed. Just before the chorus delivers its timeless message, however, a flute solo is heard which in its Oriental inspiration sounds almost like a paraphrase of the oboe flourish that introduces the 'Hindu melody' in Jules Massenet's popular opera Le Roi de Lahore.[25] And such a tasteless slip, barely tolerable in a French opera, though hardly in Wagnerian music drama, signalled in a symphony the typical disrespect of the Jew for the 'serious' German masters of the past. In other words, the Jew Mahler was doing his devilish best to trivialize the very pride of German culture.

Mahler, needless to say, was aiming for the very opposite, as he proceeded with unfailing artistic instinct to save the German tradition. Precisely in order to prevent it from succumbing to its own harmonic sophistication, he boldly drew upon whatever musical resource was likely

[24] Cf. Egon Wellesz, 'Reminiscences of Mahler', The Score, 28 (1961), 55. According to one of his closest friends and associates, 'Mahler never hid his Jewish origins. But they were no cause for joy on his part. They rather spurred and goaded him on to even higher, purer deeds': Alfred Roller, 'Die Bildnisse von Gustav Mahler', Musikblätter des Anbruch, 3 (1921), 37.

[25] Cf. Alexander L. Ringer, 'Europäische Musik im Banne der Exotik', Forum Musicologicum, 4 (Winter, 1984), 93.

to help him redress the aesthetic balance. Like Haydn, Mozart, Beethoven, and Schubert before him, he chose an essentially diatonic harmonic base for the exploration, combination, and recombination of elements from the sacred realm, Christian and non-Christian, from opera, comic as well as serious, Wagnerian drama, and, above all, the grand tradition of Central European instrumental music. What made him anathema in the eyes of Post-Romantic purists was not unexpectedly this 'bastardization' of an aesthetic world raised to the level of sacred myth and embraced by many as a valid substitute for conventional religion. From that perspective, with its strong admixture of chauvinism, Mahler and his Jewish disciples appeared to dare the gods themselves.

Aesthetic fundamentalism was a fact of musical life in imperial Germany and Austria that deserves proper consideration, if the recurring antisemitic criticism levelled at both Mahler and Schoenberg is not to be dismissed quite erroneously as but so many hate-filled manifestations of incomprehension on the part of petty men brimming with professional envy. Nothing could be further from the truth: Mahler and his spiritual descendant Schoenberg did change the direction of European, in particular Central European, music. What their most rabid foes would or could not see was that the 'pure' path of a Pfitzner led German music to a dead end. Certainly, beyond Reger there was no future. And Schoenberg's life-long admiration for the latter may well have been a function of his intuitive recognition that in his best work Reger achieved the well-nigh impossible, something worthy of the designation 'genius' that he so readily bestowed upon him. Reger himself clearly sensed the harmonic dilemma facing his generation when, as early as 1900, he composed the first of several sets of pieces for unaccompanied string instruments. Here at least the ultra-harmonist completely abandoned the bass, and thus also the very base of functional harmony, a decade before his contemporary Schoenberg proclaimed the 'emancipation of dissonance'.

While the issue was joined by many a contemporary confronting the final excesses of chromatic harmony in his own particular way, Schoenberg enjoyed the advantage of a logogenic melodic heritage perpetuated less by reform-minded cantors like Salomon Sulzer and his disciples than by the old-fashioned prayer-masters, the orthodox *ba'ale tefilla*, who chanted their daily prose-texts with often dramatic inflexions deviating rarely, if ever, from the traditional prayer-mode—the *Steiger* or underlying *maqam*. And the prayers sung in Jewish homes reflected, though inevitably at a simpler level, the same essentially rhetorical, non-metric tendencies that determined much of Schoenberg's basic musical stance, as distinguished from that of a faithful Christian disciple like Anton von Webern. What else but this deep-seated cultural trait could have induced him as early as 1911 to conclude his *Harmonielehre*, that extraordinary distillation of some twenty years of harmonic engagement as composer and teacher, with an outlook on 'tone-colour melody'? And, for that matter, what of the unusual, rhetorically punctuating effect of the lightly scored dissonant chords at the beginning of Op. 11, No. 1, reminiscent of the monodic usage of a Claudio Monteverdi? Is it really so far-fetched to suggest that in both instances Mediterranean, if not outright Oriental practices, asserted themselves at a critical historical juncture when only massive infusions of free melody and rhythm were likely to save a tradition no longer sustainable by exhausted structural procedures of Northern inspiration? That such foreign admixtures would arouse resentment among self-appointed guardians of convention in either case was to be foreseen. Schoenberg, the apostle of tradition (as distinguished from convention), harboured no more illusions in this regard than Monteverdi three centuries before him.

Viewed thus in a broader historical context, Schoenberg's unique way of restoring the primacy of melodic-rhythmic energies at the expense of functional harmony resolved in post-functional terms some of the same endemic conflicts that determined a good deal of the interaction between melody and harmony during the pre-functional stages of the figured-bass era. Nor was it sheer coincidence that this theory of harmonic relativity took shape shortly after he completed his commission of *basso continuo* realizations for a volume of early eighteenth-century music in the 'Austrian Monuments' series founded and edited by Guido Adler, one of the fathers of modern musicology as Eduard Hanslick's successor at the University of Vienna.[26] Adler, Gustav Mahler's childhood friend and his first biographer, had thought highly enough of Schoenberg to recommend him, as early as 1904, as a teacher of harmony and counterpoint for some of his most gifted students at the University, including Anton von Webern, Egon Wellesz, and Erwin Stein. These young men, in turn, made no secret of their musical research interests, in particular Renaissance polyphony, the focus of Webern's dissertation, and Eastern

---

[26] Schoenberg's work on Georg Mattias Monn's concerto for cello and orchestra and three other eighteenth-century compositions for vol. 39 of the *Denkmäler der Tonkunst in Österreich* was but the beginning of a lifelong creative involvement with music of the past. Arrangements, transcriptions, and, indeed, recompositions of pieces composed by others, including Bach and Brahms, became an integral, if intermittent, part of his subsequent output.

monophony and early monody, Wellesz's principal fields of study. Stein eventually assisted Schoenberg with the preparation of the 1921 revision of his *Harmonielehre*, where the analogy between the constitution of chords in modern music and those of the figured-bass era is made explicit for the first time: 'For it is apparent,' wrote Schoenberg, 'and will probably become increasingly clear, that we are turning to a new epoch of polyphonic style, and as in the earlier epochs, harmony will be a product of the voice leading: justified solely by the melodic lines!'[27]

Meanwhile, another Adler pupil, Ernst Kurth, had completed a thesis on the theoretical foundations of functional harmony that initiated a whole series of interrelated volumes in which Kurth explored every possible angle of his novel conception of music in terms of psychological energies. Kurth's ideas reflect the influence both of Henri Bergson's dynamic philosophy and of the Central European *Gestalt* school in psychology. But they were also remarkably in tune with contemporary musical trends, nearly all of which, in one way or another, favoured melody and rhythm as autonomous forces unfettered by strictly harmonic considerations.[28] Small wonder, under these circumstances, that the Jewish-conspiracy myth found new adherents among those who had long confused tradition with convention. For the principals involved were without exception of Jewish descent: Bergson, Koffka, Adler, and Kurth no less than Schoenberg—and of course Freud, living witnesses to that historically conditioned, characteristically Jewish disposition toward the *élan vital* in which Bergson saw the fundamental source of all existence.

This is by no means meant to suggest, however, that these and other prime movers of similar persuasion, or, for that matter, their often vociferous critics, necessarily made a conscious connection between their ancestry or upbringing and specific modes of thought and action. Quite to the contrary: Bergson proudly spoke of himself as a Frenchman; Adler remained a fervent Austrian to his dying day; Kurth became a devout Roman Catholic and Schoenberg at least nominally a Protestant, active for decades on behalf of the great German tradition in music. Still, in retrospect clear patterns emerge, separating primary from secondary

[27] Schoenberg, *Theory of Harmony*, trans. Roy E. Carter (Berkeley and Los Angeles, 1978), 389.

[28] That Schoenberg judged Kurth's writings mostly on hearsay follows from two brief comments on 'Linear Counterpoint' published in *Style and Idea* (1984 edn., 289–98). The admission 'I have not read E. Kurth's book *Der lineare Kontrapunkt*' (p. 291) speaks for itself.

elements and thus bringing to the fore cultural constants once inevitably hidden beneath a bewildering superficial array of temporarily relevant trends and counter-trends. In imperial Austria-Hungary, moreover, the nagging nationality question was likely to interfere with any meaningful discussion of religion, national character, and/or cultural roots. And so, while the unending nationality debates made and broke intellectual as well as political careers, a younger generation raised within the secure confines of established, supposedly unshakeable bourgeois verities, vented their growing unease in terms coined by the prophets of a new age—Marx, Freud, and above all Nietzsche. In that light the very word 'German', replete with ambiguity and subject to misunderstanding, seemed suspect, the more so as the ageing Emperor, officially still the all-powerful guardian of Germany's political and cultural heritage, proved no match for his Prussian rival, who, as Kaiser of a vigorous young *Reich*, now arrogated that sacred duty to himself, if not by historical right then by military might. Schoenberg was in fact barely old enough to comprehend such matters when a powerful Pan-German movement began straining at the leash to impose upon all of Central Europe the kind of Teutonic order that was to become such a frightening reality half a century later.

In this ambivalent historical context the Jewish question, precipitated by the inexorable process of Jewish assimilation, suddenly moved to the forefront of political consciousness on both sides of the German–Austrian border. By law Jews now enjoyed equal civil status as German or Austrian citizens of the 'Mosaic' faith. But unofficially, and in many instances bureaucratically as well, they were treated at best as naturalized aliens and at worst as foreign intruders. In intellectual circles too, only a minority, unafraid of possible competition, welcomed them into the ranks. The majority, anxious to preserve what they perceived to be their exclusive, rightful inheritance, tended to look upon the newcomers with an explosive mixture of fear, defiance, and contempt. Undaunted, Jewish artists and intellectuals nevertheless eagerly and often blindly embraced every opportunity to identify themselves with this culture they had admired so long from afar. Few were perceptive enough to discern the writing on the wall, even though the unprecedented violence following the assassination of Tsar Alexander II had swept thousands of East European Jewish refugees into Vienna either in transit to Britain or the United States or as eventual permanent residents. This mass migration was still in full swing when the Dreyfus trial in far-away Paris began to dominate the news in Vienna as well, thanks in large measure to the incisive reporting of one Theodor Herzl. Shortly after his return in 1896, Herzl, deeply shaken by what he had seen and heard, published *The Jewish State*, the historic essay that launched the modern Zionist movement world-wide.

To be sure, 'the Jewish question' was only one of a host of socio-political ills gnawing away at the foundations of an empire unable to contain the national aspirations of its disparate constituent populations. But, by the same token, the endemic conflict between Germans and Czechs for power in Bohemia also had direct ramifications for the Jewish minority, because ironically the Czech-speaking population resented the identification of the local urban Jews with German culture. Similar conflicts complicated the situation in Hungary, especially after the founding of the Hungarian Freedom Party in 1894, the year the Dreyfus trial got underway. Under these precarious circumstances growing numbers of Jews decided to take the ethnic bull by the horns and seek parliamentary representation as a separate national group of their own. As representatives of other parties, a few deputies of Jewish descent had figured prominently in the Reichsrat for a number of years. But in 1897, the very year his fellow Viennese Herzl founded the world Zionist movement in neutral Switzerland, Benno Staucher took his Reichsrat seat as the elected representative of the newly formed Jewish Popular Party. Internationalist leaders of Jewish origin like Victor Adler and Karl Kautsky, the co-founders of the Austrian Social Democratic Party, were thus gradually offset by equally outspoken figures espousing the Jewish national cause, whether with an eye on the ancient homeland or in hopes of becoming a recognized nationality in a new Austria, preferably transformed into a federation of semi-autonomous cultural entities.

Schoenberg was about to finish his first major work—*Verklärte Nacht*—when the social-democratic leadership, gathered in the Czech city of Brno, solemnly declared its resolve to work for just such a federated democracy. Yet that same year, 1899, Houston Chamberlain published *The Foundations of the Nineteenth Century*, a work that served more than anything else to legitimize the Pan-German movement with such disastrous, ultimately genocidal, consequences. At that point, too, 'away from Rome' became a familiar slogan among the Austrian intelligentsia, and it took barely two years for some ten thousand individuals, Jews and Catholics alike, to register their opposition to the status quo by turning Protestant, much as in the days of Martin Luther and the original 'away from Rome' movement. Among the first to follow that path was

Karl Kraus. But this dramatic gesture interfered no more with his openly proclaimed agnosticism than the decision to remain within the Jewish fold affected Arthur Schnitzler's. Otto Weininger, a pathologically self-hating convert, for his part staged a final melodramatic demonstration of his all-consuming love for German culture by committing suicide in Beethoven's last abode. Gustav Mahler, genuinely attracted to the mystical side of Christianity, defied the trend altogether and became a Roman Catholic in his thirties. Yet he never shed his Jewish cultural entity. Franz Werfel, though similarly inclined and eventually married to Mahler's widow, did not convert but instead infused much of his literary work with a mystical faith in the coming brotherhood of man, not unlike the Utopian followers of Saint-Simon during the early days of Jewish emancipation.

'Problems of Jewish alienation' have received a great deal of attention in recent years, especially in the United States, and the fact is that emancipated Jews born during the latter decades of the nineteenth century often looked askance at a heritage of which they knew little, if anything, but which nevertheless precluded their full acceptance by the non-Jewish majority. That this very real dilemma should colour their views of a world to which they aspired but which rejected them seemed inevitable. Some chose to retreat into substitute realms of their own making, centred typically on 'eros, play, and poetry'; others, loath to acknowledge their ambivalent condition, loudly proclaimed their devotion to everything German, behaving often more royally than the proverbial king himself. The more sensitive, by contrast, succumbed in alarming numbers to the pervasive aura of doom, the ominous 'lull before the storm', of which the hapless Crown Prince Rudolf had spoken just before his suicide in 1889.[29] Karl Kraus, wary of all the creative confusion surrounding him, called Austria during the period preceding the First World War the ultimate 'experiment station for the end of the world'.[30] If nothing else, the outright compulsive behaviour of quite a few of the experimenters, not to speak of their psychological victims, motivated a goodly portion of Sigmund Freud's relentless search for ways of uncovering the deepest secrets of the human psyche. A disillusioned critic like Paul Stefan, on the other hand, sensing the impending

---

[29] Pinchas E. Rosenblüth, 'Die geistigen und religiösen Strömungen in der deutschen Judenheit', in *Juden im Wilhelminischen Deutschland 1890–1914*, ed. Werner E. Mosse (Tübingen, 1979), 558.

[30] Ibid.

catastrophe, could only decry the incurable cultural decay leading to so much 'Death in Vienna'.[31]

Arnold Schoenberg, who hailed neither from an artistic nor from a professional milieu, found his way only gradually into the intellectual and quasi-intellectual circles of the Café Griensteidl (Pls. 3 and 4) and similar coffee houses, where strong positions with regard to almost anything and everything were the order of the day. Displaying little political interest or acumen in those earlier years, he kept almost pointedly aloof from current issues and conflicts. Friends and associates might embrace the Zionist cause or Utopian prescriptions for a classless society governed by humanistic rather than material ideals and pursuits; he, seemingly content with the monarchy, though not necessarily with the social order it represented, set out instead to make his single-minded contribution to what he conceived of as the great tradition of German music. The eventual defeat of the old order caused him a good deal of grief but, by the same token, reinforced the pride and determination with which he defended that tradition at its best in both word and musical deed.

That he regarded his method of composing with twelve tones as a major contribution to its post-war survival is, of course, well known, thanks to a much-cited remark to his pupil Josef Rufer. But even he may not have realized at that historic moment in 1921 that what was in the offing amounted to little less than the repolyphonization of a tradition which, in the wake of its nineteenth-century homophonic triumphs, displayed unmistakeable symptoms of an irreversible, self-destructive addiction to chromatic excesses. Only a handful of close friends and disciples, at any rate, immediately grasped the historical, as well as the purely aesthetic, significance of this unique attempt to restore polyphony to its once pre-eminent position, not by harking back to the nineteenth or eighteenth centuries in some mildly modern guise but in a stark, unabashedly twentieth-century idiom receptive to whatever was strong and viable in the immediate past. Inevitably, given the fundamentally homophonic nature of that past, it took exceptional understanding of the many-splendoured history of Western music to fathom the epochal nature of Schoenberg's seemingly irrational step, a step as selfless as it was imperative. One who did understand and share his master's conception of German music was Alban Berg. As Berg wrote to Anton von

[31] Paul Stefan, *Der Tod in Wien* (Vienna, 1912). That very year Egon Friedell, a historian of culture who was also a poet, declared: 'The true artist never found understanding in Vienna.' Cf. Walter Obermaier, 'Dokumente aus Schönbergs Wiener Zeit ...' *Arnold Schönberg Gedenkausstellung*, ed. Ernst Hilmar (Vienna, 1974), 22.

Webern in 1933, when 'the new Germany' officially banned their revered master's music as symbolic of all that was un-German, indeed anti-German, in modern art and music: 'there is but one word to characterize his musical achievements adequately: German. What I mean by German in this context I surely don't have to explain—mention of one name should suffice: Pfitzner, for example.'[32]

That particular homophonist had, of course, been among the first to denounce the 'un-German' character of Schoenberg and the many others he accused of 'musical impotence' due to their alleged inability to grasp the true nature of German culture. According to the established Wagnerian line, the Jew, though radically unfit for genuine creativity, was, by the same token, clever in hiding his sterility under various seemingly German guises. The trouble was that Schoenberg had thrown off even those last vestiges of musical assimilationism, leaving the ideologists hopelessly at sea and thus exposing himself to ever more furious abuse. To make things worse, the target of their increasingly hysterical attacks refused to be drawn into unproductive polemics. His Christian pupil Berg had counter-attacked as early as 1920 and beaten Pfitzner at his own game with a brilliant essay entitled 'The musical impotence of Hans Pfitzner's New Aesthetics'. Fifteen years later, only a few months before his untimely death, he still insisted in print that, had Handel and Bach been born in 1885 instead of 1685, surely 'the former's rootedness in the soil would have been subject to doubt as much as the latter's music would have been declared typical of cultural Bolshevism'.[33]

Schoenberg himself eschewed polemics, except where meaningful creative results were likely to ensue. He rather preferred to move forward rapidly and in a straight line, once the direction was firmly laid out. And so, in the wake of the courageous reappraisal of his Jewish roots that speaks from the exchange of letters with Wassily Kandinsky barely two years after he proudly pointed to his new method of composing as a means of ensuring the pre-eminence of German music for another century, the new course was staked out: from the spoken drama *Der biblische Weg*, begun almost immediately, to *Moses und Aron*, his crowning musico-dramatic achievement, which antedated the full onslaught of German totalitarianism by several crucial years.

The fatefully interconnected events of the early 1920s inevitably shaped not only Schoenberg's mature religious-ethical outlook but also

[32] Cf. H. F. Redlich, *Alban Berg: Versuch einer Würdigung* (Vienna, Zurich, London, 1957), 304.

[33] Cf. Willi Reich, *Alban Berg* (Vienna, 1937), 193.

the strictly musical aspects of a personal universe marked by that ineluctable sense of unity that determined everything he said, wrote, and acted upon, then and forever after. Unity, oneness, and indivisibility have been the perennial hallmarks of Jewish thought. 'One' is the watchword of the Jew as he rises in the morning, goes about his daily task, and retires in the evening. It is also the last word he pronounces before he closes his eyes for the last time. The Jewish longing for unity was at the root of 'Einstein's lifelong quest for a unified field theorem that would encompass all physical phenomena' as much as 'Marx's search for an all embracing historical method',[34] and it was the spiritual source both of Schoenberg's method of composing with twelve tones and of the analytical thought of Heinrich Schenker, who in May 1933 made note of a curious 'parallel: in the cosmos the single cause is God—in music the only cause is the *Ursatz*'.[35] Technically, Schoenberg's Piano Suite, Op. 25, completed in 1921, was the final test of his new method's structural and aesthetic validity. But in view of all that came thereafter one wonders whether things would have been the same had he not simultaneously reached the irrevocable decision to assume henceforth the full burden of his Jewishness. Thus he became a committed member of that historical people which, united under the one, unitary God, had survived millennia of enmity and persecution, a community of fate unconditionally devoted to the idea of freedom, not for its own sake but in the service of an invisible divinity that had revealed itself through deeds and called for divinely ordained deeds by and for man in return. Merely to pose such a hypothetical question, however, implies a fundamental inability to grasp the essential indivisibility of Arnold Schoenberg's life and work.

No Jewish artist leading, like Schoenberg, an undiminishedly productive life during that tragic era which witnessed both the portentous rise and the disastrous fall of European Jewry in little more than half a century was in a position to ignore the far-reaching consequences of his birth into this martyred minority, let alone Schoenberg who recognized early on that a Gentile world increasingly deprived of many of its traditional beliefs and practices was prone to turn the so-called Jewish question into a collective *idée fixe*. Never one to shrink from a challenge, however insurmountable it might appear, the composer at the very height of his creative powers resolved to confront the scourge of the age

---

[34] The formulation is Frederick V. Grunfeld's in *Prophets without Honor* (New York, 1979), 9. Grunfeld, however, sees the common denominator in a Jewish fascination with the 'never-ending solution', as exemplified in Walter Benjamin's works.

[35] Federhofer, *Heinrich Schenker*, 320.

positively, in artistic and intellectual as well as in decidedly political terms. Fully aware that true spirituality joined to an unyielding devotion to unpopular truths had been suspect even in biblical terms, let alone since then, he spurned all false illusions of peace pandered to by the modern priests of eternal bliss. Aligning himself with the visionary prophets of old, who lived and acted bereft of peace but in the certainty of an ideal future, he shunned Aaron, the practical man of experience, fact, and compromise. Instead, he chose Moses, unbending in the proclamation and defence of revealed truth yet human enough to err and pay for his error with burial in an unknown grave. And so it came to pass that, looking back upon his own forty-year trek through the modern wastelands of human passion in the service of pagan idols, Arnold Schoenberg, the selfless herald of the new music, born and raised in Austria yet a Prussian by virtue of his remarkable achievements as artist and teacher, the refugee in Paris who reached the United States on a Czech passport, the sincere, deeply grateful American citizen whose personal inspiration changed the course of musical events in the New World no less than in the Old which had forced him out, managed to uncover but two perennial denominators in his long productive life: composer and Jew.

I

Prophecy and Solitude

IN Arnold Schoenberg's personality and art, we revere above all the unyielding search for the absolute, a will-power and an ideal of perfection which his increasingly aimless and senseless contemporaries are hardly able to grasp any longer. In his devotion to the unconditional, this master of music comes perhaps closest to the old masters of the cabbala. Just as they attempted through the "Sanctification of the Name", to draw the Divine into the earthly realm, so Arnold Schoenberg endeavours, through the sanctification of the work of art, i.e. through the exclusion of all impure secondary goals (effect, success, accessibility), to draw the absolute into the world of sound. Thus he creates in the strong and courageous solitude of the mystic, beyond applause and participation, a work of sublime dialogue that will be judged properly only by a period marked by a higher degree of spirituality than ours.[1]

Thus wrote Franz Werfel over half a century ago. Indeed, it took a non-musician, a fine literary mind close to music and musicians, to pinpoint the historical and aesthetic context for the splendid isolation of Arnold Schoenberg, that curious phenomenon of a musical genius acknowledged as such by some of his worst enemies yet still widely unknown and, what is worse, unloved. Two of Werfel's formulations seem particularly apposite: 'unyielding search for the absolute' and 'devotion to the unconditional'. They certainly bear on a good deal that appears puzzling in Schoenberg's life, his artistic legacy, and his historical position. To Franz Werfel's mind these were, to be sure, truly admirable qualities, deserving of the deepest veneration, but he also recognized in them traits for which our materialist, over-sensualized world can at most muster historical respect—hardly aesthetic identification. What Werfel could not know in 1934 was that within two decades 'the strong and courageous solitude of the mystic', at least as personified in his pupil Anton von Webern, would turn out to hold tremendous attraction for a musical generation barely emerged from the crucible of the second of two global conflagrations in Schoenberg's lifetime.

Characteristically, many a post-Second World War Webernian cheer-fully dismissed Schoenberg as an acknowledged master-teacher whose

---

[1] *Arnold Schönberg zum 60. Geburtstag* (Vienna, 1934), 14.

creative achievement, unfortunately, was marred by unpardonable stylistic and structural inconsistencies. Webern's perfectionism, on the other
hand, his striving for the absolute, assumed virtually Messianic ramifications for younger men and women who associated his utterly private
universe quite naturally with the geometric abstractions of a Mondrian or
the 'cool romanticism' of a Klee, rather than with the expressionistic
fervour of his friend and teacher Schoenberg. Sophisticated musical
children of the Depression, traumatized by the firestorms of Hiroshima,
they yearned for the kind of subconscious security that exuded from a
music conceived in a spirit not so much of order as of orderliness. And as
cultural products of a technological age, they were fascinated by the inner
workings of all things, material as well as human, and revelled in the
discovery of analytical detail, especially if it was susceptible to quantita-
tive appreciation. In the end, perhaps inevitably, they proceeded with
little hesitation to lay down, in the name of Webern, their own often
distressingly rigid laws of serial composition. The aesthetic result,
needless to say, reflected very little of the 'strong and courageous solitude
of the mystic'. While seemingly foolproof structural frames of reference
offered the weak and the timid a false sense of peace, their communicative
potential was inherently limited to the point where ex post facto verbal
commentaries, explanations, and analyses often depreciated the value of
the underlying musical text to that of a mere pretext.

Arnold Schoenberg, of course, had scant regard for those who dealt
with musical art, whether his own or that of the past, primarily in terms
of 'how it is made', rather than 'what it is'. And, though by no means
averse to games in other contexts, he abhorred the very thought of music
reduced to a sonorous game, a thought so diametrically opposed to his
fundamental concept of art as the prophetic conscience of modern man.
As he saw it, music dedicated to truth must eschew all decorative
pretence.

Reflecting on the ideals of the biblical prophets of old, the late-
nineteenth-century philosopher Herrmann Cohen once pointed out that
the prophetic conscience was not incompatible with the aesthetic experience *per se* but that it was 'deeply suspicious of that one-sided
attitude of an aesthetic which is unconcerned with all moral problems of
civilization'.[2] In other words, art for art's sake, the idol of worshippers at
the altars of the religion of beauty, had no place in the prophetic scheme
of things. A good deal has been written over the past quarter of a century

---

[2] Herrmann Cohen, *Reason and Hope*, ed. Eva Jospe (New York, 1971), 110.

about the prophetic images of Schoenberg's unfinished opera *Moses und Aron*. That Schoenberg personally identified with Moses, the prophet, more readily than with Aaron, the priest, is easily demonstrated. But there can be no question either that he knew, understood, and identified with fundamental biblical notions well before he conceived his greatest stage-work that was to find its ultimate denouement in his own ostentatious act of reconversion to Judaism in 1933. A whole string of musical and verbal compositions could be cited in evidence, beginning at the very latest with the abortive Symphony of 1912, planned originally as

an oratorio on the following theme: how the man of today, who has passed through materialism, socialism, and anarchy, who was an atheist, but has still preserved a remnant of ancient beliefs (in the form of superstition)—how this modern man struggles with God (see also 'Jakob ringt' by Strindberg) and finally arrives at the point of finding God and becoming religious. How to learn to pray! This change should *not* be caused by any actions, by blows of fate, or by a love-affair. Or, at least, such things should be merely hinted at, kept in the background as motivations. And above all: the text must mirror the speech, thought, and expression of the man of today; it should deal with the problems which press upon us. For those who struggle with God in the Bible also express themselves as men of their time, speak of their own concerns, and remain at their social and spiritual level. Therefore, they are artistically strong, but cannot be put into music by a composer of today who fulfils his obligations.[3]

Today we know that Schoenberg, while still in his teens, felt compelled to reprimand his first love for her disrespectful remarks about the bible. 'As an unbeliever,' he wrote to his *chère cousine*, 'I must tell you that on the contrary there is no nonsense whatsoever in the Bible, for it deals with the most difficult questions regarding morality, law, economics and medicine in the simplest form, though admittedly often from a contemporary point of view, and the Bible generally forms the foundations of all our official institutions (excluding the railway and the telephone).'[4]

Note that young Schoenberg refers to himself as an unbeliever and that he makes no reference at all to faith, grace, or salvation. Instead, he emphasizes the relevance of biblical morality, law, and institutions, all pre-eminently within the province of the Old Testament. As far as that goes, there are striking parallels between the thoughts of the infatuated boy of fourteen and those of the mature artist of *Pierrot Lunaire*. For, like the former, the latter looked to the Bible for guidance and inspiration

[3] Schoenberg addressing Richard Dehmel, 13 Dec. 1912. Cf. Josef Rufer, *The Works of Arnold Schoenberg* (London, 1962), 117.

[4] Cf. H. H. Stuckenschmidt, *Schönberg* (Zürich, 1974), 25.

in confronting 'the problems which press upon us'. That the stages of ideological commitment and confusion outlined in the letter to Dehmel correspond quite literally to Schoenberg's own spiritual evolution goes without saying. He too had moved, however briefly, in socialist circles and had been associated with men who, like Theodor von Hartmann, his fellow contributor to Der blaue Reiter, had advocated 'anarchy in the arts'. In dire material straits he too had made his temporary sacrifices to the golden calf. And surely he, the self-confessed young 'unbeliever', had once sought modernity in the denial of God. But, like 'the man of today', with whose faith he proposed to deal in his planned oratorio, he had 'still preserved a remnant of ancient beliefs', struggled with God, and finally arrived 'at the point of finding God and becoming religious'.

Since Schoenberg abandoned his fathers' faith in 1898, before Karl Kraus, though not before Gustav Mahler, his conversion seemed no less opportunistically motivated than that of many a contemporary, anxious to acquire what Mahler later so sadly referred to as the Jew's ticket of admission to society at large. Yet Schoenberg was anything but an opportunist. And an opportunist would have chosen Roman Catholicism, the official and officially required religion of Austria, where Protestants were looked upon with only slightly less suspicion than Jews. Yet he became a Protestant, encouraged no doubt by his friend Walter Pieau, with whom he studied the Lutheran Bible in considerable detail. According to the records of the Viennese Protestant community, Pieau, an opera-singer and ardent Protestant, became his godfather, but, given Schoenberg's lifelong fierce sense of independence, it is inconceivable that the ultimate decision should not have been entirely and freely his own and for reasons already alluded to.

Among the many circumstances that may have influenced him in this very serious matter, the young composer's professional association with several workers' choruses would seem to deserve some consideration. The labour movement and the Austrian Church were sworn enemies throughout the closing decades of the Empire. And Schoenberg undoubtedly shared the deep mistrust with which those who addressed him as *Genosse* or comrade-in-arms viewed the machinations of the higher clergy in the political realm. If for no other reason, he could hardly have turned to the official faith in good conscience. And conscience was the one trait which, for better or worse, determined his every living moment from the day of his stern letter to the beloved cousin to the last words he was to compose: 'And yet I pray.' It was conscience, unyielding and unconditional, which brought him ever closer to the realization that the modern artist, if he is to retain his dignity and self-respect in a world of sham, must say the truth as he conceives it, irrespective of the consequences, whether aesthetic or personal.

The distinctly Nietzschean overtones of Schoenberg's abiding passion for truth come as no surprise to the student of European intellectual history in the early twentieth century, when countless searching young minds were spellbound by the prophet of Sils-Maria. It was Nietzsche who had formulated the modern antitheses of art and philosophy, illusion and dedication, and, last but not least, beauty and truth, and it was he who virtually alone in nineteenth-century Germany had struck the theme that was to determine so many aspects of Schoenberg's creative and personal life: self-perfection of the non-political individual as man's best hope, though admittedly a remote one, for a better world at large. Indeed, some of Nietzsche's outspoken élitist ideas not only shaped the Schoenbergian work ethic; up to a point they characterize the whole man:

The most spiritual men, as the *strongest*, find their happiness where others would find their destruction: in the labyrinth, in hardness against themselves and others, in experiments. Their joy is self-conquest: asceticism becomes in them nature, need, and instinct. Difficult tasks are a privilege to them; to play with burdens which crush others, a *recreation*. Knowledge—a form of asceticism. They are the most venerable kind of man: that does not preclude their being the most cheerful and the kindliest.[5]

In Schoenberg's *Die Jakobsleiter*, the Chosen One, incarnation of the élitest idea, exclaims:

In you is assembled whatever is the essence of all creatures. So you, as the vanguard of the spirit, which at some time draws the parts to itself, are a picture, in miniature, of the future, according to whose nature you develop. In your own advance, you lift them up too.[6]

Schoenberg and Nietzsche, the repudiator of Christian faith, grace, and salvation, did however part ways on one crucial issue. Whereas the disgruntled philosopher rejected pity as an unacceptable manifestation of human weakness, Schoenberg's Chosen One concludes:

However you despise them, you suffer for them. You suffer with them; have pity on them!

---

[5] Cf. Walter Kaufmann's excellent translation of this pertinent passage from *Der Antichrist* (1895) in his *Nietzsche* (New York, 1956), 317–18.
[6] Cf. Willi Reich, *Schoenberg: A Critical Biography* (New York, 1971), 103.

And Schoenberg, his often forbidding appearance and bitter irony notwithstanding, did suffer and was filled with pity, like all who have known the solitude of the true prophet, like Isaiah and Jeremiah, like Amos or Jonah. For he deeply believed, as they did, that

The Eternal One . . . takes account of your imperfect nature, . . . is aware of your inadequacy, . . . knows that you must fail and that your path is a long one.[7]

According to Herrmann Cohen, 'chosenness is not a mark of arrogance, it is the battle cry for divine justice'.[8] Cohen, the renowned founder of the neo-Kantian 'Marburg School' of philosophy, belonged of course to an older generation of Central Europe's assimilated Jewish intelligentsia. But not only was some of his most important work completed during Schoenberg's lifetime, his life-long efforts toward an amalgamation of Platonic and Old Testamentary concepts left demonstrable traces in Arnold Schoenberg's thoughts and attitudes. If nothing else, Cohen's writings offer a number of clues as to why the comforting sense of tragedy identified with the best in Western music is so often missing even in the most dramatic of Schoenberg's works, why in fact Schoenberg does not seem to fit into any of the neatly aligned pigeon-holes we call musical history. Clearly, he lacked the sophisticated grace of a Mendelssohn, let alone of a Mozart, the immutable faith of a Bruckner, or the ringing Wagnerian promise of salvation in death, if not in life. But what of Beethoven, especially the Beethoven of the last sonatas or quartets, the Beethoven shrugged off by most of his contemporaries and immediate successors as either a bizarre eccentric or a hopeless victim of debilitating deafness, or possibly both? Schoenberg certainly never forgot those first overwhelming insights into the spiritual potential of music, derived from some of the earliest scores in his possession: the Rasumovsky Quartets and, above all, the Great Fugue. Of the latter he said in later years that he would not have been at all surprised if listeners relatively unfamiliar with his music had mistaken this most inscrutable of Beethoven works for one of his own. And if this was so, he was surely thinking of more than such obvious technical parallels as wide intervalic skips, obsessive rhythmic patterning, and the concomitant transcendental difficulties of performance. What he no doubt sensed was a community of motivation and intent. As J. W. N. Sullivan put it in his incisive comments on the aesthetic reality of the later Beethoven:

[7] In the words of Gabriel toward the end of *Die Jakobsleiter*.
[8] Cohen, *Reason and Hope*, 116.

Beethoven does not communicate to us his perceptions or his experiences. He communicates to us the attitude based on them. We may share with him that unearthy state where the struggle ends and pain dissolves away, although we know but little of his struggle and have not experienced his pain. He lived in a universe richer than ours, in some ways better than ours, and in some ways more terrible. And yet we recognize his universe and find his attitudes towards it prophetic of our own. It is indeed our own universe, but as experienced by a consciousness which is aware of aspects of which we have but dim and transitory glimpses.[9]

Rarely, if ever, has the prophetic image in music been formulated more lucidly. For the prophet lives indeed 'in a universe richer than ours, in some ways better than ours and in some ways more terrible ... but as experienced by a consciousness which is aware of aspects of which we have but dim transitory glimpses'. And his mission is precisely to confront us with the human condition in all its terrifying ramifications as well as in its ubiquitous hopes.

According to Henri Bergson, art 'has no other objective than to obliterate the utilitarian symbols, the conventional and socially accepted generalities, indeed everything that masks reality, in order to bring us face to face with reality itself'.[10] The great Franco-Jewish philosopher offered this distinctly anti-Romantic view of the affective component in the intellectual life of modern man at a time when Arnold Schoenberg was still struggling to reconcile Wagnerian aesthetics on the one hand with Brahmsian structural procedures on the other. Wagner had spoken of harmony as a sea into which man dives 'only to yield himself again radiantly alive to the light of day'.[11] For he conceived of musical art primarily as a spiritual and ethical purge along Aristotelian lines, a cathartic experience unmatched in its purifying propensity for constant renewal. Brahms, a man of relatively few words, had little to say on the subject. But as a composer he surely acted in accordance with the credo of his contemporary Max Bruch, who once wrote that 'true art should elevate the soul and fortify the spirit, not intoxicate the senses and paralyse the powers of the mind; this continues to be my basic faith even now—that of artistic idealism'.[12] A self-styled member of an imaginary

[9] J. W. N. Sullivan, *Beethoven, His Spiritual Development* (New York, 1949), 19–20.

[10] Henri Bergson, *Œuvres*, ed. André Robinet (Paris, 1970), 462.

[11] Wagner, *Das Kunstwerk der Zukunft*, as cited in *Source Readings in Music History*, ed. Oliver Strunk (New York, 1950), 884.

[12] Cf. Alexander L. Ringer, 'Die Parthey des vernünftigen Fortschritts—Max Bruch und Friedrich Gernsheim', *Die Musikforschung*, 25 (1972), 17.

party dedicated to what he called 'reasonable progress' in music, Bruch resisted the overpowering legacy of Wagner with the determination and deliberate speed of one nurtured on Bach and Mendelssohn. The theatrical fireworks of young Richard Strauss were therefore no less abhorrent to him than the revolutionary pathos of the priest of Bayreuth.

Meanwhile, in Austria the young Mahler was embarked on his epic conquest of an aesthetic-ethical world of unprecedented complexity, designed not so much to furnish a temporary haven of escape from the woes of daily human existence as to strengthen man's rapidly fading faith in his divine potential. Mahler's was a musical 'City of God', as it were, where all men of good will might ultimately find peace and salvation. And Mahler insisted that in the end one may expect no more from the forces above than one's just deserts in accordance with one's efforts on this earth. Egon Wellesz, Arnold Schoenberg's pupil and subsequent biographer, has told how in 1907, shortly before his departure for the United States, Mahler rehearsed his Second Symphony, the 'Resurrection', with the choral ending inspired by the Klopstock ode: 'Rise, yea rise, thou shalt again.' After hours of unsatisfactory responses from an uncomprehending choir, Mahler finally shouted in despair: 'It is the wrestling of Jacob with the angel . . . and Jacob's cry to the angel: "I will not let thee go, except thou bless me." '[13] Till then, the choir members, confronted with a text of unmistakably religious implications, behaved as if in church, singing with folded hands passages that had been composed with a raised fist by a composer whose fundamental posture was that of the prophet Jeremiah: kneeling upright. Curiously enough, Arnold Schoenberg's ultimate conversion to Gustav Mahler and his artistic ideals occurred precisely in 1907. Indeed, it was upon his return from the Vienna railway station where he had gone to bid his idol farewell, that Schoenberg wrote his first song on a text by Stefan George, a song whose relentless motivic activity anticipates not only textural characteristics of the great George cycle Op. 15 but even more complex things to come.

Four years later, Gustav Mahler succumbed to his unceasing conflicts with the powers that be, on earth and in the heavens above, and his saddened protégé set out to chart his own unique course, not only with *Pierrot Lunaire*—the 'solar plexus' of early twentieth-century music, in Stravinsky's apposite terminology—but also with the projected symphony containing the first seeds of the later method of composing with twelve tones. That same year, moreover, Schoenberg picked up where he

[13] Wellesz, 'Reminiscences of Mahler', 55.

had left off with the conclusion of his *Theory of Harmony* (1911), and restated his basic philosophy on a number of important occasions, including the article devoted to 'Problems of Artistic Education', in which he formulated his stance on truth in music. While in the eyes of many truth assumes any number of guises and remains at best relative, depending on how and by whom it is conceived, Schoenberg knew only one truth, the truth not as he saw it but as he received it. For he believed deeply that 'music conveys a prophetic message revealing a higher form of life toward which mankind evolves'.[14]

In *The Stranger* Albert Camus maintains that prophets make us aware of 'the dark winds that blow back from the future'. No doubt, the prophetic message of Schoenberg's monodrama *Erwartung* could be so characterized. From the moment the symbolic heroine begins the search for her beloved in the dark recesses of the forest we find ourselves exposed to precisely such winds blowing back from the future. When that future is finally reached at the end of a half-hour that contains a lifetime, it has long since been known. But then *Erwartung* is the odyssey of alienated man doomed to a future from which there is no escape, man standing at the far side of life, unable to communicate. The quotation from Schoenberg's own song Op. 6, No. 6, 'Am Wegrand', as the drama draws to its inevitable climax, offers irrefutable proof to this effect, if such were needed at all. In the companion piece, *Die glückliche Hand*, the crucial question of *Erwartung*, 'What shall I do here alone in this endless life?', receives at least a partial, implied answer in direct response to the protagonist's material concerns: 'You poor man!—Worldly fortune! You who have the Divine in you yet covet the worldly! And cannot exist! You poor fellow!' Still, the ultimate statement had to await the ultimate drama, *Moses und Aron*, where the Lord summons Moses with the words: 'You have known the truth. You can do nothing else.'

'You can do nothing else; you have known the truth' is, of course, the central tenet of biblical prophecy: I have put before you this day both good and evil. The choice is up to you and your conscience. The prophet represents the collective conscience of a people that has known the truth yet time and again has sought to circumvent, nay deny, historical reality based on the one and only truth. The prophets of old did not inveigle their people nor try to seduce them with words of beautiful sound but little meaning. Instead, they dealt with truth as a weapon, flung at the enemy within no less than the enemy without. The Old Testament knows

---

[14] Schoenberg, *Style and Idea*, 136.

no prophets of doom, only harbingers of reality. It was this biblical axiom
with which Jonah found himself at odds. Compelled by the divine will to
bring the men of Nineveh face to face with their self-inflicted terrors, he
instinctively recoiled from doing what his own 'better' judgement could
not possibly grasp. For, like Aaron, Jonah was at heart a priest,
concerned with the 'proper' image of his people and his faith—indeed
with his personal image—rather than with the truth, irrespective of
where it might lead him. The nineteenth-century worshippers at the altar
of beauty, for their part, had exalted the artist as priest. The concept of
the artist as prophet was alien to the religion of beauty, if only because
the truth, prophetic truth, is frequently quite ugly—probing, as it must,
man's lower depths before it may hope to restore his highest ideals.
Nothing less than a complete transvaluation of artistic values was thus
required if the priestly idea was to yield to the prophetic image in music.
And it is with this Promethean act that the name of Arnold Schoenberg
will be forever associated. For this unprecedented deed, the 'conservative
revolutionary' made his sacrifices, a Moses blessed with the Word of God
but shunned by a people unwilling to shoulder its many heavy burdens.

T. S. Eliot once said that humankind cannot bear much reality, which
is merely another way of saying that humankind cannot really bear much
of itself. If for no other reason, Arnold Schoenberg, the contemporary of
Sigmund Freud, the composer whose work reflected without compromise the Bergsonian conception of the nature and function of music, was
bound to become the public victim of his own intransigence, the
intransigence of the categorical imperative 'It's not that you should, you
must.' Schoenberg himself explained that, while 'a composer speaking of
his own problems speaks at once of the problems of mankind', he
necessarily does so 'in a symbolic way, without having been able, up to
now, to develop definite vocables, expressing matters of philosophy,
economy, or problems of labor, society or morals'.[15] In short, a musical
prophet inevitably deals with truth in purely musical terms, subject to
the inherent limitations as well as the vast unexplored potential of his art.
Where Wagner, the priest, performed his feats of magic, seemingly
oblivious to temporal factors, Schoenberg, the prophet, hit hard, in-
stantly, and, if need be, in monosyllables. Where Strauss, the seducer,
sparkled and cajoled, Schoenberg emerged from his urban desert with
abrasive sonorities aimed at the sham and hypocrisy of those who
perpetually dance around the golden calf. And where Reger, though an

---

[15] Schoenberg, *Arnold Schoenberg Letters*, ed. Erwin Stein (London, 1964), 217.

authentic genius in Schoenberg's estimation, wallowed in the modulatory morass of his chromatic excesses, Schoenberg, one of the few true disciples of Bach and the later Beethoven, moved inexorably and with sharply contoured melodic-rhythmic gestures towards his logical goal. Indeed, where his own pupil Webern found solace in the intimate lyricism of a highly personal world of structural refinement, Schoenberg assaults the listener with often devastating dramatic force engendered by all manner of extreme contrasts—rhythmic, melodic, textural, and harmonic. From a psycho-historical perspective, therefore, stylistic inroads like the much-misunderstood 'emancipation of dissonance' represent but very specific aspects of a comprehensive effort to extricate music from the realm of beauty, in nineteenth-century eyes the eternal preserve of all art, for the sake of naked truth, where compromise is no longer tolerated.

'I prefer Mozart,' Walter Kaufmann declares at the end of *The Faith of a Heretic*, that moving exaltation of prophecy as a modern way of life.

Who doesn't? But one cannot live all the time in lovely music. And one cannot savor its loveliness to the full unless one has suffered much. And one cannot endure it in perpetuity. Can one endure philosophy all the time? Of course not. Even less. Can one endure prophecy all the time? Still less. That is no reason why Jeremiah ought to have kept quiet. When the false prophets cry peace, peace, one should say firmly: There is no peace.[16]

There is no peace for the Chosen One nor for Moses, and in the end Schoenberg found no more peace than Nietzsche. For the false sense of peace eagerly embraced by the many who, in Eliot's words, cannot face much reality was alien to all of them. Thus, if the emergence of Arnold Schoenberg as a mature, powerful artist did represent an actual break with the European musical tradition as it had developed over the centuries, it was not because he felt that once tonality had seemingly reached its highest chromatic potential the time had come to do away with it, not because his unquestioned propensity for logic made the dodecaphonic reorganization of pitches inevitable, nor because the abandonment of relativistic for absolute criteria imposed the emancipation of dissonance as a matter of consistency; it was because, endowed by Providence with the faculties to carry out in the aesthetic realm the dictates of his ethical convictions, this truly committed man of his time managed to give music a modern dimension determined solely by his

[16] Walter Kaufmann, *The Faith of a Heretic* (New York, 1963), 406.

philosophical concern for its ultimate prophetic message. In the wellnigh untranslatable words of T. W. Adorno:

The shocks of the unintelligible, which artistic technique provides in this its senseless age, are ultimately transformed; they illuminate a senseless world. For this goal the new music makes its sacrifices. Upon its shoulders rests all the darkness and guilt of the world. All its good fortunes stem from the recognition of misfortune; all its beauty from the denial of the illusion of beauty.[17]

[17] Theodor W. Adorno, *Philosophie der neuen Musik* (Frankfurt am Main, 1958), 126.

2

The Quest for Language: 'Oh Word . . . that I Lack'

IN early 1950, a year and a half before his death, Arnold Schoenberg told his young American colleague Halsey Stevens: 'I was never very capable of expressing my feelings or emotions in words. I do not know whether this is the reason for my doing so in music and also why I did it in painting or vice versa.'[1] Be this as it may, however, since 'I had this as an outlet, I could renounce expressing something in words', even though 'as a painter I was absolutely an amateur'. Whether or not time will uphold the composer's own appraisal of his worth as a visual artist—the critical reception of the first New York showing of a large number of his paintings in the company of such illustrious Viennese contemporaries as Gustav Klimt and Egon Schiele was rather divided—his assertion that, as a rule, words failed to do justice to his deepest feelings, would seem to be contradicted by the sheer range and quantity, not to speak of the often remarkable quality of his literary bequest. Yet his invariably ambivalent stance with regard to language was quite consistent with a unique body of creative achievement that has remained somewhat of an enigma to this day, perhaps because its underlying motivation was not so much aesthetic as philosophical in nature.

Schoenberg was of a generation blessed with a host of talents of similar cultural background and outlook who found themselves on a Central European cultural stage brimming with complex personalities in the most diverse areas of human concern: Albert Einstein and Sigmund Freud, Stefan George and Karl Kraus, Arthur Schnitzler and Martin Buber, Wassily Kandinsky and Oscar Kokoschka, Else Lasker-Schüler and Karl Wolfskehl. The last two in particular shared his personal fate in more ways than one, since they too were Jews, born and raised in Central Europe, with a burning commitment to German culture in general and the German language in particular, yet forced to end their days as

---

[1] 'Schoenberg Talks About His Paintings', *Arnold Schönberg Gedenkausstellung 1974*, ed. Ernst Hilmar (Vienna, 1974), 110.

refugees from the intellectual world they knew and loved—Lasker-Schüler finding peace in the Jewish homeland rebuilt during her lifetime, Wolfskehl down under, where everything, as far as he was concerned was upside-down. But then it may have been mere poetic justice that sent the George disciple to such an exotic far-away land as New Zealand, while 'the mother of Expressionism', who believed, with her friend Gottfried Benn, in 'going straight to the root of things', went straight to Palestine. Unlike some contemporaries of similar background, at any rate, neither Lasker-Schüler nor her fellow poet Richard Beer-Hoffmann ever forgot whence they hailed nor, for that matter, what potentially lay in store for them. And the same goes, curious as it may seem at first blush, for Arnold Schoenberg, who nominally turned to Christianity at the age of twenty-four yet never changed his basic attitude with regard to the spiritual ideals of his people, a people historically committed to being different and to enduring whatever hardships might lie in store for those determined to live and labour at the behest of a single abstract idea, the very existence of which depended by definition on men and women ready to ensure its perpetuation at any price. As Schoenberg himself put it: 'We Jews call ourselves the chosen people of the Lord and are the keepers of his promise. And we know that we were chosen only to think the thought of the one, eternal, unimaginable, invisible God through to completion, in short to keep it alive! And there is nothing that can compare with that mission . . .'[2]

Schoenberg's personal mission, and most certainly his quest for language as a crucial aspect of that mission, cannot be properly understood except in the larger context of that all-embracing mission as he understood it—indeed as it was understood by a substantial minority of his intellectual generation. Richard Beer-Hoffmann, who grappled with the problem of chosenness all his life, made it the focal issue of his *David* trilogy, a poetic drama of monumental proportions, intended, it seems, as a pointed Jewish answer to Wagner's *Ring of the Nibelung*. Like Wagner, whose ideas for the *Ring* had evolved from his interpretation of events leading to Siegfried's death, Beer-Hoffmann turned his attention first to the end of David's often tortured life, then proceeded with the Prologue, *Jacob's Dream*, in which the prophetic component in Israel's existence, embodied in the life of David, becomes the subject of a poetic description of rare linguistic strength and beauty. Martin Buber, himself approaching the end of his life, concluded his brief yet sensitive introduction to the

---

[2] Cf. Eberhard Freitag, *Schönberg* (Hamburg, 1973), 133.

collected works of Beer-Hoffmann with this paradigmatic characterization of David's path toward death: 'from the grace of having been chosen, through sin, to that higher grace accorded him who returns'.[3]

Left unfinished, the *David* trilogy shared the fate of the principal works of Arnold Schoenberg inspired by ancient Jewish lore: *Die Jakobsleiter*, begun just two years after Beer-Hoffmann completed *Jacob's Dream*, and *Moses und Aron*. The close affinities between Arnold Schoenberg, Richard Beer-Hoffmann and Martin Buber, remain to be substantiated in detail. But, if nothing else, the composer's oratorio plans of 1912 are evidence of his resolve, even then, to deal in explicitly religious terms with spiritual issues merely alluded to in his 'drama with music', *Die glückliche Hand*. While neither the oratorio nor the modified scheme for a choral symphony of truly Mahlerian proportions ever reached fruition, the latter was to have been based not only on Schoenberg's own texts but also on excerpts from both ancient and modern prophets (Isaiah, Jeremiah, Rabindranath Tagore).[4] One of the original pieces *Totentanz der Prinzipien* ('Dance of Death of all Principles'), was eventually published, together with the libretto for *Die glückliche Hand*, the unconventional *Requiem* upon the death of Mathilde Schoenberg, and, above all, the complete text of the unfinished *Jakobsleiter*, where the ideas and sentiments underlying the earlier oratorio-proposal of 1912 found their ultimate artistic crystallization. By then, to be sure, Arnold Schoenberg—the musician, philosopher, theologian, and writer—had proceeded steadily towards 'that higher grace accorded him who returns'.

Schoenberg's manifold literary activities, like his music, at first displayed the inescapable characteristics of an artistically gifted young man growing up in post-Wagnerian Europe. Leaving aside juvenilia of the sort that any half-way gifted Romantic youngster was likely, if not expected, to produce, his first creative attempt involved an opera libretto. After completing two acts based on Gustav von Schwab's popular farce *Die Schildbürger*, however, he abandoned that project for good. Among some of the other youthful fragments, one actually does point to the future. It is entitled *Aberglaube* (Superstition) and deals with a subject that was to preoccupy him all his life. Still, it was not until 1910, when he published his first aphorisms and began work on the scenario of *Die glückliche Hand*, that Schoenberg embarked fully on a literary career of

---

[3] Martin Buber, 'Geleitwort', in Richard Beer-Hoffmann, *Gesammelte Werke* (Frankfurt, 1963), 12.

[4] Cf. Josef Rufer, *The Works of Arnold Schoenberg*, 115.

prose and poetry, drama and short story, essays and criticism, and, last but not least, numerous texts for his own music.

Four poets stand out among those to whom he turned in the interim for literary and hence also musical guidance: Richard Dehmel, Maurice Maeterlinck, Stefan George, and Rainer Maria Rilke, more or less in that order. Dehmel and Maeterlinck inspired some of his finest tonal compositions. George, on the other hand, triggered the stylistic-structural breakthrough with which the name of Arnold Schoenberg has been associated ever since. However, if it is true, as he stated unequivocally himself, that George's sonorous evocations helped him a good way along the difficult road beyond the last remaining barriers of harmonic-functional convention, Rilke's intensely spiritual poetry would seem to have had an only slightly lesser share in the subsequent emergence of his new compositional 'law'. Thus Op. 22, a crucial work on the cutting-edge of pan-tonality, comprises settings of two poems from Rilke's *Book of Hours*, 'All Who Seek Thee' and 'Make Me the Guardian of Thy Realms', and one, 'Premonition', from the *Book of Images*. For the remaining song, last in the final version of the set but completed well before the others, Schoenberg relied on George's translation of Ernest Dowson's 'Seraphita'. The first two of the Rilke songs were composed in January 1915, shortly before Schoenberg's mobilization. 'Premonition', on the other hand, had to await his temporary demobilization in the autumn of 1916, and by the time he finished it a severe depression had taken hold of him.[5] For, as millions rallied around their respective flags, blessed ceremoniously in the name of the Prince of Peace but unfurled in an open spirit of hatred, Schoenberg had begun wondering with Rilke whether the world-wide 'death-dance of principles' did not also spell the death of a god fashioned in the image of man. Only the artist of genius, ordained by the divine lawgiver and supreme force of history, seemed left to carry the torch of truth into an unfathomable future. Perhaps more than anything it is this particular idea promulgated by Rilke yet remarkably in tune with traditional Jewish notions of man created in the image of God, which distinguishes 'the Chosen One' in *Die Jakobsleiter* from all the rest: from the monk, who finally recognizes the irony of self-sacrifice on the part of one who never dares expose himself to temptation; from the rebel, unwilling to condone the apparent paradoxes in the way of the Lord; from the one who thinks of himself as called upon to exalt beauty, yet in the end turns only around his own sun; and, indeed, from

---

[5] Cf. Stuckenschmidt, *Schönberg*, 223.

the one who honestly struggles for the truth but despairs at the thought that man has no way of 'sensing unspoken laws'. Only the Chosen One accepts willingly to be both 'prophet and martyr'.

Chosenness, as postulated by Schoenberg, implies total, enduring devotion to the unimaginable, invisible lawgiver. But this very idea, though quite in accordance with Jewish tradition, also entails a latent anthropomorphic problem, since the Living God revealed Himself to His people through the written word, the word of a law that was to become its lasting constitution, if not its portable homeland, across the centuries of dispersion.[6] Schoenberg proposed to resolve this admittedly vexing issue by embracing the saving power of prayer, less as a means of currying favour with the Supreme Being than as a God-granted dialogue with the higher self, the ultimate safeguard of man's spiritual dignity and self-fulfilment. As he put it in the last of his *Modern Psalms*:

> Oh Thou my God
> Thy grace has left us prayer
> As a tie, a blissful tie with Thee
> Bliss that gives us far more than fulfillment.

That very same conception of prayer permeates the final monologue of the archangel Gabriel in *Die Jakobsleiter*, a monologue that remained uncomposed because it could not be composed, just as that final work, the *Modern Psalm*, Op. 50c, was destined to break off at the words 'and yet I pray'. Prayer is man's quest for spirituality. And, even though 'God was always,' Gabriel asserts that, 'in the beginning was the spirit, the spirit of creation. And what it produced by perpetuating itself could only be less than what it was itself. That is how infinite space and infinite time came about—the finite yielded what is without end.'[7] If this is so, then surely spiritual man faces an insurmountable difficulty, and nowhere has this tragic dilemma found a more heart-rending expression in Schoenberg's work than in the final lines of Moses, about to 'sink to the ground in despair' as the second and last completed act of *Moses und Aron* draws to its inevitable conclusion:

---

[6] 'We lost our state but not our constitution; we saved it and turned it into a portable state, as it were, that gave us a measure of national autonomy in the diaspora as well.' Jakob Klatzkin, *Probleme des modernen Judentums*, 3rd rev. edn. (Berlin, 1930), 43. Klatzkin, a Schoenberg correspondent of the early 1930s, insisted also that the concept of Divine Oneness and uniqueness had generated in ancient Israel 'the idea of national unity and oneness and thus the fundamental notion of nationhood'. Ibid., 205.

[7] All translations from Schoenberg's German, unless otherwise identified, are the author's.

Inconceivable God!
Inexpressible, many-sided idea,
will you let it be so explained?
Shall Aaron, my mouth, fashion this image?
Then I have fashioned an image, too, false,
as an image must be.
Thus am I defeated!
Thus, all was but madness that
I believed before,
and can and must not be given voice.
O word, thou word, that I lack!

No other passage from Schoenberg's extensive literary output quite manages to convey with equal poignancy his own ambivalent stance with respect to verbal expression, an inherent personal problem for one so genuinely devoted to logic and unequivocal comprehension. Long before he identified the 'inconceivable God' with pure idea 'inexpressible and many-sided', as early as 1910 in fact, he had spoken of 'the work of art produced by man' as 'God's greatest creation'.[8] Yet, while struggling with the 'inexpressible and many-sided', he steadfastly trusted in the power of the word in general, and that of prayer in particular. In short, Moses, the man of pure idea, and Aaron, the communicator, reflect a spiritual dichotomy at the very roots of the Schoenbergian dialectic, which, in its ultimate synthesis of the most divergent aesthetic, ethical, and strictly religious elements, generated an entirely new concept of music as the lone prophetic voice of morality in a world of rampant materialism.

In 1909 Schoenberg swore off the last vestiges of nineteenth-century harmonic convention with that remarkable triad of works: the Piano Pieces, Op. 11, the Orchestral Pieces, Op. 16, and the 'monodrama' *Erwartung*. The year after, he pointedly defined modern art as creative man's ultimate 'cry of despair'.[9] Not unlike Edvard Munch's atavistic 'scream' of unmitigated horror, painted well before the turn of the century, Schoenberg's 'cry of despair' was directed at the sensitive few willing and able to contend with the self-inflicted misfortunes of Western civilization, uncompromisingly sacrificing, if need be, Romantic ideas of beauty to the exigencies of unforgiving truth. And it is from this characteristic perspective that he came to regard his Fifteen Songs from Stefan George's *Buch der hängenden Gärten* as a milestone in his personal

---

[8] Cf. Schoenberg, *Schöpferische Konfessionen*, 13.
[9] Ibid., 12.

artistic development. As he readily admitted in the course of that same year—1910—the requisite expressive and formal ideas had eluded him time and time again because 'I was lacking until then in both strength and self-confidence. And now that I have embarked in this direction I realize that I have broken through all the barriers of a past aesthetic.'[10]

Stefan George had served Schoenberg well on at least two hardly less crucial occasions immediately preceding the *Fifteen Songs*, Op. 15. The highly emotional farewell to his friend and protector Gustav Mahler at a Vienna railway station inspired the haunting setting of *Ich darf nicht dankend an dir niedersinken*. And George's *Litanie* and *Entrückung*, furnished the texts for the two vocal movements of his Second String Quartet, where the suggestion of total 'removal', of air from 'another planet' resulted in nothing less than the temporary abandonment of any centre of harmonic gravity. It was thus the symbolistic imagery of the poet-father of the German youth-movement which, ironic though it may seem with the hindsight of history, became the decisive catalytic agent for the new musical chemistry that was to yield some of Schoenberg's most original and penetrating compositions.

Why a composer straining for an aesthetic breakthrough should have felt attracted to a poet whose devotion to the system of Classical metres, as adapted to the German language by Goethe and Hölderlin, was axiomatic, is not easily explained, unless one believes with Karl Ehrenforth that Schoenberg, fully aware of his propensity for extraordinary achievement under contrary conditions, deliberately chose such apparent barriers only to transcend them triumphantly in his idiosyncratic creative ways.[11] Whatever the case, it does seem odd at first blush that Schoenberg should have made a careful choice of strictly metrical texts merely in order to obviate their most characteristic structural features in distinctly ametrical musical settings. Most probably he proceeded in this instance, as in so many others, in accordance with that basic conception of the 'relationship to the text' which was to be the subject of his contribution to Der blaue Reiter. There, he went to considerable lengths to defend his ostensibly ambivalent position with respect to the textual components of his own work and that of others: 'Inspired by the first words of the text,' he wrote, 'I had composed many of my songs straight through to the end without troubling myself in the slightest about the continuation of the

<hr />

[10] Ibid., 23. For a somewhat different translation of this passage from the introductory note to the first performance, 14 January 1910, see Egon Wellesz, *Arnold Schönberg* (London, n.d.), 26.

[11] Karl Heinrich Ehrenforth, *Ausdruck und Form* (Bonn, 1963), 47.

poetic events, without even grasping them in the ecstasy of composing.'[12] From such a strictly musical perspective Stefan George offered an imaginative composer unquestioned advantages. For in his poetry 'events' of the more traditional sort are interiorized to the point where they retain significance only at the behest of ever-evolving modulations of minutely differentiated moods.[13] By the same token, George's verse lends itself readily to multiple interpretations, a characteristic that must have had singular appeal for one who reacted to 'sound alone, with perfection that by analysis and synthesis could hardly have been attained, but certainly not surpassed'.[14] Hugo von Hofmannsthal once used the term *Halbgefühle*, literally 'semi-feelings' in connection with George's poetry. Schoenberg, for his part, extolled the aesthetic virtues of Kandinsky and Kokoschka, who painted 'pictures the objective theme of which is hardly more than an excuse to improvise in colors and forms', and expressed the fervent hope that 'those who ask about the texts, about the subject matter, will soon ask no more'.[15]

Stefan George's semi-abstract verse seemed thus ready-made for a musical response which, oblivious to the conventions of prosody as practised for centuries, pitted the composer's own counterpoint, as it were, against the sonorous verbal *cantus firmus* furnished by the poet. The Rhinelander George thought of himself as a faithful disciple of Stéphane Mallarmé, the French symbolist whose first name he shared and whose refined style had found such exquisite musical reflections in the work of Debussy, beginning well before *Prélude à l'après-midi d'un faune*, the very composition which in the eyes of many marks the onset of modern music. Debussy had set Mallarmé as early as 1884, shortly after his return from Russia. Three decades later he eulogized the poet with his *Trois Poèmes de Stéphane Mallarmé*, his last major work for voice and piano, of which it has been said with a good deal of justification that 'the poems present a kind of continuous enigma: the musician has tried to decipher it and to communicate it to his listeners'.[16] In composing George's *Book of the Hanging Gardens* Arnold Schoenberg apparently

---

[12] Schoenberg, *Style and Idea* (New York, 1975), 144.

[13] In the preface to the volume in which the *Das Buch der hängenden Gärten* first appeared (1898) George refers to 'mirror reflections of a soul that has sought temporary refuge in other times and places'. Cf. Albrecht Dümling, *Die fremden Klänge der hängenden Gärten* (Munich, 1981), 61.

[14] Schoenberg, *Style and Idea*, 144.

[15] Ibid., 14.

[16] Léon Vallas, *Achille-Claude Debussy* (Paris, 1944), 115.

aimed at a similar 'exegesis' of a series of poems possessed of kindred enigmatic qualities. He certainly chose his fifteen *Gesänge* carefully from the central portion of George's considerably larger poetic entity. For, as it happens, the two surrounding groups of poems, which he omitted, would have provided a discernible frame for a story-line of sorts. Schoenberg, in other words, eliminated what little exterior context George furnished, thus reinforcing the poetic enigma, as if to underscore his self-confessed inability to grasp poetic 'events' in the 'ecstasy of composing'.

As originally published, the carefully veiled story of the *Book of the Hanging Gardens* involves the rise and decline of a young Oriental potentate who, after heroic conquests, succumbs to his passion for one destined for his rival. In the end he returns, stripped of power and fame, to his prior state of political subservience. George had been partial to the *Arabian Tales of a Thousand and One Nights* from early youth on, and their influence is easily traced in the *Hanging Gardens*. But the fifteen *Gesänge* selected by Schoenberg in particular reflect also some of the general atmosphere and, in a number of specific instances, the actual phraseology of the biblical Song of Songs. Whatever his exact literary sources, though, George took advantage of the greatest possible variety of sonorous patterns to convey in the richest of verbal colours the many-splendoured facets of love blossoming, consummated, and ultimately doomed, in a social environment where individual happiness, however extraordinary and intrinsically valid, must never interfere with the established order. The true drama concealed behind the hedges of the hanging gardens is that of man forcibly alienated from himself, from society at large, and most tragically, from those most dear to him. Under these circumstances there can be no real denouement, only resignation.

Schoenberg's brief yet so crucial George period coincided with a profound personal crisis precipitated by the growing intimacy between his first wife, Mathilde Zemlinsky, and the young painter Richard Gerstl, who had attached himself to the Schoenberg circle and was in fact living in the same building while painting members of the family. Gerstl's suicide in 1908 merely exacerbated what had by then become an exceedingly complex psychological situation. Schoenberg's specific text-choices and their musical treatment reflect no doubt his intensely emotional state, at a time, moreover, when his at first hesitant attitude towards Gustav Mahler, the artist and the man, changed to total commitment. Op. 14, No. 1, *Ich darf nicht dankend an dir niedersinken* ('I may not in gratitude sink down before you'), is clearly autobiographical,

not only textually, to be sure, but also in its almost obsessive insistence on
the motivic substance generated by the initial four words. *Litanie*, on the
other hand, the third movement of the Second String Quartet, ends with
the wish 'take my love from me and give me your bliss', while *Entrückung*
desperately yearns for 'air from another planet'. And as for the personal
elements in the *Book of the Hanging Gardens*, the composer eventually
told his pupil Alban Berg, though not specifically in connection with his
Op. 15, 'everything I have written has a certain inner likeness to
myself'.[17] Needless to say, where a personality as complex and often
outright paradoxical as Schoenberg's is concerned, any such likeness
necessarily has a multitude of intricate origins and implications. Gerstl
taught Schoenberg most of what he knew in a formal way about painting
but in the process fell in love with his wife Mathilde. Unable to cope with
an intolerable triangular relationship, he committed suicide in November
1908, less than three months after Schoenberg completed *Litanie*.
George, of course, shared the striking sensitivity to visual stimulation
that manifested itself in Schoenberg's vocal output virtually from the
very outset. The beautiful setting of Richard Dehmel's *Erwartung*, Op. 2,
No. 1, is a particularly effective case in point. George's poetry abounds
with even more plentiful references to all kinds of shapes and colours
than Dehmel's and the George circle generally worshipped the fine arts.
And Schoenberg, significantly, did some of his best painting during the
two or three years following the composition of Op. 15.

George's predilection for visual metaphors was part and parcel of the
same essentially French orientation that had caused him to abandon
initial capitals in German nouns and to circumvent whenever possible the
harsher German consonants. His was, however, by no means the sole
attempt to rescue the German language from the devastating influence of
quasi-military parlance. Hugo von Hofmannsthal, mindful perhaps of
Goethe's one-time flirtation with Italian, suggested the study of Italian as
a remedy. And it was along somewhat similar lines that Schoenberg
admonished the singer Maria Schoeffer in 1913: 'Don't articulate the text
too sharply; instead bring out the musical-vocal qualities of the melodic
lines! And don't emphasize a word that my melody drops by the wayside.
Please, no "intelligent" caesurae suggested by the text. Where a comma
is needed, I have taken care of it in my composition.'[18] In other words,
Schoenberg wished to counteract some of the basic characteristics of

---

[17] *Arnold Schoenberg Letters*, ed. Erwin Stein, 143.
[18] Cf. H. H. Stuckenschmidt, *Schönberg*, 173.

conventional German declamation. A French singer might have seen little out of the ordinary in these instructions, which must have shocked one brought up with the conventional wisdom of Central European vocal training.

Schoenberg's affinity with contemporary French music speaks at least indirectly from his *Harmonielehre* ('Theory of Harmony'), which also dates from 1911. The issue, however, is not whether Debussy furnished actual models, but whether the two composers who completed their respective musical treatments of Maeterlinck's *Pelléas et Mélisande* within less than a year's time did not have much more in common aesthetically than has generally been acknowledged. That one proceeded within the established bounds of French recitative whereas the other forced the already hard-pressed limits of the German symphonic tradition close to breaking-point was in the nature of things musical in post-Wagnerian Europe. One would certainly not wish to imply that Schoenberg's Op. 15 bears more of a resemblance to the music of Debussy than George's verse to Mallarmé's. Its intense motivic continuity alone negates any such idea, and the same holds true for the pre-eminence of the piano-part as the principal carrier of musical 'events' suggested by George's poetic vision. Still, a song like 'Colloque sentimental', with which Debussy concluded his second set of Verlaine's *Fêtes galantes* in 1904, does bear certain resemblances with Schoenberg's George settings at least in general textual terms, not to speak of a basic 'relationship to the text'.

Years after completing Op. 15 Schoenberg observed that 'the musician is in a position that permits him to place himself relatively unmoved next to his text'.[19] But it was in his intimate setting of the *Hanging Gardens* that he first gave wellnigh perfect artistic shape to this decidedly aromantic stance. What Op. 15 proves so uniquely is that, precisely because he is able to place himself relatively unmoved *next* to his text, the composer manages to draw *from* that text emotional accents well beyond the reach of the spoken words, albeit spoken by the most skilful of actors. For Schoenberg, though seemingly oblivious to the metrical patterning, did take full musical advantage of the accentual properties of individual words as much as of the sonorous qualities of others.

His procedure is evident from the very beginning (Ex. 1). A true metric-melodic accent does not occur in the opening song until the first syllable of *blättergründen*. The many *sh* sounds that permeate the first five

---

[19] Schoenberg, *Texte* (Vienna, 1926), 6.

Ex. 1. Op. 15,1

men ih - re Lei - den kün - den, Fa - bel -

tie - re aus den brau - nen Schlün -

den Strah - len in die Mar - mor - be - cken spei - en, draus die klei - nen

etwas drängend

Bä - che kla - gend ei - len, ka - men Ker - zen

flüchtig

wieder beruhigend

das Ge - sträuch ent - zün - den, wei - ße For - men das Ge -

wäs - ser tei - len.

lines of the poem (*sch*, *sp*, or *st* in German), on the other hand, receive the closest possible musical attention. Thus the low B with which the vocal part begins aptly projects the sense of darkness associated with the thicket of leaves that furnishes the protection (*schutz*). Once that association has been established, its recurrence on the first syllable of *sternen* ('stars') makes its 'exegetic' point without fail. Gradually the *sh* sonority lightens, first on *schneien* ('snowing'), then rising to A flat in the same measure on *stimmen* ('voices'). After reaching its melodic climax with the A natural on *schlünden* ('apertures') it drops back to F sharp for the immediately following word *strahlen*, declining further to E on *speien* at the beginning of bar 15. By sharp contrast, the last three lines of the poem eschew *sh* sounds altogether and rely primarily on sonorous vowels, with a corresponding shift to a higher tessitura for both the voice and the piano.

Such intimate relationships between the music of George's poetry and the poetry of Schoenberg's music mark the entire cycle. Indeed, it appears that the interval of the third owes its crucial motivic importance for the whole cycle to a primary creative response to the initial *sh* sonorities typically followed by long vowels. Spontaneous action of this sort would certainly have been consistent with the composer's acknowledgement that, 'inspired by the sound of the first words of the text' he composed many of his songs 'straight through to the end'. In the case of a song cycle, one would assume, this general procedure pertained to all the constituent songs, functioning as a single entity. That the third, whether major or minor, rising or falling, has no exclusive hold on the wealth of motivic variation and development in the structural *tour de force* that is Schoenberg's Op. 15, goes without saying. Still, thirdal motion governs much of the melodic activity from the passacaglia-like bass-opening of the first song to the elaborate postlude with which the cycle concludes, in the grand tradition of Beethoven (*An die ferne Geliebte*) and Schumann (*Frauenliebe und -leben*).

Enchainments of adjacent thirds were, of course, to remain typical of Schoenberg's musical language well beyond the discovery of the 'method of composing with twelve tones related only to one another'. Yet that simple interval never retained such fundamental significance for a single extended work, except in the case of the Piano Pieces, Op. 11, the first of which was finished nine days before the completion of the last George song. In a sense Op. 11 represents, as it were, the purely instrumental side of the George coin, exceeding its vocal counterpart rather typically in the breadth and intensity of its rhetorical gestures.

The aesthetic breakthrough to which Schoenberg referred in his programme note of 1910 left none of the musical elements, let alone their interactions, untouched. Op. 15 proceeds also in this respect with the uncompromising logic that produced first the celebrated 'emancipation of dissonance' and eventually, with equal inevitability, the new twelve-tone polyphony. Thirds in every conceivable size, combination, and direction determine not only much of the melodic course of events but the harmonic infrastructure as well. Minor and major thirds in simultaneous and successive combinations account for many apparent harmonic complexities, always in conjunctions with, and in support of, purely melodic ideas, as at the beginning of the second song (Ex. 2),

Ex. 2. Op. 15,2

where an arpeggiated seventh chord (D–F–A–C♯) anticipates the principal tones of the vocal line that follows, in a manner reminiscent of the
ominous D minor triad at the onset of *Nun hast Du mir den ersten
Schmerz getan*, the recitative-like finale of Schumann's *Frauenliebe und
-leben*. The constituent elements of that minor–major seventh chord,
moreover, turn out to have ramifications far beyond the confines of this
particular song. Not only does its upper component, the augmented
triad, foreshadow an essential aspect of the cycle's harmonic idiom; the
lower D minor triad provides one of the sparse axes around which the
harmonic structure revolves. Striking examples are the tenth song, where
it furnishes the primary sonority, and the last, where it serves to stabilize
not only the prelude but also the postlude, with which the cycle pays
Schumann a final homage.

In his programmatic contribution to Der blaue Reiter Arnold Schoenberg proudly identified himself with Schopenhauer's 'wonderful
thought' that 'the composer reveals the inmost essence of the world and
utters the most profound wisdom in a language which his reason does not
understand'.[20] And it goes without saying that in so doing he also
endorsed the position of Romantics like Wordsworth and Walter Pater,
who believed, with Schopenhauer, that 'all art aspires to the condition of
music' and that music is so ideally suited for the communication of 'deep'
meanings precisely because it lacks semantic specificity. Less than a year
earlier he had sent Karl Kraus a copy of his newly published *Harmonielehre* with a personal dedication in which he confessed: 'I have perhaps
learned more from you than one is permitted to learn if one wants to
remain independent.'[21] Yet, reflecting on 'Problems in Teaching Art' at
just about the same time, he did not hesitate to cite Kraus's insistence on
language as the mother of all thought as an instance of rather problematic
reasoning, because 'feeling is already form, the idea is already the word'.[22]
And if his younger fellow-Viennese Ludwig Wittgenstein wondered how
much of a given thought actually remained discernible in the guise of
language, Schoenberg for his part was convinced that in the end language
'carries only the man who would be capable, if it did not exist, of
inventing it himself'.[23] Indeed, once the George songs had 'broken
through all barriers of a past esthetic', regarding 'the relationship to the
text' no less than in strictly musical terms, it seemed only logical to take

---

[20] Schoenberg, *Style and Idea*, 142.
[21] Schoenberg, *Schöpferische Konfessionen*, 21.
[22] Schoenberg, *Style and Idea*, 369.
[23] Ibid.

another step along the lines of the 'Melodrama' in the recently completed *Gurrelieder*. Thanks largely to the surrealistic qualities of the speechsong employed to convey the dreamlike visions of Otto Erich Hartleben's *Dreimal sieben Gedichte*, after the French of Albert Giraud, *Pierrot Lunaire* begot an entirely new musical language in which the semantic message has been uniquely sublimated. A year later, in that ultimate Schoenbergian 'cry of despair' prior to the First World War, the 'Drama with Music' *Die glückliche Hand*, verbal communication virtually ceases following the admonition of the heavenly chorus of two times six voices that man created in the divine image has no business going after material wealth at the inevitable expense of moral imperatives.

The revealing remark 'everything that I have written has a certain inner likeness to myself' appears in a letter ostensibly devoted to problems of *Moses und Aron*. No doubt almost any artist of the first order might have made the same observation. But Schoenberg's unequivocal identification with the biblical figure of Moses on the one hand, and his ostensible ambivalence towards Moses' *alter ego* Aaron on the other lend a very special significance to its direct association with the unfinished stage work in which the composer's personal dilemma found its most shattering expression. Here, as early as Scene Four of the First Act, long before the golden-calf episode, the desperate lawgiver comes to the tragic conclusion that his 'thought is powerless in Aaron's words'. In the end, in that Third Act, which, though magnificently projected, was never composed, Aaron literally becomes the prisoner of his very special capacity for speech, for interpretation. Yet, paradoxically, it is Aaron who sings throughout, whereas Moses communicates only in his speaking voice. His thoughts remain within the 'pure', 'non-material' realm of music, unsullied by compromise, whether ethical or aesthetic. Clearly, as conceived by one who admired Kraus, Kandinsky, and Kokoschka for their disavowal of 'the objective theme' in favour of modes of expression previously associated only with music, Aaron, though chosen to serve as Israel's first high priest, fails because, limited to words, he cannot but simplify and hence distort the divine message. As Moses is forced to admit:

> And the rock, even as all images,
> Obeys the word
> from which it came to be manifested.
> Thus, you won the people not for the eternal one
> but for yourself . . .

By the end of the Second Act all seems lost. As the people call upon their new god, one 'stronger than the gods of Egypt', Moses declares himself 'beaten'. Finally realizing the total inadequacy of 'Aaron, my mouth', he concludes that his awesome thoughts 'cannot and must not be spoken . . . Oh word, thou word that I lack.' At this point the music stops altogether, leaving the score in limbo. The text, of course, continues, giving Aaron a chance to defend himself. Whatever he may have done, it was for the freedom of Israel, 'that it may become a nation'. Moses exclaims: 'to serve, to serve the divine idea is the purpose of the freedom for which this folk has been chosen'. Set free at Moses' command, Aaron falls lifeless to the ground. Symbol of the word, the image, he succumbs so that the idea may survive. Whether or not one agrees with this conception theologically, dramatically Schoenberg managed thus to project with unprecedented force the essence of Israel's transcendent mission. By the same token, his failure to compose the Third Act of *Moses und Aron*, an otherwise puzzling phenomenon, assumes cultural significance of a very special order as the subconscious concomitant of his axiomatic identification with a purely spiritual idea so all-encompassing that it 'cannot and must not' be explicitly communicated.

In the spoken drama *Der biblische Weg*, written in 1926 as 'a very up-to-date treatment . . . of the story of how the Jews became a people',[24] Schoenberg combined Moses, the anthropomorphic symbol of the idea, and Aaron, its verbal manipulator, in the single figure of Max Aruns, the journalist become Zionist leader. Max Aruns is doomed to failure because for Schoenberg, at that time still nominally beyond the pale of Judaism, the biblical path, though the true path, was, in the apposite words of his early friend and companion David Bach, 'at the same time the wrong one, just as life intermingles with death'.[25] Incapacitated by his Aruns component, Max is unfit for the realization of 'the idea' as subsequently formulated by his young successor: 'We want to attain perfection of the spirit, want to be allowed to dream our dream of God — like all the peoples who put the material world behind them.' Because the immaterial world of the dream is by definition incompatible with semantic reality, this seminal drama was never published, just as *Moses und Aron* had to remain symbolically unfinished. The antecedent of both, the oratorio *Die Jakobsleiter*, was neither finished nor published during the composer's lifetime, as if to ensure that such highly personal

---

[24] *Arnold Schoenberg: Letters*, 369.

[25] Cf. Reich, *Schoenberg: A Critical Biography* (New York, 1971), 160.

philosophical concerns would in the future be subjected to non-verbal, purely musical treatment. *Die Jakobsleiter* was bound to remain in limbo, not because any 'newly found possibilities' precluded its completion, but because the new method of composing with twelve tones was the abstract embodiment of the oratorio's spiritual quest. Hence, too, it would seem, the decision to publish its text separately. The unresolved aesthetic-ethical dilemma posed by the opera *Moses und Aron* in turn led, a decade later, to the restoration of traditional structural procedures with due regard for the inherent requirements of 'the new method'. Schoenberg put the crux of the matter in so many words when on 20 July 1922 he wrote to Kandinsky that, had it not been for the kind of religion that motivated his *Jacobsleiter*, he surely would have succumbed to the years of struggle for a totally new approach, having forsaken the relative security of the old: 'For a man for whom ideas have been everything that means nothing less than the total collapse of things, unless he has come to find support, in ever increasing measure, in a belief in something higher, beyond.'[26]

Seen in this light, as a historical stepping stone, the significance of Op. 15 exceeds even that of an unqualifiedly brilliant artistic realization of a 'new expressive and formal ideal'. For, once the text no longer acts as a limiting factor in the creative process but, on the contrary, serves to evoke meanings ostensibly unrelated to its explicit semantic content, music becomes 'absolute' in the deepest sense of that much-abused term, pointing indeed to 'something higher, beyond'. Henceforth Schoenberg no longer attempted to give musical expression to a chosen text in all its poetic detail; he sought rather to find intrinsically musical ways for the conveyance of meaning beyond the power of words. And *Pierrot Lunaire* offered the perfect initial opportunity. Encouraged by the terms of the commission to relegate the text to a speaking voice, he turned it into a mere pretext. As he told Marya Freund, one of its early interpreters, who wondered about audience reactions: 'If they were musical, not a single one of them would give a damn for the words. Instead they would go away whistling the tunes.'[27] Be this as it may, the passacaglia of 'Nacht' and the crab canon of 'Mondfleck' are surely instances of philosophical discourse through musical structure in the long tradition of spiritual music from Guillaume de Machaut, Josquin des Prés, and Johann Sebastian Bach.

The extent to which Schoenberg came to regard musical structure and

[26] *Arnold Schoenberg Letters*, 71.

[27] Ibid., 82.

texture as the highest potentialization of the written word is illustrated by a comment he made in 1945 in connection with the *Genesis Prelude*, his contribution to the collective work of a group of *émigré* composers which also included Igor Stravinsky and Darius Milhaud. Faced with the task of reflecting musically on the act of creation, he explained, he had decided to employ a large orchestra and a choir singing wordless melismatic passages in a manner so intricate as 'to give an idea of the "technical" difficulties at the creation of the world'.[28]

Thus it appears that Arnold Schoenberg's unceasing quest for language formed an intrinsic aspect, a logical function, of both his essentially prophetic self-image and his specific artistic genius. Early on, Schoenberg no doubt agreed with his friend and comrade-in-arms Karl Kraus that 'in the beginning was the word'. But he clearly realized before long that in the end there will always be music, the very source of language, as not only Paul Hindemith believed. If it could be said that Kraus 'carried out his mission with true priestly devotion', in the manner of Aaron, Schoenberg single-mindedly pursued the path of the pure idea, like Moses—to the discomfort not only of the musical Pharaohs of his time but of some leading figures among his own people as well. Historically, the idea as transcendent abstraction, accounts in no small measure for the oft-cited 'Jewish problem', a problem created long ago by a Christian civilization committed for its part to the word in all its seductive concreteness.

The biblical Moses was not allowed to enter the Promised Land; instead he vanished in the serene solitude of a desert mountain, his grave unmarked, unknown, so that only the divine idea to which he dedicated his long, troubled life might be remembered. The ashes of Arnold Schoenberg were returned to Vienna, his place of birth and the seat of an evil far greater than anything the ancient Hebrews endured in Pharaonic Egypt. And yet Schoenberg, this twentieth-century Moses who prophesied the abstract idea to a people—nay a world—hopelessly caught in the web of its own materialistic words and concrete images, who managed to carry modern music to the very threshold of complete freedom, circumscribed only by such functional laws as will always be needed to fully endow human achievement with lasting meaning, lives on equally unseen and largely unheeded, still the supreme musical symbol of the pure idea.

[28] Reich, *Schoenberg: A Critical Biography*, 215.

3

Idea and Realization:
The Path of the Bible

DER biblische Weg occupies a very special position in Arnold Schoenberg's personal history and creative evolution, not only because of its obvious ramifications for Moses und Aron but also as a crucial philosophical statement made at a critical juncture in his professional career, the fruit of a long, often agonizing reappraisal of his origins, loyalties, priorities, and goals. Schoenberg and his family had moved to Berlin in January 1926. The play was begun in May, and the first draft completed three weeks later, in June. On 27 May Schoenberg was sworn in as a Prussian official in charge of one of the three master-classes in composition at the Prussian Academy of the Arts. This occurred after months of agitation against his appointment, including anti-Semitic attacks of a sort new even for him, who was hardly a stranger to racial slurs. The worst of these attacks, particularly regrettable since it emanated from the pen of the editor of a respected musical journal, had come as early as October 1925 in the Zeitschrift für Musik, the monthly that could claim Felix Mendelssohn's friend Robert Schumann as its founder.[1] Alfred Heuss, a musical scholar of merit, forswore the usual personal vilifications in favour of a historical analysis that took for granted the validity of racial theories current at that time and on that basis concluded that the appointment in question amounted to nothing less than a concerted attempt to overthrow everything that 'true' Germans held sacred in art.

Those in the know had little trouble detecting echoes of the customary intimations of a Jewish conspiracy. Leo Kestenberg, the music specialist in the Prussian Ministry of Culture, was a Jew and one born in Hungary to boot. He had come to Berlin as a student of Ferruccio Busoni, and when his beloved master died in July 1924 Kestenberg, whose task included recommendations for such top appointments, could think of none better equipped than Schoenberg to assume the Busoni succession as a teacher of composition in Prussia's most prestigious institution.[2] The

---

[1] Dr Alfred Heuss, 'Arnold Schönberg: Preussischer Kompositionslehrer', Zeitschrift für Musik, 92/10 (Oct. 1925), 583–5. For a full English translation see app. A.

[2] Leo Kestenberg, Bewegte Zeiten (Wolfenbüttel and Zurich, 1961), 54–5.

self-appointed keepers of the German cultural Grail were outraged. Without as much as mentioning the fact that it was Kestenberg who had seen to the previous appointment of Hans Pfitzner, Schoenberg's antipode and sworn enemy, they sounded the alarm. Had Paul Bekker, the powerful critic of Jewish origin, not promoted Busoni, Schoenberg, and Stravinsky as prime movers of the 'new' music? Jews, foreigners, and national half-breeds could not be allowed to take over!

Schoenberg was unshaken. His trauma had come years earlier, in 1921, when he and his family had been driven from their summer retreat in Austria because the village of Mattsee wished to remain strictly 'Aryan'. And in the spring of 1923, with the radical Right hunting Jews freely in German streets, he had engaged his long-time friend Wassily Kandinsky in an exchange of letters which, though quite ill-considered, had given him the opportunity to come to terms with his heritage and contingent obligations in ways that were to have far-reaching consequences for his life's work. A decade later, about to leave Europe for good, he recalled that his as yet unstaged play was 'conceived in 1922 or '23 at the latest'.[3] Walter Rathenau fell victim to assassins in 1922 and Britain, about to assume its League of Nations mandate over Palestine, issued a White Paper severely limiting the wartime promise of the Balfour Declaration which had endorsed the creation of a Jewish homeland in Palestine, where Jews from the four corners of the earth might enjoy physical safety as well as the psychological solace of a life of dignity and self-respect. At the turn of the century Theodor Herzl had gloomily predicted that

In Russia they'll simply confiscate from above. In Germany they'll make special laws, once the Kaiser finds it impossible to get along with the *Reichstag*. In Austria they'll be intimidated by the mob and deliver the Jews to it. Thus we'll be chased from these countries, and in those where we'll seek refuge, they'll murder us.[4]

By 1923, in the wake of Adolf Hitler's abortive Munich Putsch, it seemed obvious to Arnold Schoenberg that Herzl's dire warnings were rapidly turning into frightful political reality. And with racial prejudice by no means limited to Germany but alive throughout the Continent, a Jewish national home became an even greater concern than it had been prior to the world war that so unsettled the sorely tried masses of Europe.

[3] Cf. Schoenberg's letter of 16 Oct. 1933 to Alban Berg, *Arnold Schoenberg Letters*, 184.

[4] Theodor Herzl on 13 June 1895 in the draft of his address to the Rothschilds, as quoted in C. H. Beck, *Geschichte der Juden* (Munich, 1983), 175.

It is hardly surprising under these circumstances that Jewish settlement in Palestine aroused considerable interest in both literary and political circles during the inter-war period, the more so as the reports of what had already been accomplished by the Zionist pioneers under conditions of extreme hardship blatantly contradicted some of the anti-Semites' favourite stereotypes. In short, Schoenberg was not alone in broaching the subject creatively and passionately. What set him apart from many others was his insistence on the biblical premise that in order to possess the land the Jewish people must be willing and ready to accept ethical responsibilities on a par with those of their forefathers at Sinai. They must, in other words, be prepared to take 'the path of the Bible'. Given that willingness, Schoenberg believed, 'the idea of providing a home for the Jews implies already its realization'. For, as he noted upon completion of the second version of what was then still called *Sprich zu dem Felsen* ('Speak to the Rock'): 'From a good thought everything else flows forth as a matter of course.'[5]

In *Der biblische Weg* Schoenberg set out to explore 'the possibility of creating a (new) homeland for the Jews', with due regard to the enormous problems involved, whether material, political, psychological, or cultural. To this end the play 'employs all the theatrical means necessary'. But 'the character of the protagonists, or their fate, philosophy, economics, technology, religion, general human concerns, politics, etc.', though seemingly occupying centre stage, are 'to be viewed only as a means. All that is touched upon only to demonstrate what difficulties must be overcome and what the possibilities are.'[6] In other words, *Der biblische Weg* was conceived from the outset as a piece of propaganda, and its author insisted that it be regarded as such. Propaganda for a good cause, he believed, was nothing to be ashamed of; it had in fact been part and parcel of his life, in word and deed, ever since he and Zemlinsky founded the Society of Creative Musicians, in Vienna in 1904, with the stated purpose of fostering performances of modern music and keeping 'the public constantly informed about the current state of musical composition'.[7] Its post-war counterpart, the Association for Private Musical Performances, actually announced major events as propaganda-concerts.

---

[5] The autograph in question is listed in Josef Rufer, *The Works of Arnold Schoenberg* under E 14.

[6] Ibid. All passages from *Der biblische Weg*, including the speech by Max Aruns reproduced in app. B, are quoted here in translations prepared by this writer.

[7] For a complete translation of the pertinent circular see Willi Reich, *Schoenberg: A critical biography*, 16–19. The passage in question appears in italics on p. 19.

Ideological propaganda on and through the public stage had, of course, a long and by no means undistinguished history. In the mid-twenties in Berlin, however, it set the prevailing tone not merely of the political cabaret and the 'agit-prop' theatre of Erwin Piscator, Caspar Neher, and others who took their cues from early Soviet-Russian experiments along these lines. Bertolt Brecht's concept of 'epic theatre' was also beginning to make an impact, as was indeed *Zeitoper* of the sort favoured for a while by young composers like Paul Hindemith and Kurt Weill.[8] Visually, propaganda posters, frequently of considerable artistic merit, were dotting the urban landscape throughout the short lifespan of the Weimar Republic, especially during that fragile political creature's unending succession of election campaigns. As a propaganda play *Der biblische Weg* was thus truly a child of the times. And as such it inevitably shared some of the inherent handicaps as well, including lengthy exchanges concerning relatively abstruse subject-matter, apt to slow the pace of events and to reduce dramatic tension.

But if Schoenberg's unique non-musical work for the theatre suffers from certain weaknesses closely tied to its original purpose, its place in the total scheme of things and thoughts Schoenbergian remains none the less secure, if only because of its germinal importance for the composer's later whole-hearted engagement in the politics of Jewish survival. The idea of mobilizing the financial resources of world Jewry on behalf of fellow Jews in immediate physical danger was admittedly anything but new. It had been at the heart of Theodor Herzl's extensive dealings with the Hirschs, Rothschilds, and other reigning philanthropists of his day. And even before then Moses Hess, the German-Jewish socialist whose influence ranged clear across from Marx to Herzl, had advocated the purchase of Palestine, by means of a huge public subscription, as a haven for Jews.[9] Hess, moreover, made his proposal at the very moment when most German Jews were just beginning to enjoy the fruits of full citizenship. Barely three generations later, what Hess feared, seemingly against all odds, did come to pass: born into an era of incipient racism, the much-touted German–Jewish symbiosis was snuffed out even before it reached full maturity.

Schoenberg may never have read *Rom und Jerusalem*. Much of what Hess had to say in this, his principal work, should have appealed to him, however, in particular the trenchant distinctions Hess made between

---

[8] See Ch. 7.

[9] Cf. Shlomo Avineri, *Moses Hess: Prophet of Communism and Zionism* (New York and London, 1985), 230.

Christian beliefs and attitudes and the Jewish experience. For while it is undoubtedly true that Herzl's visionary novel *Alt-Neuland* found lively echoes in *Der biblische Weg*, spiritually the play explores areas rather beyond the grasp of Herzl, the political journalist, but by the same token close to the heart and mind of the social philosopher Hess raised, unlike Herzl, as an orthodox Jew. Admittedly Hess abandoned ritualistic practice early in life and never resumed it. But then Schoenberg was nominally a Protestant when he wrote the play in which the creation of a modern Jewish commonwealth is made contingent on its commitment to the ancient biblical ideals for which thousands paid with their lives through millennia of persecution.

Schoenberg's steadfast conviction that a nation's security is above all a function of its military strength received a further boost in 1925, when Vladimir Jabotinsky rejoined the Zionist struggle, now as head of his own revisionist party, on the premiss that in a world contemptuous of the weak only the strong are prone to gain and preserve their independence. Schoenberg was in full agreement and in his play sided emphatically with the revisionist leader, except on the question of a temporary alternative to Palestine. Painfully aware of the defeat of the Uganda proposal, to which he ascribed—with some justification—Herzl's premature death in 1904, he advocated an interim solution, if necessary, and modelled his imaginary country Ammongäa after British-held Uganda, where large-scale Jewish settlement had been envisaged. Max Aruns, that curiously composite figure, clearly thinks of it, as had Herzl, primarily as an expedient, but appears mindful also of the forty years it took those on the original path of the Bible to reach the promised land.[10]

Both Schoenberg's own abiding interest in physical fitness and discipline and the rising popularity of Zionist sports organizations— *Maccabi*, *Hakoah*, and the revisionist *Betar*—may account for the setting of the dramatic conclusion of the First Act in a sports arena.[11] The very existence of such clubs, not to mention the competitive performance of many a top athlete, flew in the faces of those who never ceased to depict Jews as endemically decadent, physically no less than mentally. And as a passionate tennis-player himself, the composer remained a life-long adherent of the doctrine *mens sana in corpore sano*—a healthy mind in a healthy body. Theodor Herzl had pinned great hopes on technology for

[10] As late as Oct. 1933 Schoenberg maintained that he 'never said I am a Zionist, but that I want to found a Jewish Unity Party'. See *The Arnold Schoenberg–Hans Nachod Collection*, ed. John A. Kimmen Jr. (Detroit, 1979), 36.

[11] For Aruns's pertinent speech see app. B.

the conquest of the barren land of Palestine, and Schoenberg made it a focal issue as well, though mostly in terms of its military potential. But excessive reliance on its supposed blessings actually leads to the undoing of Aruns and of much of his ambitious project. The magic weapon designed to guarantee the people's security vanishes, an aeroplane carrying crucial aid crashes, and the ensuing crisis leaves no doubt but that the future lies rather with strength of mind and purity of heart.

That technology stands here in large measure for materialism emerges from the agonizing discussion between Aruns and Asseino, the prophetic figure whom Aruns consults on questions of religious law and its role in New Palestine. While Asseino stresses the lasting value of ancient tradition, Aruns takes the liberal position of modern 'progressive' Judaism, which has sought to comply with the spirit rather than the letter of Jewish law. Thus, when Aruns argues in favour of new Sabbath laws—because 'a people of today cannot extinguish the blast-furnaces every Friday and close down its power stations'—Asseino's retort goes straight to the heart of the issue. 'Once again', he tells the pragmatic man of action, 'your materialism leads to betrayal of the idea . . . What you ask of me amounts to a request by Aaron that Moses lend his agreement and assistance to the erection of the golden calf.' How could the chosen of the Lord yield to purely material considerations?

He told you (fourth book of Moses, chapter 20, verse 8): 'Speak to the rock before their eyes, that it bring forth water!' But you had no faith in the spirit; you did not speak to the rock, instead (verse 11) 'you hit the rock twice with your staff'. You tied the emergence of the Jewish people to material strength, to the powers of a machine. Hence, like Moses (verse 12) who because of this sin was not allowed to enter the promised land, you, too, will not reach your goal.

Aruns insists that the transformation of the people into a military power violates neither Mosaic law nor 'the purity of the idea'. Following rabbinic precedent he offers a different interpretation of Asseino's biblical references by combining them with passages from another chapter of the Torah. But to no avail. Asseino remains adamant, and Aruns concedes: 'If I am beaten now, I am forever beaten. Then the idea itself was wrong, everything a mistake, and for that I must atone.' Urged to save himself for the sake of the community, for the idea, he declares: 'We Jews are a people of martyrs and cling tenaciously to life in order to save it for our idea. We have always known how to die for it. We would no longer be alive had we not risked for it, had we shunned death for its sake.' The problem thus is and remains the realization of the idea in ways and by means that will not destroy it in the process, an almost insurmountable task. For, as Asseino reiterates,

'the idea conceived in bliss, born of pain, raised under privation, tolerates no material realization, just as God permits no *representation*. He who commits himself to the idea must either renounce any attempt of realization or be content with a reality he would not wish to experience. That is why anyone who must live for an idea becomes a martyr; that is why others will enjoy the fruits of his labours; that is why he is never allowed to enter the promised land himself, can never derive benefits from its realization.'

The burden of the ancient 'belief in the one, unitary, immortal, eternal, unimaginable God' is shouldered in the end by Guido, the Joshua of Schoenberg's version. Like Joshua, Guido has only one thought: to see to it that the Jewish people living within safe borders will finally be able to determine their own destiny. As he puts it in his concluding monologue, 'we want to make sure that nobody can compel us to do anything, that nobody can prevent us from doing something'. Not in order to dominate others, if only because 'we have enough work with ourselves', but so as to be able to 'spiritualize our existence, detach ourselves from all that is material'. First, however, the people will have to 'learn to think the idea of the one, eternal, unimaginable God'. Once that by no means simple challenge has been met, once the spirit has overcome matter, they will be allowed to dream their dream of God—'like all the ancient peoples who put the material world behind them'.

Schoenberg's self-conscious disclaimer notwithstanding, the three acts of his play contain a good deal of the human, all too human: personality conflicts, jealousies, betrayals and hypocrisy, ambition and incompetence. But all that is overshadowed by the idea of redemption. Once Aruns has reached the conviction that freedom lies only along the path of the Bible, that 'the Bible shows the way to liberation', the rest follows as a matter of course. This dictum, repeated several times in the course of the play, might well be regarded as Schoenberg's personal motto, representative of a fundamental attitude that affected whatever he did or said. Its Old Testamentary roots are self-evident: the Lord rests on the seventh day, and, in keeping with the principle of *imitatio dei*, man is commanded to keep the Sabbath holy; hence too the sabbatical year, ensuring the release of slaves, and the jubilee year, releasing the land from its servitude to man. One divine decision brings in its wake blessings to the individual, to society at large, and indeed to nature. In the words of Leviticus 19:2, 'Ye shall be holy; for I the Lord your God am holy.' In the words of

Moses in the First Act of the opera that owed so much to the spoken drama, 'inexorable law of thought compels fulfilment'.

Fulfilment is, needless to say, the haunting goal of every creative effort. And Schoenberg undoubtedly made the Jewish spiritual dilemma his own. He certainly identified the artist's responsibility with that of the Jewish people. As he noted on 23 July 1927, upon completion of the second draft of *Der biblische Weg*, 'the communication of an idea involves in most cases a reduction to comprehensibility'. The musical idea, however, as Schoenberg conceived of it, was not merely a theme from which everything else 'flows forth' but 'the totality of a piece . . . the idea which its creator wanted to present'.[12] Like the divine idea of creation, 'it must be moulded, formulated, developed, elaborated, carried through and pursued to its very end'.[13] In other words, the composer, like his divine model, is expected to envisage at the outset the entire complex of problems inherent in the idea and its realization. Which is precisely why the theme of a musical work must be 'so constructed that it already contains within itself these many figures through which the many-sided presentation of the idea is made possible'.[14]

In *Der biblische Weg* Max Aruns succumbs tragically to the liabilities inherent in his Aaron component. In the later opera Aaron is explicitly referred to as 'the mouth of the idea and its destroyer', a metaphor no doubt for the modern performer as well, whose musical realization plays havoc with the composer's intent. Ideally, composer and performer ought to be one and the same person, but, Schoenberg seems to imply, that is not the way it usually works out, even though the public may think otherwise. Kaphira, Ammongää's ambassador, hails Aruns as a man 'possessed of the strength and the courage to persist in his idea in the face of opposition from the entire world . . . the man of success, who is not merely capable of conceiving an idea but has the stamina and the good fortune to realize it'. That, surely was the way Schoenberg saw himself. Even his nemesis, Alfred Heuss, had to admit that he 'was and is honest, just as every fanatic is honest, and there is in fact nothing objectionable in his person'.[15] Still, few friends, let alone foes, were perceptive and sensitive enough to appreciate his utter devotion to ideas for their own sake in the full knowledge that, as he stressed in his notes for the play, such devotion may demand the ultimate sacrifice. As far as that goes, 'the

---

[12] Schoenberg, 'New Music, Outmoded Music, Style and Idea', in *Style and Idea*, 123.

[13] Ibid., 124.

[14] Note on 'Darstellung des Gedankens', cf. Rufer, *The Works of Arnold Schoenberg*, 140.

[15] Heuss, 'Arnold Schönberg: Prussischer Kompositionslehrer', 594.

seemingly fortuitous death of Aruns turns out to be in accordance with established law'.[16] And the same holds for art and intellectual pursuits: 'he who really uses his brain for thinking can only be possessed of one desire: to resolve his task. He cannot let external conditions exert influence upon the results of his thinking . . . One thinks only for the sake of one's idea. And thus art can be created only for its own sake.'[17]

If this be typical of 'Jewish fanaticism', Alfred Heuss and company certainly scored a point. Where they proved utterly, indeed disastrously, wrong was in their assumption that 'the idea' was to undermine the past of German music and dominate its future. Unlike the man they loathed, they argued with the aggressive fury of the weak, not the inner strength of martyrs. Prejudice born of fear is often the ultimate fruit of ignorance, the mother of myth; and ignorance with regard to Jews and Judaism has been and remains a pervasive phenomenon, the historical bequest of centuries of forced ghettoization. The scholarly editor of the *Zeitschrift für Musik*, for one, could hardly be expected to have much firsthand knowledge of any of those furtive bearded figures in long black caftans who had begun to stream into Central Europe, impoverished refugees from pogrom-ridden Russia, eking out a living in some of the poorest quarters of the major cities. If anything, their clannish behaviour seemed to confirm that a viable culture had to be rooted in native soil, had to be *bodenständig*. Conventional wisdom had it that these alien elements typified the rootless, eternal, wandering Jew. No matter that their forebears had lived in the same village or *Shtetl* for generations, long before the compulsory settlement in 'the Pale', decreed by a nineteenth-century Russian Pharaoh. As for the modern, emancipated Jews—the Schnitzlers and Freuds, the Mahlers and Schoenbergs—the fact is that few indigenous Austrians could lay more legitimate claims to life and work in the imperial and royal capital than they whose families came from some of the most creative and industrious parts of the far-flung realm of the Habsburgs. Characteristically, Heuss tried to divide and conquer, covering himself all the while against accusations of anti-Semitism by insisting on the specious distinction between 'rooted' and 'rootless' Jews. That callous procedure was unlikely to fool even the most gullible of Jews and hardly any of their sworn enemies. If, on the other hand, he really believed what he wrote, one can only marvel at a professional historian so blinded by prejudice that he could not conceive, let alone acknowledge, the existence of a dynamic culture 'anchored' in

---

[16] Rufer, *The Works of Arnold Schoenberg*, E14.
[17] Schoenberg, *Style and Idea*, 124.

living traditions, as opposed to a conventional culture 'rooted' in physical space.

Physical concreteness admittedly holds considerably wider appeal than timeless abstraction. As Aaron found out to his detriment at Sinai, most people must be able to see in order to believe. Christians eager to convert a continent and then a world chose the Cross as a visible symbol of death and resurrection. And the small minority unwilling to let go of the one, unitary, unimaginable, eternal God has suffered the gruesome consequences ever since. Under these circumstances determination became a question of survival but it hardly constituted fanaticism, with the mindless behaviour this usually entails. As for Schoenberg's tendency to cull the very last possibilities from 'a narrow premiss', the good Dr Heuss was nearly correct: his only mistake was to confuse 'single' with 'narrow'. To draw exclusively upon the single premiss of the unitary Lord of Creation has certainly been a hallmark of the 'Jewish spirit' through the ages, though by no means only in music. Nor could they who followed the path of the Bible remain stationary for any length of time, given their unique and anything but 'narrow' premiss. For, as the Hebrew Bible makes abundantly clear, as soon as the divine cloud lifts, the Holy Ark must be carried forward on the way to the promised land.

The avowed self-reliance which so disturbed Heuss in Schoenberg had no more to do with 'fanaticism' than with any lack of a sense of a 'strong German past in himself'. Quite to the contrary. Possessed of a far greater analytical understanding of what constituted the essence of that past than Heuss, Pfitzner, and the rest of the conservative camp, Schoenberg willingly assumed the onerous historical task of building forth upon that very past which, as Heuss was forced to admit, had fallen on hard times. In that process Schoenberg put his trust not in himself but, like Moses in the desert, in Him whom he called 'the supreme commander'. Fanaticism became rather the province of those 'German attitudes' which, according to Heuss, spawn progress by definition, eschewing all violence. No doubt the Pharaoh of *Exodus* harboured similar illusions.

In view of the fact that Heuss launched his ominous attack in the October 1925 issue of his monthly, a model of German punctuality, it is perfectly possible that it reached Schoenberg before the end of the previous month. Given the general political climate of the day, however, not to speak of the composer's personal experiences during the immediately preceding years, the exact sequence of events hardly matters. His creative response, at any rate, couched most appropriately in strict twelve-tone terms, came on the last day of September: the first of the

Four Pieces for Mixed Choir, Op. 27, *Unentrinnbar* ('No Escape') draws indeed every last 'inescapable' consequence from a single but comprehensive musical premiss. And textually, no answer could have been more dignified and to the point than Schoenberg's own underlying poem.[18]

> Brave are they who accomplish deeds
> beyond the limits of their courage.
>
> They possess the strength to conceive their mission,
> and the character not to be able to refuse.
>
> If a God was so unkind as to grant them insight into their condition,
> they are hardly to be envied.
>
> And that is why they suffer envy.

[18] Offered here in this writer's translation.

4

Creation, Unity, and Law

THE idea that the laws of man as well as those of nature must be governed by the essence and will of the one, unitary God is almost axiomatically Old Testamentary. It clearly follows from the story of Creation as told in the very first chapter of Genesis, and it has been basic to Jewish thought ever since. Arnold Schoenberg, for one, took it for granted and turned it into the guiding principle of his own creative approach and achievements. In the area of musical theory it found its first comprehensive expression in that vast, often free-wheeling compendium of the practice and remaining potential of functional harmony, the *Harmonielehre* of 1911. Compositionally it generated, a decade later, the 'method of composing with twelve tones'. And in the field of politics it caused Schoenberg to call, in the early 1930s, for a Jewish Unity Party, to fend off the evil designs of the new Nazi rulers.

The proposition that either the 'emancipation of dissonance' or the dodecaphonic mode of composition, let alone both, might be indebted to the medieval concept of *imitatio dei*, the imitation of God, is likely to strike modern secular minds as rather questionable, if not thoroughly outlandish. Even so, in the case of Schoenberg, who never failed to listen carefully to his 'supreme commander', the historic mandate 'Ye shall be holy; for I the Lord your god am holy', produced a virtual identity of art and religion, with significant consequences, down to the smallest technical detail, for his creative thought and procedures. That it was at the root of his ever more intense commitment to the people, his people, chosen to proclaim the unity of the Lord of Creation against all historical odds, goes without saying. As Schoenberg saw it, quite in keeping with Jewish tradition, this alone was the reason and purpose of Israel's chosenness, a chosenness, moreover, freely chosen and thus psychologically more powerfully binding than any set of obligations dictated from above. A well-known Jewish saying has it that 'the world was created for the sake of the choice of him who chooses'.[1] In the play *Der biblische Weg* Schoenberg explored the ramifications of that premiss

---

[1] Cf. Martin Buber, *On Judaism*, ed. Nahum N. Glatzer (New York, 1967), 81.

for twentieth-century Jews facing a hostile Gentile world in their search
for institutional and material conditions permitting them to live and work
in peace and quiet in accordance with those ancient ideals, whose
aesthetic realization, in turn, engaged the composer in a lifelong quest for
laws ensuring musical unity and coherence.

That abiding concern with problems of structure informed not only
his oral teaching; it also governed the bulk of his theoretical writings,
both published and unpublished. Among those that never appeared in
print during his lifetime, a series of interconnected fragments committed
to paper over a period of nearly forty years bears ample testimony to
the remarkable continuity of Schoenberg's thinking with regard to the
configurational interaction of all the constituent elements of a musical
work and its contingent significance for meaningful musical understanding. Characteristically, even though a treatise on 'composing with
independent voices' conceived in 1911—probably as the contrapuntal
counterpart to the *Harmonielehre*—barely went beyond the planning
stage, the extant preliminary sketches indicate that it would have turned
into anything but a conventional textbook. It seems that Schoenberg
intended to dispense with the customary rules in a single chapter, in
order to proceed with such fundamental aesthetic issues as a given work's
purpose, the importance of intrinsic unity, pertinent laws and definitions,
principles of instruction in these matters, etc.[2] And when, years later, he
prepared himself for his duties at the Prussian Academy, having long
since mastered the method of composing with twelve tones, designed
precisely for optimal unity in a non-tonal idiom, he turned his attention
once again to the same general questions.

The year, of course, was 1926. He had just finished the first draft of
Der biblische Weg and now confronted the practical realities of his new
position. But even when such was not the case, as in April 1917, during
the incubation period of *Die Jakobsleiter*, theoretical considerations of
coherence mysteriously cropped up. And, characteristically, the essay in
question, which deals with understanding as a function of the 'recognition of similarities', was filed years later with yet another attempt 'to find
the rules of form which govern musical works by raising the question of
coherence'.[3] The latter dates from 1925, and it would appear that, far
from responding merely to immediate didactic needs, Schoenberg seized
the opportunity to reiterate his belief that all good music is 'based on

---

[2] Rufer, *The Works of Arnold Schoenberg*, 135.
[3] Ibid., 137.

knowledge and realization that come from musical logic',[4] at a time when his dodecaphonic music was widely denounced as the product of a chaotic, if not totally deranged, mind. Thus defending the method of composing with twelve tones in terms of unifying properties comparable to those entrusted to tonality in music based on functional harmony, he consistently cited musical logic as the only valid common denominator and declared, with justifiable pride: 'I do not teach my students "twelve-tone composition" but "composition" in the sense of musical logic.'[5]

Ironically, but no doubt also inevitably, Schoenberg's many detractors managed to draw comfort from this tireless pursuit of logical processes for the sake of unity and coherence. Did it not confirm for all and sundry their long-standing charge of 'Jewish intellectualism' in music? Was it not obvious that this brazen display of Jewish sophistry was motivated by utter contempt for the glories of German art on the part of one racially incapable of delving into its soulful depths? Schoenberg's erstwhile student and assistant Erwin Stein retorted angrily that 'depth' implied precisely a sense of those 'connections and relationships that do not appear at the surface'.[6] It was Beethoven who had taught music how to think, and that historic step could no longer be reversed. Beethoven's entire manner, 'his motivic and thematic procedures, his tonal disposi-tions, everything demonstrates unmistakably that music is not sonorous forms but tonal ideas in motion'.[7] Schoenberg merely translated Beet-hoven's 'idea-principle' into language, whether tonal or non-tonal, commensurate with what he wished to convey. But this idiosyncratic trait was precisely what confused even some of his best friends, as did no doubt the unending stream of theoretical material. As late as June 1946, about to complete both *Structural Functions of Harmony* and the concise *Fundamentals of Musical Composition*, he produced yet another set of notes on the structural possibilities and implicit laws of contrapuntal textures.

Unlike some who knew him in his earlier days—his childhood friend David Bach, for example, or Wassily Kandinsky—Schoenberg's later supporters, and many a critic too, proved so intrigued by his novel

[4] Ibid., 140.

[5] Ibid.

[6] Erwin Stein, 'Das gedankliche Prinzip in Beethovens Musik und seine Auswirkung bei Schönberg', *Anbruch*, 9 (March, 1927), 117. For a concise discussion of the fruits of two decades of Schoenbergian concerns with 'the idea' in music, see Alexander Goehr, 'Schoenberg's "Gedanke" Manuscript', *JASI* II, 1 (Oct., 1977), 4–25; also, Rudolf Stephan, 'Der musikalische Gedanke bei Schönberg', *ÖMZ* 37/10 (Oct., 1982), 530–40.

[7] Erwin Stein, 'Das gedankliche Prinzip', 118.

technique of composition that they rarely took the trouble to delve into its historical, let alone its spiritual, roots. Not until the post-Second World War revelations of *Moses und Aron* and *Ein Überlebender aus Warschau* did it become customary, indeed fashionable, to broach the Schoenberg problem in—at times quite inappropriate—religious terms. Meanwhile, the composer began to resent that growing body of twelve-tone analyses which, as he warned his long-time associate and brother-in-law, Rudolf Kolisch, in the summer of 1932, could at best reveal something of *how* a piece was made but never what it *is*.[8] Thinking of himself essentially as a twelve-tone *composer*, he hated the designation *twelve-tone* composer, unlike his old rival Josef Matthias Hauer, who had become a virtual prisoner of his own hermetically closed system and to whom composition was, in Schoenberg's estimation, 'only of secondary importance'.[9]

Typical of those sympathetic to his endeavours but viewing them from a strictly secular perspective was the dialectician Theodor Wiesengrund-Adorno, who, as a student of Alban Berg, contributed regularly to *Anbruch*, the progressive musical periodical sponsored by Universal-Edition. Adorno eventually served as Thomas Mann's musical adviser when the great German author, in the Californian exile he shared with both Schoenberg and Adorno, was writing *Doktor Faustus*. The central figure of that monumental novel, the composer Adrian Leverkühn, seemed in many ways patterned after Arnold Schoenberg, who, upon reading it shortly after the war's end, reacted bitterly to what he called 'Andreas Leverkühn's 12-tone Goulash', a mere conglomeration of some well-known stereotypes about his own work. Leverkühn, he noted, was

one of those amateurs who believe composing with twelve tones means nothing else but always using the basic set or its inversions. In fact, the meaning of this rule should be expressed in another manner. It should be: None of the twelve tones must appear without the order of the basic set or its derivatives. But to think that obeyance to this rule produces a composition, is as childish or amateurish or laymanish as to suppose avoidance of other forbiddings suffices to create music. For instance avoidance of parallel fifths or octaves. These rules are only restrictive. You must be able to produce music in spite of those severe restrictions.[10]

When all is said and done, he added in 1948, musical composition turns out to be

[8] *Arnold Schoenberg Letters*, 164.
[9] Ibid., 165.
[10] Rufer, *The Works of Arnold Schoenberg*, 142.

a secret science . . . a science which cannot be taught at all. It is inborn or it is not there. This is also the reason why Thomas Mann's Adrian Leverkühn does not know the essentials of composing with twelve tones. All he knows has been told him by Mr. Adorno who knows only the little I was able to tell my pupils. The real fact will probably remain secret science until there is one who inherits it by virtue of an unsolicited gift.[11]

The dialectics of freedom and constraint, universal law and human creativity, have been basic to Jewish thought at least since the revelation at Sinai—some might say since Adam and Eve. They are certainly inseparable from the concept of the one, unitary God as the invisible 'first cause' and ultimate source not only of nature but also of history. Christianity tends to stress man's fall from grace and the contingent loss of paradise as inexorable consequences of his original claim to knowledge and personal choice. In this view, shared officially by most denominations, sin came into this world as a function of the desire for freedom. Most modern Christians might not quite put it this way, but that is another matter, one that has in fact troubled theologians for some time. Jews, at any rate, tend to think of man's first effective act of rebellion rather as the onset of history, an act no doubt foreseen by the Creator, since without it there would be none to serve Him. Nor, of course, would there be any divine law guiding the descendants of those original 'sinners' who had the will and ability to change their own condition—for a blessing and a curse—precisely because He created them in His image.

Once man left timeless Eden behind him and became a historical being—so Hasidic Jews in particular would argue—a dialectical relationship with God inevitably ensued, one of mutual dependence. Man has depended upon his Creator from the beginning for commands that have ensured both his physical existence and his spiritual welfare. But if He has time and again shown mercy to His chosen people, it is not in the last instance because its continued existence is living testimony to His omnipotence. The God of the Hebrew Scriptures does not deny the existence of other 'gods', pretenders to divinity thriving on the people's gullibility. Quite to the contrary: the Bible refers repeatedly to the 'gods which you have known', most of which the people in fact created themselves. By contrast the One 'from whom all else flows forth' remains unknown, except that through revelation His essence is embodied in the Law, the one and only valid law. Deuteronomy 11: 26–8 tells of the

---

[11] Schoenberg, 'The Blessing of the Dressing', *Style and Idea*, 386.

historical decision facing the children of Israel poised on the banks of the river Jordan prior to the conquest of Canaan:

Behold, I have set before you this day a blessing and a curse; a blessing if you shall hearken unto the commandments of the Lord your God, which I command you this day; and the curse, if you shall not hearken unto the commandments of the Lord your God, but turn aside out of the way which I command you this day, to go after other gods which you have known.

Decades earlier, barely escaped from the rigours of Egypt, their fathers had made an even more difficult choice when at Mount Sinai Moses 'called for the elders of the people, and set before them all these words which the Lord commanded him. And all the people answered together, and said: "all that the Lord has spoken, we will do." '

Jewish peoplehood was and is based on that Covenant, and a covenant, whether between man and man or God and man, implies mutual obligations freely incurred, with due consideration of relative advantages and disadvantages. In the event this entailed the voluntary subjection, though admittedly after ample warnings of the likely dire consequences of non-acceptance, to exceptionally stringent laws binding on countless generations yet to be born. Only after the people had 'chosen' to conclude the Covenant were they to be known as the chosen of the Lord. And such was the legal burden, with its host of practical ramifications for the future, that it took forty years of hardship, abounding with protracted remonstrations and hesitations, before they proved ready for it. Then, however, they did a rather extraordinary thing, declaring their willingness not, as might be expected, to listen and act but, if need be, to act first and listen afterwards. And in so doing they established a lasting characteristic of Jewish behaviour. In Judaism it is the deed committed in good faith which ultimately counts, not the thought. Even the teaching of the Law, upon which Jewish historical continuity has so largely depended through the ages, has little merit, according to some sages, unless it is designed so as to affect action in the spirit of *Mitzvah*, the divinely ordained deed. Jewish notions of freedom are thus inseparable from concrete obligations toward one's fellow man in accordance with divine law, which is precisely how Arnold Schoenberg understood 'chosenness'. As Moses puts it in the third, uncomposed, act of *Moses und Aron*: 'to serve, to serve the divine idea, that is the freedom for which this people has been chosen.'

Explication, paraphrase, and interpretation of the Law, both written and oral, have been at the heart of Jewish intellectual activity for some two millennia, stimulating not only relatively abstract philosophical discourse but discussions of everyday practical concerns from physical health to business ethics. Living up to the letter as well as to the spirit of the Law was literally a question of life and death for thousands, from the days of the Emperor Hadrian to the Great Inquisition and well beyond. And it was, by the same token, the motivating force behind the unbroken collective will to go on living in a hostile Christian environment that ranked individual faith far above a code of law which, though God-given, had been all but superseded by the sacrifice of His only-begotten son, whose death, the Gospels seemed to imply, it actually precipitated. As far as Jewish tradition is concerned, fulfilling the demands of a *Mitzvah* requires no momentary sense of devotion; the decisive element is its punctilious execution. Consequently the Jewish conception of prayer also differs rather substantially from its Christian counterparts. For one, Hebrew liturgy minimizes individual requests for personal favours. Instead it abounds with collective expressions of grateful submission to the divine will as codified in biblical law and revealed throughout Jewish history. When pious Jews appeal to their Lord, it is typically not so much for personal grace as for 'knowledge, insight, and understanding' of His law at the behest of a just world, a true fellowship of men created in the image of their Creator. In short the Law reigns supreme in Judaism, because it alone vouchsafes true morality, in keeping with the command 'Ye shall be holy; for I the Lord your God am holy.' From this all-encompassing idea all the rest 'flows forth', as Arnold Schoenberg so clearly understood. It was indeed a teacher in the great rabbinic tradition who, in the wake of the Nazi seizure of power, declared with justifiable pride: 'Whoever was my pupil gained a serious and moral concept of art which, if he knows how to maintain it, will do him honour in all circumstances of life.'[12]

Some twenty years earlier, well before the guns of August shattered what few illusions his fellow contributors to Der blaue Reiter had left, Theodor von Hartmann had called for nothing less than total anarchy in the arts, in the hope of effecting the kind of *tabula rasa* which the war, to the cheers of fellow artists like Franz Marc, quickly brought about.[13] Arnold Schoenberg, by stark contrast, was utterly shocked by such patent lack of faith in man's ability and will to determine his own failure constructively and with characteristic determination he chose the very

---

[12] Rufer, *The Works of Arnold Schoenberg*, 209.
[13] See Ch. 2, n. 1.

opposite path, away from the fleshpots and diseases of the modern
equivalents of Pharaonic Egypt. Having tried in vain, with every musical
and musico-dramatic means at his disposal, to awaken a mindless society
to the gruesome realities behind the façade of pre-war cultural glitter,
Schoenberg embarked on a solitary forty-year trek of his own, undaunted
by the shifting sands of post-war politics, let alone the perennial taunts of
the musical reactionaries. 'Unyielding law of thought compels fulfilment', Moses exclaims in the second scene of *Moses und Aron*. For
Schoenberg, as for Moses, fulfilment came but decades after the law was
received and accepted, irrefutable evidence of the creative logic of
consistently positive, structural thought, employed not for its own sake
but at the behest of the 'supreme commander'. As far as this latter-day
musical prophet was concerned, the rules of non-tonal polyphonic
composition emanated from that

power behind the human mind, which produces miracles for which we do not
deserve credit ... if one has done his duty with the utmost sincerity and has
worked out everything as near to perfection as he is capable of doing, then the
Almighty presents him with a gift, with additional features of beauty such as he
never could have produced by his talents alone.[14]

In the last years of his life, Schoenberg attached considerable importance to the fact that the twelve chromatic pitches appeared in a specific
thematic order for the first time in the Scherzo 'The Joy of Life',
intended for the large-scale symphony project that left manifold traces in
the equally unfinished oratorio.[15] That magnificent torso, in turn, begins
with a striking hexachordal ostinato which introduces and then underscores the opening lines of the Archangel Gabriel:

> Whether right or left,
> Forward or backward,
> Uphill or downhill,
> One must go on without asking
> What lies behind or ahead.[16]

[14] Schoenberg, 'My Evolution', in *Style and Idea*, 85–6.

[15] Ibid., 88 ff.

[16] Curiously, Richard Wagner used virtually identical language to describe his own
attitude: 'those like myself', he told Mathilde Wesendonk in 1860, 'look neither to the right
nor the left, neither forwards nor backwards. Time and the world are nothing to us. Only
one thing matters to us and determines our actions, namely, the necessity to release what is
within us.' Cf. Walter Salmen, 'Social Obligations of the Emancipated Musician in the
Nineteenth Century', in Walter Salmen (ed.), *The Social Status of the Professional Musician
from the Middle Ages to the Nineteenth Century* (New York, 1983), 271.

This poetic evocation of dodecaphonic procedures couched in biblical phraseology points perhaps more directly than anything else to the true roots of Arnold Schoenberg's most talked-about achievement. The 'method' of course, evolved precisely during the years following the war-enforced suspension of work on the oratorio. In short, it appears that Gabriel's ethical message found its aesthetic realization in a compositional system specifically devised for maximal variety within the constraints of a single unifying idea from which 'all else flows forth as a matter of course'. In the oratorio, Gabriel goes on to say that in order to fulfil his earthly task man does not have to be privy to every secret. What counts is not the degree of one's knowledge but the measure and effectiveness of one's deeds. Fraught though it obviously is with countless dangers and difficulties, human existence does reward those who humbly accept their calling and in so doing give substance to the eternal laws promulgated by the Creator.

That the composer was by no means unaware of the inner connection between the philosophical *Leitmotiv* of *Die Jakobsleiter* and a unified-field theory equating musical time and space, is confirmed by his observation that '*the unity of musical space demands an absolute and unitary perception.*' In this space, as in Swedenborg's heaven (described in Balzac's *Seraphita*) there is no absolute down, no right or left, no forward or backward.'[17] The Princeton University lecture of 1934, in which this revealing passage first occurred, opened quite unexpectedly with an explicit reference to the divine act of creation, followed by the admonition that 'the concept of creator and creation should be formed in harmony with the Divine Model'. In divine creation, Schoenberg reminded his listeners, 'there were no details to be carried out later; "There was light" at once and in its ultimate perfection'.[18] Four years later he prefaced his *Kol Nidre*, commissioned by a Los Angeles temple for the eve of *Yom Kippur*, the most solemn hour in the Jewish liturgical calendar, with an anything but customary evocation of the creation of the world. Once again unity, law, and coherence became the watchwords, musically as well as theologically.

After intensive study and analysis of the traditional *Kol Nidre* tune, Schoenberg concluded that this most hallowed of Jewish melodies 'is no melody as such' but consists of 'a number of melismas which resemble each other up to a point without, however, being identical; also, they do

---

[17] Schoenberg, 'Composition with Twelve Tones', in *Style and Idea*, 223.
[18] Ibid., 215.

not always appear in the same order'.[19] The motivic material, in other words, is subject to both variation and rotation. Armed with this perceptive appraisal of a melody preserved throughout the generations both in the synagogue and—possibly longer—in Catalan folklore, he proceeded to treat it in accordance with the principle of 'developing variation' so basic to dodecaphonic music. Thus this purely tonal composition solidly anchored in G minor has come to symbolize also the creative unity of all his work, whether tonal or non-tonal, religious or ostensibly secular, and going back to the days when the Viennese Jewish youth had stepped on to the path of that past master of the developing variation, Johannes Brahms.

Indeed, as if to demonstrate the essential unity of all of Schoenberg's musical thought, the *Kol Nidre* is based on virtually the same material as the Fourth String Quartet, Op. 37, completed some two years earlier. There, to be sure, it serves dodecaphonic purposes and does so admirably. Yet the broad rhetorical gestures of the quartet, the Largo in particular, come closer in general spirit and actual musical details to traditional Jewish high-holiday recitatives than does the accompanied declamation of the Reform Rabbi in the melodrama sections of the *Kol Nidre*. Jewish Reform Temples do as a rule frown upon the more passionate behaviour of orthodox worshippers. But in the case of Schoenberg's Op. 39 this very circumstance also opened the way for as personal a testimony of faith as any in the history of music. In the course of his preparatory investigations the composer had come across information that struck a sensitive autobiographical nerve well beyond the inevitable childhood associations with the holiest of holidays. For he had been led to believe that the much-misunderstood and hence often suppressed text originated in early medieval Spain and pertained in the first instance to those who, like himself,

had willingly or unwillingly (apparently), gone over to Christianity—and who, therefore, were supposedly excluded from the Jewish community—might, on this day, once more became reconciled to their God; all other vows and promises were to be dissolved.[20]

The American Jewish Reform Prayer Book, anxious not to offend, had eliminated the original prayer as early as 1894. It took over eighty years and the murder of one-third of the Jewish people for the Reform powers that be to restore it. But individual rabbis and congregations catering to

[19] Rufer, *The Works of Arnold Schoenberg*, 67.
[20] Ibid.

the universal emotions attached to it often preferred their own versions or substituted kindred readings from other sources. One such rabbi, attempting to save its spirit, if not necessarily the letter, was Jacob Sonderling in Los Angeles, who not only commissioned the piece but also drafted the introductory recitation. It was this introduction, with its traditional references to the light of Creation, sown for all the righteous on earth, which Schoenberg, deeply moved by the historical and personal implications of the ancient ritual, turned into a reaffirmation of his own lasting indebtedness to that light which illuminates the creative path of every 'meek and modest mortal' and the repentant sinner as well. In Schoenberg's critical revision, the Rabbi's somewhat flowery metaphors became a forceful homage to God, the creator of light, who 'about to make the world, crushed that light to atoms'. Those 'myriads of sparks are hidden in our world', waiting to be fanned into the flame of human creativity in the image of the 'One, Everlasting, Unseen, Unfathomable'. To do full musical justice to the elemental power of this awesome thought Schoenberg felt he had to 'vitriolize away the cello-sentimentality of the Bruchs, etc., and to give this DECREE the dignity of a law, of an edict. I think', he told Paul Dessau, 'that I have succeeded in this.'[21]

If he did succeed with such apparent ease, it may well have been because the identifying motive of the *Kol Nidre* was anything but a new element in his by no means very extensive mix of melodic resources (Ex. 3). Like all primarily polyphonic composers, Schoenberg could do with surprisingly little motivic material. Basic interval combinations— like the second cum third, govern his works in one variant or another from *Verklärte Nacht* to the Fourth Quartet and beyond. And since the descending minor second and major third nucleus which, in the Fourth Quartet, generates countless contrapuntal artifices in accordance with the method of composing with twelve tones is heard also at the beginning of the *Kol Nidre* tune, only to be followed immediately by its retrograde, Schoenberg made the most of that happy coincidence. Which is not to assert, however, that he had this particular tune in mind while working on his quartet, any more than Beethoven did when he based his last quartets on essentially the same material. After all, the descending upper tetrachord of the harmonic minor had served Beethoven well way back in the first movement of his C minor String Trio, Op. 9, thus rendering irrelevant all speculation concerning the possible impact of his alleged studies of synagogue melodies in connection with an unrealized

[21] Ibid.

Ex. 3. Table of Motives

Kol Nidre (after Pedrell, Catalan. Songs No. 267)

Kol Nidre (after Baer, Ba-al Tefillah No. 1301) in Schoenberg's key

Schoenberg Op. 39

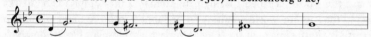

Schoenberg Op. 37, Largo

Beethoven Op. 9,3, Allegro can spirito

Beethoven Op. 131

Schoenberg Op. 11

Schoenberg Op. 30, Intermezzo

Schoenberg Op. 7

later

commission for the dedication of the first official Jewish synagogue in Vienna's Seitenstettengasse in 1826.[22]

Not only Beethoven himself but most nineteenth-century Beethovenians, including Franz Liszt and César Franck, favoured such motivic alignments of seconds and thirds, which form a common bond between the most disparate compositions, Franck's Symphonic Variations no less than Schoenberg's Piano Piece, Op. 11, No. 1 (1909), or his Third and Fourth Quartets (1927 and 1936), and even, in a but slightly different arrangement, his First Quartet, Op. 7 (1905), a copy of which he dedicated to his pupil Karl Horwitz with these characteristic words:

Do not try to learn anything from this, but rather from Mozart, Beethoven, and Brahms! Then you will perhaps find much in this work that is worthy of notice.[23]

He might have added that its central melodic ideas hark back to medieval chant and permeate works of Josquin des Prés, Palestrina, J. S. Bach, and many others who gave structural preference to melodic-rhythmic forces at the expense, though not necessarily to the detriment, of functional harmony. Indeed in its pentatonic guises the same combination of intervals held sway over quite a few of Claude Debussy's quasi-modal harmonic excursions well before it found its way into Schoenberg's transcendent chromaticism. Inevitably, even the greatest artist's *unentrinnbares Denkgesetz* operates within the constraints of equally inescapable forces of history.

As the Bible tells it in Exod. 3, the Lord warned Moses 'out of the Midst of the bush ... Draw not nigh hither; put off thy shoes from thy feet, for the place whereon thou standest is holy ground.' Schoenberg, whose *Moses und Aron* was the ultimate fruit of earlier plans for a separate 'Burning Bush' cantata, made this very scene the starting point of his opera. But in so doing he also introduced some significant modifications. It is Moses who speaks first and, whereas in the biblical account the Lord identifies himself as 'the God of thy father, the God of Abraham, the God of Isaac, and the God of Jacob', here Moses, anticipating later events, addresses Him already as 'One, Eternal, Omnipresent, Invisible and Unimaginable'. The Lord, for His part, far from sounding a stern admonition, invites the weary Moses, as any Oriental host would, first to 'take off your shoes, you have come a long

[22] Cf. Alexander L. Ringer, 'Salomon Sulzer, Joseph Mainzer and the Romantic a cappella Movement', *Studia Musicologica*, 2 (1969), 357.

[23] *Schoenberg, Berg, Webern—The String Quartets, A Documentary Study*, ed. Ursula von Rauchhaupt (Hamburg, 1971), 14.

way'. Only then does He remind him: 'you stand on ground that is holy.' Whereupon Moses, now referring in proper biblical terms to the God of his fathers, asks to be relieved of the burden in store for him, because 'I am old ... Let me tend my sheep quietly.' In the end he has no choice, because 'you have seen the horrors'. Thus events and ideas scattered throughout the Book of Exodus have been compressed into a few pregnant sentences. And this is exactly what happened to Genesis in the *Kol Nidre* ten years later.

By the time he recognized that he 'could even base a whole opera, *Moses und Aron*, solely on one set' Schoenberg too had 'come a long way'.[24] He too had put his faith singlemindedly in the One, Unitary God as the eternal model for man created in His image. And, like Moses, he had smitten many idols of the perpetrators of man's inhumanity to man. Long since painfully disabused of his last illusions about the world around him, he logically resolved to pursue the biblical path all the way to that holy ground where the chosen are called upon to become co-creators in the perpetual act of creation. It has been said that the Jew, history's 'specialist in alienation', has little alternative, if he is to survive, but to 'create the Zion he must return to'.[25] But having built his own artistic facsimile of the historical Zion squarely on the solid cornerstones of binding musical laws, Schoenberg felt no less lonely than Moses after Sinai:

While composing for me had been a pleasure, now it became a duty. I knew I had to fulfil a task: I had to express what was necessary to be expressed and I had the duty of developing my ideas for the sake of progress in music, whether I liked it or not.[26]

It was the 'duty' to create a timeless *musica humana*, following only the dictates of 'inner necessity' and at the risk of violating fashionable tenets of the *musica instrumentalis* of his time, which forced him literally to pave his own way, aided at best by a few faithful disciples. And in so doing he found himself in the distinguished company of equally notorious fellow Jews like Albert Einstein and Sigmund Freud. But Schoenberg, who so admired the biblical Moses, also knew about the vainglory and inexorable tragedy awaiting those chosen to be 'a light unto the nations' (Isa. 49: 6). Precisely because he undertook his mission in this 'light', however, he

[24] Schoenberg, *Style and Idea*, 224.
[25] Allen Guttmann, 'Jewish Radicals, Jewish Writers', *American Scholar*, 32/4 (autumn, 1963), 571.
[26] Schoenberg, 'How One Becomes Lonely', in *Style and Idea*, 53.

managed to prevail against all odds, undeterred, though not unscathed, by racial hatred in his earlier years and, for that matter, sudden exile later in life. By the same token, it was this peculiarly Jewish attitude which incurred him the enmity of post-Romantic souls sorely offended in their Christian humility by one who was not only unusually outspoken but, it appeared, supremely arrogant, self-serving, and, worse, outright heretical. Barely given the benefit of doubt, even where his unending search for coherent musical thought might have been expected to find sympathetic responses, he was virtually forced into an intransigent stance much like that of the biblical communicator of the divine law, facing showdowns with the motley crowd that worshipped the golden calf to be sure, but also with his brother Aaron, his *alter ego*, endowed with powers of sweet speech which the Lord in His all-encompassing wisdom had refused him.

Hans Swarowsky, the lamented conductor, once called his teacher Schoenberg 'an artist whose free inventiveness followed an inner compulsion towards logical necessity'.[27] The ultimate aesthetic-ethical result, one might argue, was that, given Beethoven's essentially Christian ideal of music in the service of 'inner and outer peace', Schoenberg devoted his long creative life to music to the cause of 'inner and outer law', in keeping with the Old Testamentary notion that peace will thrive only where the God-given Law unreservedly obtains. It was the bitter bane of his existence that, of all things, his devotion to ancient monotheistic doctrine should cause both uncomprehending critics and the broader public to condemn the most genuinely human composer of the twentieth century as a fanatic worshipper at the idolatrous altars of sterile reason. Nothing could have been further from the truth, if only because so much of his philosophical baggage, a life-long admiration for Schopenhauer in particular, was part and parcel of the Wagnerian inheritance of his generation, just as his analytical bent never ceased to be stimulated by Bach and Beethoven, the twin musical heroes of the Romantic age. The spiritual strength embodied in his strikingly prophetic self-image he certainly acquired in the course of his extended journey along the path of the Bible. Like his personal hero Moses, Arnold Schoenberg faced a 'stiff-necked people'. And he too had to wait forty years before at least a substantial minority yielded to the force of his convictions as a matter of logical and historical necessity.

[27] Hans Swarowsky, 'Zur Einführung', in E. Hilmar (ed.), *Arnold Schönberg Gedenkausstellung*, 46.

5

Relevance and the Future of Opera: Arnold Schoenberg and Kurt Weill

BORN of crisis rather than revolution, a fragile child not so much of inexorable historical change as of political misalliance, the Weimar Republic never quite managed to outgrow its traumatic infancy, not even when, for a short period immediately preceding its catastrophic decline, it miraculously mustered the formidable strength of the condemned man compressing the creative energies of a lifetime into what little time he has left. Crisis was indeed endemic to Germany's short-lived experiment in democracy. Nor was the crisis-mentality alien to the arts, which, frenzied by daily injections of journalistic sensationalism, became the paradigmatic tumbling-grounds of radical forces from both Left and Right, favourite battlefields of the breeders of anarchy and the defenders of civil law and order. Opera had reflected, and often anticipated, socio-political change virtually from its early seventeenth-century beginnings as a public art. But since it traditionally catered to a variety of cultural elites—whether aristocratic or bourgeois—out for an evening of edifying entertainment, its actual existence had never been seriously threatened. However in the wake of the great blood-letting that was the First World War, faced with unprecedented ideologically inspired expectations and ever-increasing competition from the new media of film and radio, opera, an aesthetically ambivalent genre almost by definition, appeared to have reached the very end of its post-Wagnerian rope. By the middle twenties the 'operatic crisis' was a broadly acknowledged cultural concern discussed in literally hundreds of literary exercises—scholarly, artistic, and, above all, journalistic.

In December 1927 the *Neue Wiener Zeitung* asked Arnold Schoenberg, among others, to comment on 'The Future of Opera' as he saw it. Schoenberg replied that the issue was, in his eyes, inextricably tied up with the serious challenges to all established forms of dramatic expression posed by the rapid technological advances of the post-war era. The cinema, which had fascinated him from the outset, was perhaps the most crucial factor, because it could provide 'all that theater offers, except speech'.[1] When, less than a year later, speech and music joined the cinematographic arsenal, Schoenberg was quick to perceive both opportunities and the inherent dangers for composers and play-wrights. In the meantime he felt that the cinema, without ensuring 'the future of opera' as such, had removed from the traditional stage any further responsibilities toward the mass public, leaving it free to serve the more exclusive needs of the minority that will never 'be satisfied wholly and exclusively by what everyone can understand'.[2]

To be understood by many, ideas need expressing in a particular way. Nature decrees that the essence of any such mode of expression must be a basic decrease in the tempo at which things happen. Clearly one may not leave gaps in the action, during which many of the audience would have to think out for themselves what was missing. All the conclusions that the listener is to draw must be explicitly stated, clearly and at length. Endless time would have to be spent on this, and one could hardly spend so much time in order to arrive at certain extreme conclusions that follow from complicated and deep ideas. So it is self-evident that art which treats deeper ideas cannot address itself to the many. 'Art for everyone': anyone regarding that as possible is unaware how 'everyone' is constituted and how art is constituted. So here, in the end, art and success will yet again have to part company.[3]

Given the matchless visual effects that accounted for so much of the general fascination with moving pictures, not to speak of the fact that 'color film will soon be here, too', the composer, who had called for colour and light crescendos in his opera *Die glückliche Hand* some fifteen years earlier, now wondered how much of an opera-public would soon be left 'unless a new path is found', a path away from the easy access and understandability of the film in the direction of 'the depth where riddles lie'. To remain viable in an age of technology, he concluded, 'opera will have to be an opera of musical ideas'.[4]

Schoenberg committed these reflections to paper while holidaying on the French Riviera at a time of intense dramatic preoccupations. Having devoted much of the preceding year to his play *Der biblische Weg*, he turned his full attention to *Moses und Aron*, in the hope of completing the text soon without substantial interruptions. Yet in the autumn of 1928 he stopped everything and, with extraordinary dispatch, wrote his solitary

[1] Schoenberg, 'The Future of Opera', in *Style and Idea*, 336.
[2] Ibid., 337.
[3] Ibid., 336.
[4] Ibid., 337.

comic opera *Von heute auf morgen*. Why one so deeply immersed in biblical subject-matter should suddenly turn to such a frivolous libretto, rather hastily concocted by his wife, would seem to elude reasonable explanation, were it not for the virtually irresistible challenges presented at the very beginning of that final boom season by *Die Dreigroschenoper* of Bertolt Brecht and Kurt Weill, which began its triumphant course on 31 August, and by *Friederike*, Franz Lehar's thoroughly romanticized version of an episode in the love-life of Goethe, which had its Berlin première on 4 October. Three weeks later Schoenberg plunged into his one and only contribution to the sprawling field of 'relevant' opera. That the Lehar connection was by no means fortuitous follows from his strong recommendation that the role of the *Sänger* be confided to 'a tenor capable of singing especially beautifully, smoothly, sweetly and express-ively—something like Tauber',[5] the public idol as leading man in opera, operetta, and soon film as well. Nor was Lehar very far from Schoen-berg's mind when, a few years thereafter, he commented extensively on the concept of 'epic opera', as exemplified in the next joint effort by Brecht and Weill, *Aufstieg und Fall der Stadt Mahagonny*. Meanwhile he wanted it understood that in his own opera 'behind these simple events something else is hidden; that these everyday characters and happenings are being used to show how above and beyond this simple story of a marriage, the so-called modern, the merely modish exists but "from today till tomorrow", from a shaky hand to a greedy mouth—not only in marriage, but no less in art, in politics and in attitudes toward life'.

Their obvious artistic and political differences notwithstanding, Kurt Weill and Arnold Schoenberg did not really stand as far apart as might appear at first blush. Although Weill belonged to a younger generation, both were products of the emancipated Jewry of Central Europe that contributed so mightily to socio-political as well as to artistic change. Ultimately they suffered the same persecution and exile. But before the forces of darkness assumed full control, each in his own inimitable way responded creatively to the moral dilemmas that racked Germany's ominously unstable exercise in democracy.

Weill arrived in Berlin the very year the Republic was declared. In 1920, after initial study with Humperdinck and a short interlude as a small-town conductor, he was admitted to Busoni's master-class in composition at the Prussian Academy of the Arts. In 1923, the very year Schoenberg discovered that there was no escape from one's Jewish

---

[5] Cf. Rufer, *The Works of Arnold Schoenberg*, 55.

heritage, Weill, the son of a Dessau cantor, completed his formal studies with a stunning choral setting of portions of the Lamentations of Jeremiah, the biblical prophet who witnessed the destruction of Jerusalem. This, needless to say, was before he discovered the surrealistic theatre of Georg Kaiser or, for that matter, the work of Stravinsky and the 'new objectivity', and well before his growing concern with the fate of the culturally and economically deprived masses steered his creative energies in quite different directions. Not till 1935 when in exile in France, did he return to the Old Testament, as composer of the score for *The Eternal Road*, Max Reinhardt's grandiose staging of Franz Werfel's *Der Weg der Verheißung*, an evening-filling historical pageant that not only recalled Schoenberg's *Der biblische Weg* in its very title but reached its theatrical climax, like *Moses und Aron*, with an orgiastic dance around the golden calf.[6]

Schoenberg, to be sure, had struggled with the theme of spiritual decay in the face of naked materialism ever since *Die glückliche Hand*. But that complex if brief work, though written before the First World War, saw German footlights only in 1928, the year of *Die Dreigroschenoper*. By then its author had succeeded Busoni in Berlin. And Busoni's pupil Weill, who shared his master's early admiration for Schoenberg, was nearing the end of his tenure as chief columnist and critic for the German broadcasting corporation's weekly publication. In four years of intense journalistic activity, cut short, ironically, by the triumph of *Die Dreigroschenoper*, Weill had rarely missed an opportunity to draw attention to Schoenberg as the foremost composer of his time. Indeed, as early as 28 February 1926, previewing one of the regular *Hour of the Living* programmes, he extolled Schoenberg as one whom

broad circles of the public continue to regard as a kind of scarecrow, the despicable generator of the current 'corruption' in music, while actually his style grows quite organically out of the music of the nineteenth century; he merely draws the last consequences from the style of Wagnerian chromaticism, which he advances to the highest degree of differentiation; in so doing he arrives at a 'colour melody' that represents affective developments in every tender shade. True, spurning all concessions, he proceeds with the straightforwardness of the fanatic who looks upon success in his lifetime almost as evidence of regression in his art.

---

[6] Marc Blitzstein, reporting from France at the time, ventured the opinion that Weill's latest score, the title of which he translates as 'The Road to Promise', was both his 'best score, and also his most uneven'. Cf. Marc Blitzstein, 'Theater-Music in Paris', *Modern Music*, 12 (1935), 132–3.

But even his opponents are forced to recognize in him the purest, noblest artistic personality and the most forceful spiritual force in musical life today.[7]

In May 1927 Weill celebrated the Berlin Academy's broadcast of *Pelleas und Melisande* under Schoenberg's own direction as 'a truly festive hour'.[8] And when *Pierrot Lunaire* was performed in Frankfurt later that year, he reiterated that its 'decisive significance for the musical development of the last decades is recognized even by Schoenberg's enemies'.[9] Moreover, 'in the conciseness of its expressive means and in the tremendous intensity of its musical language' *Pierrot* seemed, as it were, predestined for broadcasting. If there was a parting of the ways with Schoenberg, it was primarily over Stravinsky, whose strident post-war homophony appealed to Weill, as did 'the grotesque ironic-element that is represented in Stravinsky without any doubt more strongly than in anyone else'.[10] Stravinsky's Octet and Symphonies for Winds, in particular, left unmistakable traces in Weill's Concerto for Violin and Winds, premièred—characteristically—in Paris, the musical dominion of Stravinsky, Honegger, and Milhaud, in 1925. Eight years later, when the now internationally famous composer of the *Dreigroschenoper* escaped to France just ahead of the Gestapo, Paris theatres vied for the honour of staging his new ballet, *Die sieben Todsünden*. Schoenberg, to be sure, had done a great deal for French music through repeated performances of Debussy, Ravel, Milhaud, and others at his Vienna *Privataufführungen* shortly after the First World War; but once he had gained full possession of his method of composing with twelve tones he tended to look 'neither left nor right', whereas Weill doggedly kept his stylistic options open. By the mid-twenties, no doubt under French influence, Weill had turned to jazz as a catalyst for a process of aesthetic fusion that was to produce a unique body of new music perhaps no less significant yet quite unlike that of Schoenberg, who had no more use for such American imports than for Weill's strong socialist leanings. And, needless to say, Weill, who had barely left school when the guns of August finally fell silent, was committed to international understanding through music, whereas Schoenberg prided himself on his particular contribution to the German musical heritage.

---

[7] Cf. Kurt Weill, *Ausgewählte Schriften*, ed. David Drew (Frankfurt, 1975), 119.
[8] Ibid., 123.
[9] Ibid., 124.
[10] Ibid.

The journalistic controversy which erupted in 1926—primarily over *Jonny spielt auf*, Ernst Krenek's sensational 'jazz opera'—received additional impetus almost immediately when Busoni's posthumous work *Doktor Faust*, completed by his pupil Philip Jarnach, was staged in Dresden that same year. Steadfast in his loyalty to his beloved master, Weill decided to join the fray with a 'commitment to opera' of his own, pointing, in keeping with Busoni's teaching, to Mozart as the supreme musical dramatist, who even in his instrumental music never left 'the temple of the stage', but who by the same token let purely musical considerations determine much of the dramatic course of events. If nothing else, contemporary composers could learn from Mozart a 'glass-like clarity and inner tension of musical diction'; above all Mozart had shown that opera is generally at its best as a 'most precious vessel filled with every possible musical form and genre'.[11]

Having thus gone on record in favour of Mozart as the supreme source of inspiration for his generation, Weill proceeded to link 'the renewal of operatic form' directly to Busoni's *Faust*. While acknowledging the difficulties that any intrinsically polyphonic composer encounters in attempting to come to grips with musico-dramatic conflict, he contended that in *Doktor Faust* polyphony was dramatically mandated, 'like the Turkish colouration of the *Abduction*, like Spanish rhythm in *Carmen*, and its only function is that of representing the work's principal figure in all shades of feeling become sound'.[12] In other words Busoni understood that the 'renewal of operatic form' depended on the strictest adherence to, and enforcement of, 'the purely musical generation of form through the medium of the stage'. Needless to say, it was this essentially anti-Wagnerian conception of the musical theatre which guided Weill's own hand as he proceeded toward his distinctive brand of 'relevant' opera predicated on the novel doctrine of 'the gestic character of music'.

Though hardly for the same reasons, the Schoenberg circle was clearly moving in similar directions.[13] The *Wozzeck* fragments performed in Frankfurt in 1924, a year before the opera's much-delayed Berlin

---

[11] Kurt Weill, 'Bekenntnis zur Oper', in H. Heinsheimer and P. Stefan (eds.), *25 Jahre Neue Musik: Jahrbuch der Universal-Edition* (Vienna, Leipzig, and New York, 1926), 228.

[12] Kurt Weill, 'Busonis "Faust" und die Erneuerung der Opernform', *Anbruch*, 60 (1927), 54.

[13] Reminiscing about *Die Glückliche Hand* Schoenberg explained in March 1928: 'For quite some time I had been preoccupied with a concept which I actually believed to be the only one permitting a musician to express himself in the theater. In my private vernacular I referred to it as: *making music with the means of the stage*.' Schöenberg, *Gesammelte Schriften*, i, ed. Ivan Vojtech (Frankfurt, 1976), 236.

première, had confirmed that a non-tonal dramatic idiom was not necessarily incompatible with the Classical-Romantic structural tradition. Indeed Alban Berg made a special point of his reliance on strict formal patterns for both symbolic and specific dramatic purposes, citing in particular the chorale-prelude in the tavern scene of the Second Act, 'a caricature in the truest sense of that word, which manifests itself also in its musical treatment'.[14] This scene undoubtedly loomed large in Weill's mind when he conceived the exquisite Second Act duet for *Mahagonny* along very similar lines. As for 'the future of opera', Berg soon lost patience with the constant search for new idioms and procedures. All he asked was 'the opportunity to enhance good theatre with beautiful music, or—better still—to make beautiful music in such a manner that good theatre results nevertheless'.[15] Berg might therefore conceivably have managed to bridge the rapidly widening gap between Weill and Schoenberg—who was to remember *Wozzeck* so audibly in *Moses und Aron*—had not Weill, buoyed by the frenetic career of *Die Dreigroschenoper*, chosen at the crucial moment to regale his Berlin fans with a journalist prank, published during the 1928 Christmas holiday under the title 'The Musician Weill' (see Fig. 2), that made light of everything Schoenberg held dear. Although it was by no means aimed at him, Schoenberg was shocked by such schoolboyish tomfoolery on the part of a young colleague brazen enough to deal with serious aesthetic issues in the comic manner of a typical German secondary-school lesson, parodied down to the last detail, including the typical conditioning ritual of 'Get up—sit down—get up', etc. preceding the lesson proper. In the interests of a better understanding of the Schoenbergian reaction, the substance of the article follows in translation.[16]

During the last hour we spoke of the transformation of opera into music drama, and I explained to you the notion of the complete work of art. So that nobody has any excuses, I'll write on the blackboard once more the names of

> Richard Wagner
> Richard Strauss.

Now we come to a new chapter. You'll remember that I read to you from the texts of Wagner. They always dealt with gods and heroes and curious concepts

[14] Alban Berg, 'Die musikalischen Formen in meiner Oper "Wozzeck"', *Die Musik*, 16 (1924), 587.

[15] Alban Berg, "Das Opernproblem", reprinted from *Neue Musikzeitung*, 16 (1928) in Willi Reich (ed.), *Alban Berg*, 174.

[16] The newspaper clipping with Schoenberg's extensive annotations forms part of the Arnold Schoenberg Institute collection in Los Angeles (Rufer D 114).

like forest murmur, magic fire, knights of the Grail, etc., which you found rather strange. Then there were some difficult thought-processes, which you were unable to follow, and also certain things that you could not yet comprehend and which are as yet none of your business. None of this was of much interest to you. You rather busy yourselves with technical questions, with airplanes, automobiles, radio installations, and bridge construction, and as reading material you prefer sports news.

Write down!: The time of gods and heroes is past.

I played you excerpts from the music of Wagner and his successors. You have seen for yourselves that there are so many notes in this music, I could not even reach them all. You would have liked to sing along with an occasional melody, but that proved impossible. You also noticed that this music tended to make you sleepy or had an intoxicating effect like alcohol or other drugs. But you don't want to be put to sleep. You want to hear music you can comprehend without special explanations, music you can readily absorb and sing with relative ease. Nor, in all probability, do you any longer understand why your parents should attend concerts from time to time. For that is a habit generated by social conditions characteristic of the last century but for which your generation lacks any basis. Today there are again broad areas of great concern, and if music cannot be placed in the service of society as a whole, it forfeits its rights to exist in the world today.

Write down!: Music is no longer a matter of the few.

The musicians of today have made this sentence their own. Their music, therefore, is simpler, clearer and more transparent. It no longer wishes to represent philosophies, it does not want to depict exterior events, nor does it intend to generate specific sentiments, instead they (the musicians?) seek to restore music to its original mission, its original significance. You can think of it in this fashion: once musicians obtained everything they had imagined in their most daring dreams, they started again from scratch.

Write down!: Kurt Weill makes the attempt to start from scratch in the realm of musical theatre.

He has reached the conclusion that opera cannot be allowed to perpetuate its self-centred romantic existence in an atmosphere incompatible with the times. He wants to get to the point where opera finds its place in the general development of the contemporary theatre, where the operatic figures become once again real human beings who speak a language understood by all. He has, therefore, joined that theatrical movement which most explicitly meets the artistic demands of our time, that founded by Bertolt Brecht—open parenthesis: Bertolt Brecht, the originator of epic drama—close parenthesis. Weill has recognized that this movement offers the musician a wealth of new, surprising tasks. Brecht and Weill have examined the question of the proper role of music in the theatre. They have come to the realization that music should not promote or underscore the action on stage, that it fulfills its genuine function only when it breaks the action at appropriate moments. Make a note of the most important result of Weill's work to date, the term gestic character of music with which we'll deal in detail next year in a special course after those of you who intend to become professional critics will have left us.

Get up!: We shall now sing no. 16.

The article concludes with the first eight measures of song 16 from *Die Dreigroschenoper*, 'Der Mensch lebt durch den Kopf', according to which 'man's reliance on his head does not suffice, try if you like, living off your head are mostly lice!'

Berlin's leading newspaper, the *Berliner Tageblatt*, had asked a number of *Prominente*, including Heinrich Mann, Otto Klemperer, and the critic Alfred Kerr, to contribute to its 1928 Christmas issue a concise description of their work in terms an intelligent twelve-year-old would understand.[17] Only Weill made a joke of it, and Schoenberg, for one, had no use for his rather crass humour. But neither was he prepared to dismiss 'the musician Weill' as a mere prankster. In his characteristic fashion he carefully underlined the most offensive passages, systematically numbered others, and filled the margins with his biting comments. How was such impudence to be explained if not as a deliberate ploy to obscure the issues by substituting absurdities for sorely missing logic? Unlike Anton Webern, who, under the impact of early traumatic experiences with the theatre, adhered heart and soul to the Romantic doctrine of the 'purity of music', Schoenberg was no aesthetic puritan. Instead, ever conscious, though not necessarily indulgent, of human folly, he continually searched for new comprehensive forms of musico-dramatic expression even in the film age, indeed precisely because the cinema had produced some radically new modes of articulation. Unlike Busoni, who, as he recalled much later, had generated the notion that operatic music 'must not express what is expressed in the action', Schoenberg remained steadfast in his belief that 'opera is principally the product of four factors: the text, the music, the stage, and the singer', and that 'none of these ought to disregard what the others do'. That younger composers had seized upon some of his own pre-war experiments as a licence to indulge in all sorts of mindless exaggerations was surely not his responsibility: 'when I had asked not to add external expression and illustration, they understood that expression and illustration were out,

[17] Cf. David Drew, 'To the Editor', *Kurt Weill Newsletter*, 5/2 (autumn 1987), 3.

that there should be no relation whatsoever to the text ... what nonsense!'[18]

Although the Busoni pupil Weill had catered to non-committal relationships between text, music, and action even in his earliest dramatic efforts, Schoenberg, recognizing his great gifts, had followed his at first rather modest career with benevolent interest. But when *Die Dreigroschenoper* quite unexpectedly swept everything before it, one so thoroughly suspicious of popular success as Schoenberg felt constrained to ask: 'What has he accomplished in the end? He has restored 3/4 time.' Weill's newspaper-piece, thriving as it did on *non-sequiturs* and glib assertiveness, could not but reinforce Schoenberg's keen disappointment. Yet it seems that at times Schoenberg found it difficult to desist from the very stance that so appalled him. Thus playing on the linguistic sanction of the same German word for 'opening up' and 'putting on', he cleverly speculated that the teacher (Weill) quite likely asked his pupils to 'open a parenthesis because with him everything was a put-on (*Aufmachung*)'. In a more serious vein, he ponders Weill's reference to an 'atmosphere alien to the times'. How is one supposed to take this? 'Are there time-related cucumbers, fountain pen inks, shoe pastes ... ?' Weill's wholesale condemnation of opera 'of the romantic variety' is ridiculed with all sorts of tongue-in-cheek remarks. The passage 'you also noticed that this music tended to make you sleepy' leads him to observe that in all likelihood the boys fell asleep before noticing anything:

The one who noticed was Mr. Kurt Weill; he did take notice and resolved never again to copy ten times as punishment the kind of music that causes boys to fall asleep. Instead, he decided to start from scratch, where one can copy freely behind the back of the teacher, who won't notice and whom one does not have to put to sleep or drown in alcohol.

The crux of the matter for Schoenberg was the contention that music should always be understood as soon as it is heard. Does this imply that in fact 'one is supposed to talk only about matters which the most stupid can understand?' That those alleged areas of current interest to the masses offer opportunities for good earnings without much hard work is 'something that Mr Weill understandably passes over in silence'. Surely none could blame the boys for preferring sports-news to the epic dramas of Mr Brecht?

I only hope the time is not too distant when youth will consider it offensive that one writes for them as if they were idiots ... one can express oneself in a very

[18] Schoenberg, 'This Is my Fault', in *Style and Idea*, 146.

popular manner without having to behave idiotically. In the end those commu-
nally-oriented artists will have addressed their idiocies only to each other. When
all is said and done, art for art's sake has simply been replaced by *l'art pour les
artistes*, music for the initiated, who pretend to be uninitiated so as to make sure
nobody notices that that's what they really are.

I can truthfully say that I have often discussed very sophisticated matters with
simple people who were intelligent though unlearned, conceding nothing save
certain terms which I could not employ without some explanation and the fact
that I could not express myself all too concisely. Stupid people, whether learned
or not, have never understood me, and there isn't a chance that they would, even
if I spoke to them like Weill.

Characteristically, Schoenberg does not leave it at that but adds a
postscript of a far more positive nature:

There can never be any question in matters of the mind—and there precisely lies
the fundamental difference between creative and commercial activity—of arrang-
ing things in such a way as to suit a definite purpose; rather, a thought must be
couched in whatever form suits it best, in the clearest and most comprehensive
fashion, and so that all the consequences to which it gives rise flow from it
effortlessly, indeed almost inevitably. And that is why one can't ask of musical art
what Mr. Weill (for once, I want to speak seriously about these things) has in
mind. Perhaps things will make more sense to him if I get Aljechin or Lasker to
resolve that from now they'll play only such [chess] matches as are within the
comprehension of people generally, or let Einstein discover no other physical or
astronomical laws.

It stands to reason that decisions of this sort do not depend upon the inventors
themselves; for they do only what the good Lord commands. He, however, has
deliberately left so much in the dark that those working under His orders can at
most enlighten each other. Of course once things are taken in hand by those
pledged to obey only the orders of the people at large, they are bound to improve!

In a last rejoinder at the bottom of the page, Schoenberg expresses
serious doubts about ideological purity in a profit-oriented environment.
In the words of one, perhaps apocryphal, publisher: 'At current interest-
rates communal art alone offers financially rewarding possibilities.'

Weill might well have agreed, if only because he had maintained all
along that the contemporary musical theatre was entitled at the very least
to the kind of financial incentives that had been largely responsible for
the formidable growth of commercial music. As he stated unequivocally a
few weeks later, in January 1929, nothing was more important to Brecht
and himself than 'this first successful penetration of a consumer industry
which until now has been the exclusive preserve of an entirely different

sort of musician and author. With the *Dreigroschenoper* we get through to a public which either did not know us at all or at any rate denied us the ability to generate interest among members of an audience way beyond the limits of the musical and operatic public.'[19]

That Weill did not have material gain alone in mind goes without saying. But there was a strong feeling in his circles that those who made artistic contributions to the well-being of society were entitled to commensurate rewards as a matter of course. Indeed *Die Dreigroschen-oper* was but one manifestation of 'a movement that comprises virtually all of the younger musicians: the renunciation of the *l'art pour l'art* perspective, the turning away from individualistic principles of art, the film music idea, the connection with the young music movement, the significance of the musical means of expression related to all of this— these are but different steps along the same path.[20] In short, what Weill rejected was not the concept of a consumer-industry as such but the poor quality of its products; and he was confident that his collaboration with Brecht would effectively restore, under totally different social, political, and economic circumstances, a measure of that quality which the aristocratic and bourgeois pasts had taken for granted.

It was at the behest of this socio-musical idea that Weill felt he had to 'start from scratch'. There was no place in the democratic musical theatre for 'romantic opera ... conceived in moments of creative ecstasy' and stressing irrational elements to the point where, in its ultimate Wagnerian transformation, 'it renounced the representation of man altogether'. Nor did Weill see a viable alternative in 'that form of musical theatre which employs a text only as a pretence for free, uninhibited musical enjoy-ment', so that 'the music contributes even less to the development of the dramatic idea than in the music drama'. Opera was bound to remain an anomaly until 'the gestic character of music' was permitted once again to determine its overall structure as well as the minutest dramatic detail.

Now it is well known that music is entirely devoid of psychological faculties or powers of characterization. But music does have one potential of decisive significance for the representation of man on the stage: it can render the *Gestus* that clarifies the stage event, it can even create a sort of fundamental *Gestus* through which it forces the actor into a specific attitude precluding any doubt and

---

[19] Kurt Weill, 'Korrespondenz über Dreigroschenoper', *Anbruch*, 11 (1929), 24. For a slightly different translation see Ulrich Weisstein (ed.), *The Essence of Opera* (New York, 1969), 331.

[20] Ibid.

any misunderstanding concerning the event in question; ideally, it will fix the *Gestus* so strongly that faulty representation of a given event is no longer a possibility. Every attentive theatre-goer knows how many false tones, how many hypocritical movements accompany even the simplest and most natural of human actions on stage. Music has the possibility to tie down the underlying tones and the underlying *Gestus* of an event in ways that eliminate the danger of wrong interpretation yet leave the actor plenty of opportunity for the deployment of his own personal manner. Needless to say, gestic music is in no way bound to the text, and Mozart's music owes its dramatic import, even outside the realm of opera proper, precisely to the fact that it never surrenders its gestic character.[21]

But exactly what is it that music can do to enforce its gestic character? For one, it can fix speech accents, syllable lengths, and pauses, so as to neutralize the most common sources of actors' mistakes. The creative musician will always go beyond mere text-based rhythmic fixation and establish a very special relationship between word and meaning. In other words, textual considerations 'constrain the opera composer no more than such formal schemes as fugue, sonata, or rondo pinned down the classical master'. Not only Mozart, the most obvious case in point, but also Bach, especially in the recitatives of his Passions, Beethoven in *Fidelio*, and, more recently, Offenbach and Bizet, have shown that there is room for every kind of melodic expansion and rhythmic or harmonic differentiation, as long as the musical tension-curve is motivated by the gestic course of events. Thus there is nothing to prevent the melodic embellishment of a single syllable, provided it is justified in terms of a gestic rest at that particular moment. In conclusion Weill cites the ritornello from *Mahagonny*, 'Oh, Moon of Alabama', derived from a simple melody contributed by Bertolt Brecht, which, though admittedly primitive, had nevertheless proved more than adequate for the determination of the intended *Gestus*. Weill's far more sophisticated version 'in no way altered its majestic character, even though its appearance was drastically changed'. Brecht regarded the *Gestus* concept as nothing less than an aesthetic breakthrough, opening up entirely new vistas for writers as well as composers. For his part, Weill, acting in the same spirit of collective responsibility, lost no time in adapting Brecht's doctrines of 'epic theatre' to the requirements of 'relevant opera'.

Yet in the end, socio-aesthetic theory had to yield to socio-artistic practice in the 1920s in Germany, just as it had in England two centuries

---

[21] Kurt Weill, 'Über den gestischen Charakter der Musik', *Die Musik*, 21 (1929), 420–1. Erich Albrecht's full translation of this crucial piece in *Tulane Drama Review*, 6 (1961), 28–32, is somewhat less than satisfactory, as suggested by its very title 'Gestus in Music'.

earlier. And since 'epic opera', as conceived by Brecht and Weill, accomplished little by way of direct, didactic communication, others— Hindemith and Krenek foremost among them—were promoting still another genre, the *Lehrstück* or musical teaching-piece, thus further complicating the ongoing debate over 'relevant opera'. Structurally the *Lehrstück* favoured the greatest informality, if not always outright indeterminacy. While Krenek argued that proper representation of the 'here and now' required medley-like groupings of loosely ordered numbers, Hindemith advocated essentially an *ad libitum* approach permitting not only various arrangements of the component parts but actual omissions as well, provided such appeared to be required by the specific context of a given performance. Nothing could have been further from the Schoenbergian aesthetic, of course, and he acidly commented that 'if music is frozen architecture, then the potpourri is frozen coffee table gossip, instability caught in the act, a parody of all logical thinking'.[22] But Weill too sensed danger. As usual closer to Schoenberg with respect to structural issues than his musical generation at large, he was concerned above all that such pieces might deal with daily events yet neglect their underlying relationships: 'One does not show the man of today as he really is, one wants to photograph him instead of offering him the mirror in which he can see himself.'[23] In its radical manifestations the *Lehrstück* offered little more than 'contemporary subject-matter in an outdated theatrical form'. The larger issues of the time—political ambitions, war, capitalism, inflation, and revolution—demanded a 'new over-all form of the theatre', well beyond that exemplified by *Die Dreigroschenoper*, which represented a preliminary, though in itself significant, step toward the realization of the many 'new and strong' possibilities of gestic music. As a case in point he cited the revitalized role of the chorus, which adds so substantially to the dramatic range of *Aufstieg und Fall der Stadt Mahagonny*, the first and perhaps last work in which large-scale operatic design and socio-political relevance managed to coexist at the behest of both.

Possibly because he felt by no means very sure in matters of musical style and structure, Brecht decided that his most recent joint venture with Weill deserved some rather thorough commentary, for the benefit not so much of the public, which was expected to react instinctively, as of the

[22] Schoenberg, 'Glosses on the Theories of Others', in *Style and Idea*, 313.

[23] Kurt Weill, 'Aktuelles Theater', reprinted from *Melos*, 8 (1924) in *Melos*, 37 (1970), 277.

critics, who were bound to be no less perplexed by its novelty than those who had confronted Wagner's *Ring* half a century earlier. And, in order to make sure that his theoretical formulations would indeed withstand close scrutiny from every point of view, he enlisted the aid of his friend Peter Suhrkamp. Quite probably, Schoenberg read the resulting statement of the principles of 'epic opera' when it first appeared, although he reacted in writing only in July 1931, following the appearance in the *Vossische Zeitung* of a summary by H. H. Stuckenschmidt, published while Schoenberg was on holiday in French Switzerland, struggling with the wellnigh insurmountable problems of *Moses und Aron*.

For all we know, the composer's extensive analysis of Brecht's categorical distinctions between 'dramatic' and 'epic' opera owes its existence primarily to the opportunity it offered for a meticulous test of his own musico-dramatic premisses. At any rate, though acknowledging at the very outset his inability to check on the accuracy of Brecht's 'guidelines' as reported by Stuckenschmidt, he also mentions that they sound vaguely familiar and that, indeed, he must have read them before. But why, he asks, did a man of Brecht's stature have to enlist the assistance of a certain Peter Suhrkamp ('Who is he?'). What is one to make of the peculiar circumstance that 'even if Kurt Weill did not collaborate, it took two nevertheless to produce this brew'? Schoenberg suspends the torrent of his questions just enough to render the offending guidelines as conveyed by Stuckenschmidt.[24]

Dramatic Opera	Epic Opera
The music serves	The music mediates
Music heightens the text	Interprets the text
Music illustrates	Anticipates the text
Music provides the physical situation	Takes a position
	Renders the attitude

Are these mere ideal postulates, Schoenberg wonders, or the fruits of Brecht's analysis of existing categories? How is one expected to reconcile such seemingly contradictory statements as 'asserts the text' and 'the music serves'? Assuming that the remaining lines are meant to suggest the various ways in which music 'serves' in 'dramatic' opera (heightening the text, asserting it, etc.), how then is it to render an attitude, take a

[24] Schoenberg's manuscript (Rufer E 12) is entitled 'Stuckenschmidt-Brecht Operngesetze'. All quotations below, unless identified otherwise, refer to this document. H. H. Stuckenschmidt's actual title was 'Brecht, Operngesetze: Anmerkungen zur Oper'. For John Willett's translation of Brecht's 'Anmerkungen zur Oper Aufstieg und Fall der Stadt Mahagonny' see U. Weisstein (ed.), *The Essence of Opera*, 334–44.

position, and mediate all at the same time in its 'epic' counterpart, 'since he who mediates cannot possibly take a position of his *own* but instead must take his place between two each of whom *insists* on a different position'? How can one come to a mutual understanding where fundamental issues are stated in such a questionable manner? Although he states with a touch of exasperation that 'one doesn't really know where to begin', Schoenberg not only makes a beginning but keeps going. For the questions raised by Brecht touched him directly, as he was struggling to complete *Moses und Aron*, and called for immediate specific responses.

Needless to say, one so passionately committed to logic and lucidity in presentation was bound to find Brecht's manner no less disconcerting than Weill's, since both tended to treat historical issues al fresco, with little regard for meaningful distinctions in matters of detail. Weill's quite untenable identification of all nineteenth-century opera with Wagnerian music-drama and its 'gods and heroes' was matched, as far as that goes, by Brecht's highly idiosyncratic use of an established term like 'drama'. How could opera be anything but dramatic? Schoenberg suspected that the underlying problem was 'once again colloquial language, which understands "dramatic" to relate only to fighting and murder', even though every schoolboy is aware of the real issue: whether the acting takes place before our eyes or is left to our imagination. Because dramatic action precludes lengthy explanations of whatever may be necessary for a proper understanding of the plot, it relies on visual complementation. Its inherent 'lack of time, however, must be a function of the plot itself: if not, it is difficult to see why everything has to go so fast, considering how much better it would be to read it or hear it presented slowly'. In other words, truly dramatic material will be explosive in nature and abound with exciting events. Whether or not such material is also suited for epic representation depends, all things being equal, on the ability of the narrator, his capacity to arouse the imagination sufficiently without visual support.

While Schoenberg regarded any and all such considerations as 'elementary', he recognized that 'today one deals with concepts and terminology in accordance with the possibilities and demands of merchants and newspapers'. Hence, he assumed, Brecht was simply forced to engage the eye as well, which explained his famous posters. Those ubiquitous props of the contemporary theatre by and large replaced the monologues and dialogues to which the traditional theatre entrusted the important issues. Reducing all such integral dramatic elements to the bare minimum,

Brecht indulged in 'primitiveness, which offers virtually no advantages, except that it looks today as if it were *new*: in all probability this is what the theatre was like at the very beginning'. Which, it would seem, was what Weill had in mind when he decided to 'start from scratch'. By contrast Schoenberg, who acknowledged 'making sense of the action where the sung word cannot be perceived' as a perennial operatic problem, felt that more recent experience offered plenty of guidance and inspiration.

In the past, composers sought by and large extraneous solutions for this fundamental operatic dilemma, employing recitatives, spoken dialogues, changes in scenery, movement, lighting, etc. In all probability it will always be difficult to do the right thing in these matters, which, however, lose much of their importance anyway, as soon as a creative musician, in response to a dramatic situation comes up with a good musical figure, a good motive: for the musician the joy of a beautiful, interesting figure will always be greater than his sadness over the fate of the greatest hero. For therein lies the real problem of opera: the effects of music are hardly influenced by the will (this skirts Schopenhauer), and when it is strong, it is stronger than any real event. An example: Fidelio third act. Who really cares about the chorus's exaltation over the liberation of Florestan thanks to Leonore? One must distinguish: it is certainly possible to rejoice over the liberation *itself*, but here the members of the choir are the ones who rejoice, and they don't interest me at all. And yet there are few theatrical pieces of music which time and again make an effect comparable to this march-like choral setting 'Hail this day, hail this hour!' I could well imagine that the chorus would impress me in exactly the same fashion were it to accompany Pizzaro's revenge with Rocco's help and with Leonore abandoning the desperate Florestan in order to start an affair with Pizzaro.

Quite obviously nothing in the twenty years since he made his fundamental contribution to Der blaue Reiter had given Schoenberg cause to change his mind on 'the relationship to the text'. In a postscript to his notes to Brecht's notes he in fact points to that very article which, he admits regretfully, had misled younger composers like Hindemith who actually tried to compose operas 'without paying any attention whatsoever to the stage'. All he had meant to convey was what he still believed, i.e. the inherent incompatibility of events on stage and in the orchestra-pit is 'a problem of effect, not cause ... while the effect will always be ambivalent, the conception must be unitary, i.e. *the composer must be sparked by the text*, must create the illusion that he actually gives expression to that which happens on the stage'. In 'Glosses on the Theories of Others' the same thought is expressed even more graphically:

'An opera is a whole, conceived unitarily. It comes about as does any fruit of the womb—an apple, a pear, or a child—as a whole, in a single act of procreation.'[25]

As he comments item by item on the Brecht–Weill guidelines 'translated into German', Schoenberg unwittingly enters into a revealing dialogue, less, it would appear, with his antagonists, who act as convenient foils, than with himself:

The music mediates:
> That is very difficult: mediates between this and that; or it mediates as it communicates; Probably the latter, hence:
>> The music communicates the text; but that is something the text itself does; thus: the music communicates something of the text which it alone, without this mediation, cannot communicate.

Perhaps this is the emotional content, the *élan*, the character of some romantic sentimental quality. Thus:
> *The music communicates things which the text won't or cannot say.*

One surely doesn't have it easy with this Brecht: Is that what he means or not? At any rate it is said in riddles.

Perhaps he means:
'The music interprets the text' in that sense?

But then he says:
'The music anticipates the text.' This would seem to require an addition. Something like . . . draws conclusions or possibly supplies information (mediates) yielded by the interpreted text.

'Takes a position' could signify, for example, that, where the text communicates something sad, it 'takes a position' by taking (for ex.) a different position; by poking fun at the sadness, parodying it, making it ridiculous, in short by *expressing* (thus expression after all!!!) something different than the text; taking a position, as conceived here, would be an illustration of the opposite through its expression. (One could of course also say that it illustrates the sentiments of one having a different perspective.)

'Renders the attitude.'—in this connection I can only say: that seems to relate to something quite similar to the preceding. In view of the 'Drei-Groschen-"Oper"' I can hardly imagine anything else.

In this context it must be said first of all that Brecht's viewpoint implies not only that music *expresses* 'something' but that it expresses something *concrete*.

Thus—and that would be an interesting result of the struggle against romanticism, against expressive music—he has definitely *expressive music* in mind.

Except that he insists it express 'something else'.

But that creates the following situation:

In the past the author of the text intended his text to produce a sentimental or

---

[25] Schoenberg, 'Glosses on the Theories of Others', in *Style and Idea*, 314.

whatever effect, and a composer was obliged to compose so as to obtain such a sentimental or whatever effect. But now we have a poet who—and that is where the knot becomes hopelessly entangled—looks to express that which the poet meant but did not say, or perhaps also, what he actually said but did not really mean—the main thing is: that text and music stand in their contradictory relationship. This is the way it is, I suppose, and that is certainly the impression one gains: Messrs Brecht and followers do not want to be taken seriously, which is something that would not have occurred to me in the first place. If that is not 'vieux jeu,' Saint Offenbach, Saint Nestroy, Saint Johann Strauss, librettists all the way down to Knepler (the 'poet' and thinker who gives Lehar his wings), then it can only be modern.

But then Schoenberg never made a secret of his contempt for the 'so-called modern', which in the letter to Steinberg he identified with the 'merely modish', existing 'from today till tomorrow; from a shaky hand to a greedy mouth'. Years earlier, in his Three Satires for Mixed Chorus, Op. 28, he had ridiculed 'the little Modernsky' whose 'versatility' and 'new Classicism' affected the German 'moderns' of the 1920s so decisively, whose L'Histoire du soldat, as Ernst Bloch, the philosopher who was also among the more perceptive critics of the period, once observed, represented in fact 'the original good music made of refuse, dreams, and rags'.[26] That L'Histoire could not have been written without the precedent of Pierrot Lunaire in no way affects its basic incompatibility with the Schoenbergian aesthetic.

Arnold Schoenberg's own single entry into the arena of 'relevant' opera was signed and completed '1. Jänner 1929'.[27] Given the nature and substance of his one-sided intellectual bout with that very concept the week before, Von heute auf morgen would seem to derive its true relevance precisely from the criticism of 'relevance' in art, which its strict reliance on the method of composing with twelve tones metaphorically implies. This admittedly somewhat abstruse work thus represents a historical event of the first magnitude, a necessary stepping-stone, as it were, from

[25] Ibid.

[26] Ernst Bloch, 'Lied der Seräuber-Jenny in der "Dreigroschenoper"', Anbruch 11 (1929), 127. Bloch's felicitous phrase also aptly characterizes parts of Weill's Mahagonny--Songspiel, which preceded the Dreigroschenoper by one year and was subsequently expanded into the evening-filling Mahagonny opera. In the Songspiel the spirit of Pierrot Lunaire has, as it were, been filtered through L'Histoire du soldat, then gone through the crucible of American jazz as represented in particular by Paul Whiteman and his band, whose appearances at the Große Schauspielhaus in Berlin in June 1926 created a sensation, if not an outright crisis, among some younger German composers.

[27] Rufer, The Works of Arnold Schoenberg, 53.

the fleshpots of modern society to that desert where pure ideas eternally prevail. Unlike Weill, caught in an ill-fated ideological propaganda war, Schoenberg attempted to give his sorely tried contemporaries sustenance in the grand tradition of the ancients, dramatizing basic conflicts that have beset human kind from time immemorial. Whereas Weill felt moved by the socio-economic crisis of his time to depict human folly at its most decadent, and in often deliberately absurd fashion at that, Schoenberg attacked the cultural dilemmas of Western civilization at their very roots. Where Weill turned to Charlie Chaplin's universally admired 'Gold Rush' for his 'epic' masterpiece *Aufstieg und Fall der Stadt Mahagonny*, Schoenberg in *Moses und Aron* seized upon the Book of Exodus as a paradigm for the perennial dichotomy of raw materialism and its ubiquitous companions fear and alienation on the one hand, and, on the other, the ideal of a spiritual peoplehood contingent on unremitting courage and self-denial. In thus responding creatively to the challenge of a particularly ambivalent stage in Germany's often confused and confusing history, Schoenberg and Weill not only carried to different, uniquely personal heights the momentum of German opera from *Wozzeck*, that most shattering of musico-dramatic testimonies to man's inhumanity to man, to *Lulu*, where the culture of narcissism raises its ugly head; they also shaped the twin foundations of whatever viable opera the future might yet hold in store.

6

Dance on a Volcano:
Von heute auf morgen

AMONG the many strikingly revealing popular songs that enjoyed popularity in the early days of the Weimar Republic, one in particular stands out in historical perspective. It is entitled 'Hiawatha', and its first line reads: 'Everybody dances even if he doesn't quite know why, because, it seems, all are as yet a wee bit high.' Whereupon a rousing chorus, cast in the typical Berlin lingo of the day, describes a scene familiar to all at the time:

> Lights out! Pull your knife!
> Beat him to a pulp.
> Free the streets!
> Close the windows.
> Quick, get off your balconies.

In the wake of the largely democratic revolution of 1918 and its sundry Fascist postludes, a song like 'Hiawatha' afforded the average citizen a vicarious sense of participation in the same seemingly momentous yet so tragically bungled series of events which caused the satirist Tucholsky to comment wrily that 'due to unfavourable weather conditions, the German revolution has been relegated to music'.[1] But if the progressive German intelligentsia chuckled knowingly at Tucholsky's hard-hitting political wit, many a member of the traditional artistic establishment was rapidly slipping into the kind of paranoia that signalled the ascent of Hitlerism. Hans Pfitzner, the ultra-nationalist composer and symbol of Aryan musical genius, was so thoroughly frightened by the post-war music of Busoni, Schreker, Schoenberg, and Hindemith, he could hardly find words enough to condemn this 'artistic parallel to Bolshevism'.[2] Even before a runaway inflation of unprecedented proportions destroyed what little the war had left of Germany's socio-economic foundations, the musical battle-lines were clearly drawn. In counteracting the forces of

[1] Cf. Hans Erman, *Berliner Geschichten, Geschichte Berlins* (Herrenalb, 1966), 440.
[2] Ibid., 434.

reaction, however, the younger generation was no less drastically divided:
there were those who firmly believed that only a good dose of humour
could assuage what was anything but a laughable situation; and there
were others, more radically inclined, who insisted on periodic shock
treatments designed to bring their fellow countrymen face to face with
the very real threat to human decency posed by the various obscurantist
harbingers of doom whose post-Wagnerian pretensions capitalized on the
ubiquitous Romantic tendency towards exaggerated self-pity and ultimate self-destruction. That the first decade of the Weimar Republic
earned the historical epithet of a golden age, with a good deal of
justification, was due in large measure to the uncanny combination of
social consciousness and artistic creativity which characterized both
these—at times strongly antagonistic—camps, whose brilliant achievements accounted for the extraordinary position of the capital city of
Berlin in the artistic life not merely of the young Republic but of the
entire continent, after it rose from the ashes of war.

For historical reasons too well known to be repeated here, German-
speaking Central Europe had long been free of cultural domination by a
single seat of political power. Hence, whereas French music and art were
inextricably bound up with the fortunes of Paris, nineteenth-century
Germany took pride in such fiercely competing centres as Mannheim,
Hamburg, Munich, Leipzig, and Weimar. Not until 1870 did the
movement towards an intellectual capital for the whole of Germany gain
significant momentum, a movement consolidated during the decade
preceding the First World War and fully completed only after the war's
disastrous conclusion. Musically, the rapid emergence of Berlin sealed
the fate of Vienna, its fading rival, even though the Viennese, past
masters of nostalgia, somehow managed to keep up appearances well into
the 1930s. For centuries Vienna had exerted its magnetic force upon
musicians and patrons of music from the four corners of the Austrian
realm. Now Republican Berlin became the cosmopolitan centre of
attraction for gifted men and women from central, eastern, and northern
Europe. But, more than any other distinct group, it was the Jewish
minority, whether established or recently arrived, which transformed this
city of merchants and manufacturers into the twentieth century's avant-
garde Mecca at the Spree.

Writing in 1928, a beacon year for the democratic German theatre
between the two world wars, Arnold Zweig explained the amazing
contributions of Jewish actors to the German stage: 'The Jew is in
essence a Mediterranean being; among the peoples of the north a

southeastern phenomenon, he defines his behaviour, his inner tension, his tension release, in Mediterranean terms.'[3] Like other Mediter-raneans—Spaniards, Greeks, or Arabs—Zweig maintained, the Jew is fundamentally a speaker: 'He thinks with his ear. He hears sentences as he thinks and when he writes; His writing is an inner speech. The tempo of his sentences and their organization are frequently rhetorical in nature . . . He is the born actor, not because he has so many egos, like a neurotic, but because he has taken such firm hold of his own ego that he can assume others temporarily at will . . .'[4] Needless to say the sociological and psychological factors accounting for the prominence of artists and intellectuals of Jewish descent in the Weimar Republic were both manifold and complex. Politically, Jews had been in the forefront of the German Socialist movement from the days of Ferdinand Lassalle and, somewhat later, of Eduard Bernstein and Otto Landsberg, partly for general humanitarian reasons and as a matter of enlightened self-interest: 'the socialist principle sternly eschewed anti-Semitism, and this was often decisive to an increasingly harassed Jewish community.'[5] Whatever their exact motivations, in November 1918 a number of ideologically well-versed Jewish Socialists were ready and able to fill a substantial portion of the political vacuum created by the overthrow of the imperial regime. In addition, and perhaps more decisively, the widespread social *malaise* and psychological maladjustment that marked the post-war era struck familiar chords among a people who, after centuries of discrimina-tion and outright oppression, had become Europe's leading specialists in alienation.[6] Psycho-historically, Franz Kafka's fascination with estrange-ment in all its debilitating variety was but the most intense literary reflection of the protracted minority trauma of the 'mice nation', as Kafka called the Jews in *Josephine the Songstress*.

Alienation, to be sure, begets any number of often contradictory attitudes: the bitter type of humour identified in the nineteenth century with the satirical verses of the self-exiled Heinrich Heine no less than the

[3] Arnold Zweig, *Juden auf der deutschen Bühne* (Berlin, 1928), 22.

[4] Ibid., 22–3. As for the Jewish propensity for satire, Zweig commented: 'Not one to take himself seriously, anything but a solemn crocodile, as long as he is left alone in his natural skin, he does not act solemnly with others either; a polemicist who aims his arrows laughingly like Heine, like Kerr and such, capable of wrathful laughter about the evils of his time, in whose default he fervently believes, because, man of the sea and the market place, he has seen the ways of many different people.' Ibid., 25.

[5] Howard M. Sachar, *The Course of Modern Jewish History* (Cleveland, 1958), 286.

[6] The characterization 'specialist in alienation' is Isaac Rosenfeld's. Cf. Guttmann, *American Scholar*, 32/4 (autumn, 1963), 570.

musical parodies of Jacques Offenbach, the son of a German Jewish cantor, who dominated French comic opera. Towards the end of his life Offenbach devoted his remaining energies increasingly to serious musical drama, but the spirit of his ever-topical operettas was perpetuated in late nineteenth-century French cabaret, which in turn inspired both the Berlin Überbrettl and the Chat Noir where Rudolf Nelson, the ruling cabaret-master of the Weimar Republic, earned his early musical laurels. Born Rudolph Lewinsohn in 1878, Nelson, who had appeared publicly in the 1880s as a child-prodigy playing Chopin and Liszt, was dismissed from the Berlin Academy of Music when he presented his composition teacher with a waltz instead of the required canon. The shocked professor's last words, 'man, you belong in a nightclub', were prophetic. The notorious waltz quickly earned first prize in a contest sponsored by an entertainment magazine, and Nelson was launched on a long career which, after first contacts with *Kleinkunst* at the Überbrettl and subsequent employment with several of its various imitators, led straight to the Kurfürstendamm, and, decades later, survived even the Nazi onslaught.[7]

Paradoxically, early German cabaret enjoyed the active support not only of prominent members of the aristocracy but of the imperial family as well. Zum Faun, where Nelson obtained his first job as composer-in-residence, was owned by Baron von Ensberg. In 1903 none other than Prince Joachim Albrecht of Prussia offered Nelson the musical director-ship of a small theatre under his personal patronage. Nelson, however, had little taste for such close ties with representatives of the reigning élite and eagerly seized the opportunity of starting an independent establish-ment with Paul Schneider-Duncker, an actor who, having fallen in love with cabaret in Paris, shared Nelson's passion for informal communica-tion between stage and audience. In order to engage the audience more directly in a theatrical experience, Nelson and his partner decided to expand the role of the traditional master of ceremonies, the *conférencier*, in terms both of the element of time allotted to him and of the nature of his discourse, which then assumed unprecedented literary qualities and socio-political overtones. Inevitably, Berlin cabaret, as virtually created by Nelson, left its lasting imprint on German theatre at large. As if to symbolize this historical task, Dr Arthur Pserhofer, imported from Vienna to serve as Nelson's principal *conférencier*, brought with him

---

[7] The author is indebted to Mr Herbert Nelson of New York City for information concerning his late father's theatrical career.

Alexander Moissi, the singing guitar-player who later became one of Germany's most celebrated serious actors. When, in 1907, Nelson dissolved his partnership with Schneider-Duncker and opened his own Chat Noir, Pserhofer was replaced by Dr Fritz Grünbaum, a literary descendant of Heine, who set the tone and pace of intellectual satire that was to dominate the cabaret of the twenties from Trude Hesterberg's Wilde Bühne to Werner Fink's Katakombe.

The pervasive significance of the cabaret as a breeding- and training-ground for actors, singers, librettists, and composers, even visual artists, can hardly be overestimated. Not only Moissi but Friedrich Kayssler and Max Reinhardt too began their careers as cabaret artists. And it may well have been his early close contact with the audience in a cabaret symbolically named Sound and Smoke which later prompted Reinhardt to acquire an abandoned circus-building for the first European theatre-in-the-round (or almost in the round) and, similarly, to stage *Everyman* in the Salzburg town square. In short, as counter-theatre the cabaret affected even theatrical ventures otherwise quite removed from its physical and spiritual ambience.

Like the rest of the German theatre, Berlin cabaret undoubtedly reached its artistic and financial peak in 1928, the climactic year of the German economic boom. Kurt Robitschek, the director of the leading Kabarett der Komiker, responded appropriately by moving into a new and much larger house designed by Erich Mendelsohn, one of the Republic's most celebrated architects. To commemorate this signal occasion, Robitschek invited Walter Trier, the well-known cartoonist, to illustrate the cover of the special issue of the house-organ and pro-gramme-booklet *Die Frechheit* and asked a number of prominent critics to contribute their views on the nature of good cabaret. There was widespread agreement that the cabaret represented an autonomous form of art with its own intrinsic ideal and requirements. As Max Hermann put it:

With the theatre the cabaret shares the stage, with the musical show a certain *souplesse* and variety as well as compressed instant effects. But the stage events in the cabaret must have something of improvised play. The pieces presented must engender humour that rises like a rocket, whirls along in a jiffy, and does not suffer from long breath. Cabaret has an edge over the musical show because of its genuine wit, wit characterized by a degree of superiority and mobility found nowhere else: unencumbered by claims of eternal validity, responding to timely issues forcefully, even rebelliously, with generous caricature, aggressively, impro-vising comments, whipping up controversy. The basic formula is something like this: sharply contoured art of the moment spiced with a goodly amount of change, irreverent and unsentimental, full of colour and surprise . . . no gilded show and no accelerated theatre but rather something quite different, an altogether separate world.[8]

While Robitschek was agonizing over the completion of his new home, helping with manual labour himself on occasion to minimize delays, the Renaissance Theatre hosted a show, put together by Bruno Arno, which featured a cross-section of characteristic cabaret topics in typical rapid-fire succession, effectively linked by the jazzy sounds of Sid Kay's Fellows, perhaps the most popular theatre band of the period. There was a futuristic skit depicting the successful moon-landing of a German rocketship whose occupants claimed the moon as a German colony and then radioed the former Kaiser this clever play on words: *Wie Euer Majestät suchten wir das Weite*. In another scene, the paramilitary branches of the major political parties, usually locked in ferocious street-battles, appeared on stage in their respective uniforms, linked in brotherly song: *Wer will unter die Soldaten*. Nor was Erwin Piscator, the famous leftist director, exempt from ridicule. He, who that year made such abundant use of conveyor-belts in his staging of *The Adventures of the Good Soldier Schwejk*, was the obvious target of a Faust parody showing Faust and his disciple Wagner on their famous walk, which, however, quickly deteriorated into an athletic competition, due to mechanical malfunctioning. The extent to which the proliferation of political parties with often ill-defined ideologies tickled the humorous nerve of *Kleinkunst* artists is shown graphically in the sophisticated programme covers of yet another show, featuring the Hungarian-born actor Szöke Szekall, later of Hollywood fame. Red is the primary colour worn by a barely-dressed girl, representing no doubt the Republic in all its blatant nakedness. But the girl's concertina and the star-studded background turn the overall colour-scheme into the very opposite: imperial black, white, and red.

If *Kleinkunst* thus displayed a distinct physiognomy, whether from a political or histrionic point of view, the same was surely true of its musical qualities. The leading *Kleinkunst* musicians were seasoned professionals whose thorough knowledge of musical literature in general

[8] *Die Frechheit*, 4/9 (Sept. 1928), 11. The author gratefully acknowledges the invaluable assistance of Mr S. Petruschka of Jerusalem, founder and director of Sid Kay's Fellows, the prominent Berlin jazz band of the 1920s and early 1930s. Mr Petruschka not only offered his invaluable personal collection of newspaper reviews for examination but made available for photographic reproduction copies of rare programme booklets.

was as far-reaching in its consequences as their often highly individualistic assimilation of traditional techniques of composition. In 1901/2 none
other than Arnold Schoenberg worked for Ernst von Wolzogen's Buntes
Theater.[9] As for Nelson, following his inglorious departure from the
Royal Academy, he had studied with Gustav Holländer, director of the
Stern Conservatory, on a scholarship provided by three Berlin bankers
eager to further such an obvious talent. A private institution directed by
the Holländer family for two generations, the Stern Conservatory was
distinguished by a liberal stance to the point where, as early as 1911, it
had offered Arnold Schoenberg its podium for a highly successful lecture
series. Friedrich Holländer, on the other hand, Gustav Holländer's
nephew, became a mainstay of Berlin cabaret, together with Werner
Heymann, Bronislaw Kaper, Mischa Spoliansky, and eventually Willy
Rosen, all of whom, except for Rosen, who was killed by the Nazis,
wound up in Hollywood shortly before the Second World War. Friedrich
Holländer, already famous as the composer of Marlene Dietrich's songs
in *Der blaue Engel*, managed to write the music for a total of one hundred
and sixty-five German and American films.[10]

The film industry was not the only force inimical to the cabaret with its
characteristically intimate atmosphere. By the mid-twenties, Broadway-
inspired shows with lavish sets, fancy costumes, and plenty of 'cheese-
cake' made much money for Eric Charell, a shrewd producer who, after
bringing Paul Whiteman and his orchestra to Berlin, crowned his
youthful career with the 'immortal' *White Horse Inn*. And then there was
Berlin operetta, almost totally identified for a while with Fritzi Massary
and Richard Tauber, who sang Franz Lehar's sparkling scores from
Viennese poverty to Berlin riches. Still, the more thoughtful members of
Berlin's growing musico-theatrical colony remained wary of the euphoric
atmosphere created by the rapid economic rehabilitation of Weimar
Germany from the mid-twenties on. An eloquent minority, they refused
to be fooled by one-sided material gains and expressed their deep sense of
frustration at the many unresolved social and political problems temporarily obscured by Germany's first economic 'miracle'. It is thus more
than mere coincidence that the basic tenets of the Berlin cabaret began to

[9] Ironically, Schoenberg was introduced to von Wolzogen by Oscar Strauss, the
company's regular musical director—who would not himself appear on *Kol Nidre*, the eve
of the Jewish Day of Atonement—during the series of guest performances that von
Wolzogen's Überbrettl gave in Vienna in September 1901. Cf. Stuckenschmidt, *Schoenberg: His Life, World and Work* (London, 1977), 49.

[10] Herman Behr, *Die goldenen zwanziger Jahre* (Hamburg, 1964), 94.

influence the 'serious' musical stage at about the same time that its more superficial characteristics found their way into musical shows, operettas, and motion pictures.

In the early twenties, Kurt Tucholsky, bitter-sweet and sharp-tongued as ever, wrote for Nelson. A few years later, Georg Kaiser provided the texts for Kurt Weill's *Der Protagonist* and *The Tsar has his Picture Taken*, the former tragic, the latter utterly grotesque. By 1928, at the very height of the economic boom, Bertolt Brecht co-operated with Weill on their hit *Die Dreigroschenoper*, shortly after Berlin witnessed the unforgettable première of the stage adaptation of Hasek's satirical novel *The Adventures of the Good Soldier Schwejk*, directed by Erwin Piscator in his best 'epic' manner and designed by George Grosz. Piscator had managed to make effective use of photomontage as a replacement for traditional stage scenery, and Grosz was enthused. 'What new possibilities for the artist who wants to speak to the masses at large,' he exclaimed, 'wishy-washy impressionism will not do. The lines have to be "filmic", clear, simple, and not too thin (to allow superimpositions); besides, the lines have to be hard, somewhat like the drawings and woodcuts in the gothic block-books, or the lapidary stone-carvings on the pyramids.'[11]

These traits are discernible also in the musical aesthetic of Kurt Weill, as exemplified in both *Die Dreigroschenoper* and *Aufstieg und Fall der Stadt Mahagonny*. In each of these two works the *conférencier* of the cabaret has been retained: as the Street Singer in the former, as the Speaker in the latter. And each in its own way makes abundant use of the kind of musico-poetic entity to which the German cabaret artists themselves referred with the English term 'song', in contra-distinction to the German 'Lied'. English, eventually also American, influences were generally strong in the world of *Kleinkunst*. The stage-names of many of the principal artists, including Nelson, are no less indicative of this fact than Brecht's choice of a two-hundred-year-old English model for his topical morality play. In *Mahagonny*, America provides the frame of reference. Needless to say, the story of *Mahagonny* views American society from the most critical European perspective of the 1920s in terms of the money-dominated free-for-all prohibition. Whether or not the Alaskan memories of the four male protagonists, all lumberjacks, were inspired by the enormously successful showing of Charlie Chaplin's film *Gold Rush*, which ran in Berlin for years from 1925 on, Chaplinesque

---

[11] Cf. Herbert Knust, 'Grosz' Contribution to the Berlin Schwejk Performance of 1928', in *Theatrical Drawings and Watercolours by George Grosz* (Cambridge, Mass., 1973).

satire and exaggeration permeate the entire work except for the ubiquitous underdog, who is depicted here as brutally self-indulgent rather
than pathetic. *Mahagonny* was projected as an 'epic' opera rather than as
a traditional 'dramatic' opera, and this very break with operatic tradition
was bound to make a socio-political point. Gustav Brecher had conducted the first performances in March 1930 in Leipzig with trained
opera singers. Brecht and Weill were therefore determined to recruit for
Berlin a number of singing cabaret-actors. Their choices included the
young Lotte Lenya as Jenny, Trude Hesterberg as the widow Begbick,
and Harold Paulsen as Jim. Except for the latter, all had distinctly non-
operatic voices and thus reinforced the general ideal implied by Georg
Grosz when he wrote that 'the lines have to be "filmic", clear and simple,
and not too thin'.

Parody in *Mahagonny* is for the most part of a purely musical nature,
limited to often incongruous allusions to tunes and procedures of implied
symbolic value. Characteristic instances are the figurated chorale ('Haltet
euch aufrecht'), clearly inspired by the two armoured men in Mozart's
Magic Flute; the male quartet ('Auf nach Mahagonny'), which cites the
bridesmaids' chorus from Weber's *Freischütz* to the words *Schöner,
grüner Mond von Alabama*; the bar-room piano-solo rendition of 'The
Maiden's Prayer' at the beginning of the 'Here-You-May Tavern' scene,
which prompts one of the lumberjacks to exclaim nostalgically, 'What
truly eternal art'; and the parody of conventional operatic declamation in
the first ensemble following the Hurricane Fugue, with the constant
repetition of the word 'Wo' in the two lines:

> Wo ist eine Mauer, die mich verbirgt?
> Wo ist eine Höhle, die mich aufnimmt?

In addition there are musical references to the type of kitchen-maid song
that served Weill as a lasting source of inspiration, and to all sorts of
modern ballroom dances. Actual jazz rhythms underline the words
'money alone does not produce sensuality', and jazz-related combinations
of instruments, including guitar, saxophone, and percussion, are heard
throughout, as are various march patterns inspired by popular Socialist
labour songs, many of which were subsequently taken over by the Nazi
movement.

Die Dreigroschenoper, as Weill observed in 1929, had managed to break
'into the entertainment industry, which was hitherto reserved for a
completely different type of writer and composer'.[12] *Mahagonny*, though

---

[12] See Ulrich Weisstein (ed.), *The Essence of Opera*, 331.

infinitely more complex, effectively maintained that momentum. Still, its historical roots, like those of the cabaret, were not so much German as French. After the Russian emigrant Stravinsky, it was the young Darius Milhaud who, fascinated by the music of the New World, introduced the sounds and textures of popular bands into the post-war theatre and concert-hall. But while the Milhauds, Poulencs, Wieners, and Français produced a succession of fluffy parodies, bitter satire prevailed in Germany not only in the output of 'democratically' inclined artists like Weill, Eisler, and Dessau. During the twenties, even the 'élitist' Arnold Schoenberg, indulged in sophisticated satire in works as divergent as the Serenade, Op. 24, the one-act opera *Von heute auf morgen*, Op. 32, and the *Sechs Stücke für Männerchor*, Op. 35 (written in 1930, the year of *Mahagonny*). His Op. 28 is clearly entitled *Drei Satiren für gemengten Chor*. Schoenberg, however, pointed his arrows at both ethical and aesthetic targets, whereas for Weill and other musical representatives of the political left, the aesthetic issues merely reflected the state of society at large. Commenting on his comic opera in his letter of 4 October 1929 to William Steinberg, Schoenberg specifically refers to 'the disgusting slapstick which is rampant in Berlin'.[13] If he mentions Richard Tauber as a model for his self-satisfied tenor, it is because the opera is 'vocally conceived from A to Z'. There are, in fact, only short orchestral interludes. And 'the singing and acting must always remain dignified'. There must be no exaggeration whatever: 'Better colourless than crude . . .'[14]

Schoenberg's topical reference to Richard Tauber, undisputedly the most successful German tenor of the 1920s, bears on one of the most characteristic traits of artistic life in Weimar Berlin: the virtual inter-changeability of its component parts and figures. Tauber had made a remarkable career in traditional opera and held the coveted title *Kammer-sänger*. But the public revered him above all as the incomparable interpreter of that prolific type of Berlin musical stage-production between the wars, operetta. Few composers of these stunning visual and musical affairs came originally from Berlin: Lehar, Brodsky, and Paul Abraham, perhaps the most gifted of the younger generation, were of Hungarian origin. Kollo was of Polish descent, Stolz came from Vienna. Like their 'serious' fellow musicians, they had been attracted to a capital which had grown from 1.8 million inhabitants in 1900 to more than four million, following the unification of its innumerable small boroughs, and

[13] See Rufer, 55.   [14] Ibid., 56.

1. Interior of the Seitenstettengasse Synagogue in Vienna's First District

2. The Café Griensteidl in 1896, from the Michaelerplatz towards the Herrengasse

3. Interior of the Café Griensteidl

4. Otto Dix, *Großstadt* (Big City), 1927–8

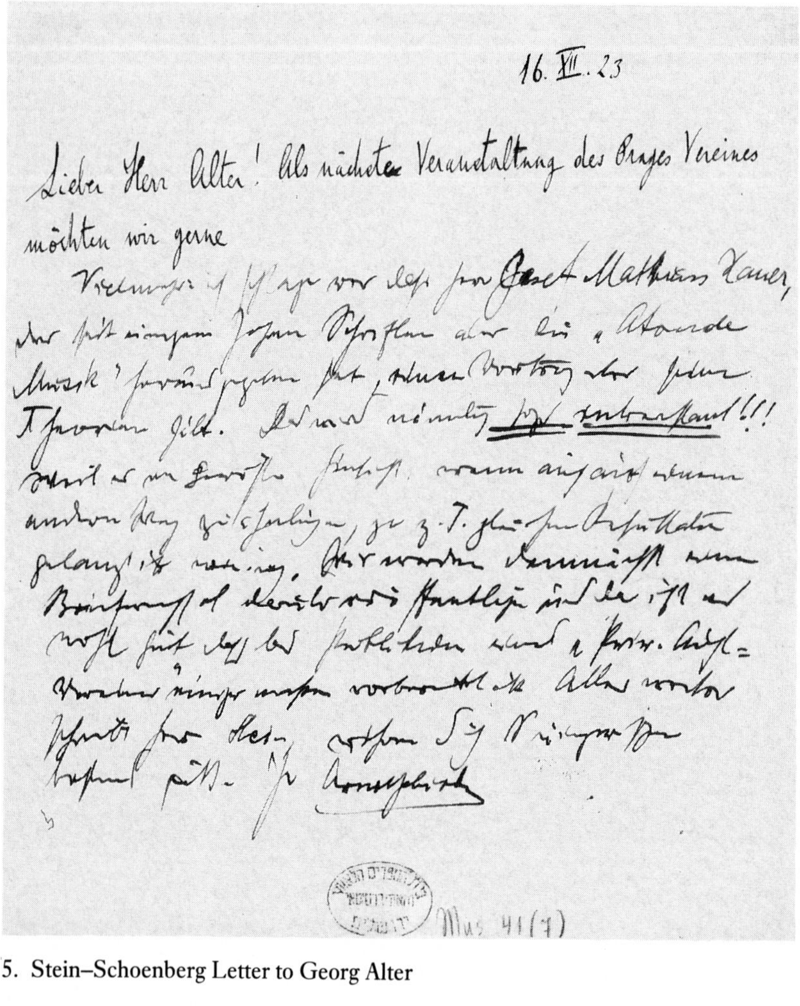
16. XII. 23

Lieber Herr Alter! Als nächste Veranstaltung des Prager Vereines möchten wir gerne

… Josef Matthias Hauer, …

5. Stein–Schoenberg Letter to Georg Alter

Also lieber Herr Alter, bitte teilen Sie mir mit, wann dieser Abend sein kann. Womöglich bald, Hauer geht es materiell elend. Selbstverständlich ~~braucht~~ kann dieser Abend ein einzelner sein.

Bitte geben Sie mir nach Darmstadt Antwort, wo ich bis 3. Januar sein werde.

Mit besten Gruss

Ihr Einstein

6. The First Schoenberg Family at Traunkirchen, 1922 (Photograph by Georg Alter)

7. Schoenberg at Traunkirchen (Photograph by Georg Alter)

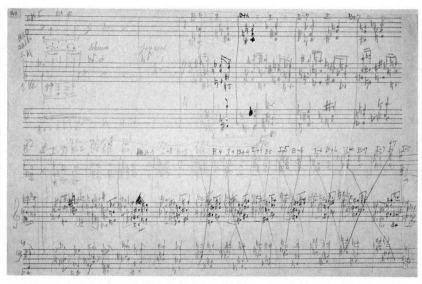

8. Sketch for *A Survivor from Warsaw*

which had first-rate theatres like the Metropol and the Admiralspalast, specifically devoted to operetta. Not only did they find production-facilities and personnel unmatched anywhere else; even more attractive was the free interaction of all the media: opera, operetta, cabaret, film, and the legitimate theatre. In this musical showman's paradise, the Berlin State Opera proudly permitted its prize tenor to perform at the Metropol, or even in motion pictures, once sound pictures had become practicable. And such popular cabaret-based actors as Paulsen or Hester-berg moved with equal ease from one type of entertainment to the next, including a serious evening-filling work like *Mahagonny*. This was feasible because all concerned were outstanding performers who, inevi-table rivalries and jealousies notwithstanding, basically respected each other. Moreover, the very concept of democracy as promulgated in the Weimar Republic forced the levelling of traditional aesthetic distinctions identified with specific social classes. Above all, Berlin was no longer a strictly German centre of musical activity but had advanced to a position of uncontested world leadership, to the great chagrin of provincial nationalistic and chauvinistic forces, which regarded the capital of the Reich as the ultimate Babylon (cf. Pl. 4).

Nothing, however, disturbed the perpetrators of the *Dolchstoss legende* quite so much as the veritable dance-mania which had seized the Republic, to the point where the 'people of poets and musicians' seemed in mortal danger of losing its racially unblemished soul. The only dance-steps compatible with the reactionary concept of German honour were those of stylized military marches and of Franz Lehar's 'imperial' waltzes, conjuring up the 'good old days' of the alliance of Central Powers. The pervasive impact of jazz and American popular music was regarded as incontrovertible, barbaric evidence that Germany was succumbing to the evils of racial impurity, both Semitic and Black.

The response from the Left, unfortunately, was no more than half-hearted, as might be expected from a house sorely divided against itself. Dressed in the appealing guise of catchy songs, its social criticism remained largely at the surface. Instead of dealing with the growing *malaise* of a republic moving from an unprecedented boom into a fearful economic depression, cabaret artists and assorted song-writers contented themselves with allusions to the more hilarious aspects of what was unquestionably a rapidly deteriorating situation. Sometimes they actually gave aid and comfort to the enemy, as did, for example, Peter Kreuder with a song entitled 'Der Kleine Wolf' in which the lyricist Grünbaum, himself of Jewish descent, poked fun at the pathetic figure of a little

Jewish merchant from Olmütz come to town to seek new fortunes and a good time. Rudolf Nelson, to the extent to which he did not merely belabour the traditional *risqué* subjects, limited himself to journalistic themes of the more sensational variety, such as Professor Piccard's pioneering balloon-ascent into the stratosphere, or the capital's intolerable traffic problems. Even so, his patter-song about Piccard does imply that such scientific exploits do little for the multitude whose toil and misery supports them, and his defence of the pedestrian, whose rights are violated every day by motorized superpowers, is clearly a parable calling upon the many individuals threatened by extinction in a technological mass society to band together in 'rebellion'. Pedestrians are referred to as *Großstadtinfanterie*, and the show which featured this bouncy big-city lament was pointedly called *The Red Thread*.

At this superficial level, social criticism remained integral to Berlin musical theatre even beyond 1933. As a matter of fact, the word *Rebellion*, which figures so prominently in the Nelson song, returned with unmistakeable topical implications as late as 1938 in the Gustaf Gründgens film *Tanz auf dem Vulkan*. Here the protagonist, an actor of the time of the French Revolution, played, ironically, by the Goering protégé Gründgens, incites his fellow citizens to rebellion with a rousing song, 'Die Nacht ist nicht allein zum Schlafen da', as bystanders whisper: 'He must be crazy.' And, as if to make a special point of the survival of such an occasional vestige of the democratic theatre, the composer of the film's score was none other than Theo Mackeben, the excellent band-leader, who had premièred Weill's *Dreigroschenoper* exactly a decade earlier under different, though anything but stable, circumstances.

As regards the fascinating case of *Staatsschauspieler* Gründgens, the leftist actor who became the histrionic pride of the Third Reich, Klaus Mann has dealt exhaustively with this live Mephisto in a 1936 novel that could not be published in Germany until just a few years ago.[15] Extremely talented as an actor, director, cabaret artist and producer, the ethnically and religiously unencumbered Gründgens was simply a born 'survivor'. Max Adalbert, his cabaret partner in earlier Weimar days, used to sing: 'Perhaps in time one gets accustomed to the times.' And it was this basic philosophy of accommodation which defeated the democratic musical theatre before it had any real opportunity to explore its vast socio-political potential. Even so, Werner Finck, one of the few leading non-Jews in German *Kleinkunst*, who survived the Nazi years

---

[15] Klaus Mann, *Mephisto* (Amsterdam, 1936).

heroically both on stage and in and out of gaol, had every reason to recall with pride the prophetic words he had spoken at the opening of his Katakombe in 1929: 'Two thousand years ago the catacomb was a place of refuge for the first Christians, today it offers shelter to the last.'[16]

'Man is an abyss; one feels dizzy looking down into it', Alban Berg laments in *Wozzeck*, where man's inhumanity to man is symbolized by the behaviour of members of the same military caste that had aroused the ire of Büchner nearly a century earlier. Not surprisingly, those who for four dehumanizing years had looked into that very abyss more deeply than any other generation prior to the Second World War chose, with few exceptions, to forget, whiling away in one continuous revel time miraculously gained. That the volcano into which they preferred not to look should finally erupt while their dance proceeded frantically on its edge was a foregone historical conclusion. On 28 January 1933 the prominent figures of stage and screen gathered once more for their annual night-long gala, the Berlin *Presseball*. Richard Tauber, accompanied by Gitta Alpar, his charming partner in many a Lehar operetta, toasted his Gentile competitor, Marcel Wittrisch, while the unsinkable Gründgens wooed General Kurt von Schleicher and the many other political dancing-masters present. Two nights later, on 30 January 1933, the volcano spewed forth its brown lava, and its fires burned bright in the *Wilhelmstraße*: Hitler was in power.

[16] Erman, *Berliner Geschichten, Geschichte Berlins*, 443. Once, when a heckler hurled 'Jew boy' at him, Finck retorted 'You are mistaken, I only look that intelligent' (ibid., 444).

7

Unity and Strength: The Politics of Jewish Survival

EARLY in August of that fateful year 1933, Anton Webern received a letter from Arnold Schoenberg which so upset and confused him that he immediately sent it on to Alben Berg for his reaction. Webern, distraught and unable to cope with the events that had driven his friend and teacher into exile, had written to Schoenberg in Paris that, in his opinion the best personal policy in such trying times was to keep as busy as possible. And Schoenberg quite agreed, adding that he had been subjected to fourteen years of preparation 'for what has now happened'.[1] Then, however, he exploded the bombshell that hit his erstwhile pupils with such devastating force: 'even though with difficulty and a good deal of vacillation', he wrote, he had finally managed to cut himself off for good 'from all that tied me to the Occident'. Those who knew him well should not really be surprised, for already his play *Der biblische Weg* had been part and parcel of an organic process that had merely been accelerated by the inevitable course of history: 'I could not say more about it at that time, but in it I have shown the ways in which a national Zionism can become active. And now that I have also returned officially to the Jewish religious community . . . it is my intention to take an active part in endeavors of this kind. I regard that as more important than my art, and I am determined—if I am suited to such activities—to do nothing in the future but work for the Jewish national cause.' Having found sympathetic ears in Paris, he was now thinking of a 'long tour of America which could perhaps turn into a world tour, to persuade people to help the Jews in Germany'. Past experience had shown that he was more persuasive orally than in print; that a great deal depended 'not only on my actual words, but on the way I say them—something very hard to reproduce'. Hence even such pressing and relevant tasks as the completion of *Moses und Aron* and the revision

---

[1] Quoted here from Willi Reich, *Schoenberg: A Critical Biography*, 189–90. Cf. also H. H. Stuckenschmidt, *Schoenberg: His Life, World and Work*, 368–70.

of *Der biblische Weg* might have to be temporarily shelved. Given the political emergency, it was more important for him to make his voice heard at the impending Zionist Congress in Prague, possibly also the World Jewish Congress in Geneva.

If in the end he attended neither event, it was primarily because he quickly parted ways with the official Jewish leadership over the economic boycott of Germany, a method of retaliation to which he was to remain unalterably opposed, considering it both undignified and ineffective. Convinced that the Jewish people had no choice but to rely on their own inner and outer resources rather than get involved in the national and international politics of their respective host countries, he proceeded to formulate a set of comprehensive but specific plans for the resettlement of German Jewry, all the while pressuring prominent fellow Jews into promises of active support. Yet he was neither untruthful nor inconsistent when, a few short months before his death, in an admittedly somewhat pathetic disclaimer prepared during the loyalty-oath controversy at the University of California, he called himself 'at least as conservative as Edison and Ford have been'. True, as a young man he had sided with the Viennese Social Democrats who were then the only ones to fight 'for an extension of the right of suffrage'. But, 'before I was 25, I had already discovered the difference between me and a laborer; I then found out that I was a *bourgeois* and turned away from all political contacts'.[2]

It does not really matter whether the myth of the apolitical Schoenberg was generated by this episode, dating from a period when he had reason to fear that the long arm of the inquisition might ultimately reach also those who, like himself, had long since retired. Nor is this the place to deal with Schoenberg's alleged 'betrayal of the working class'.[3] More important in the present context is the composer's assertion that, had he devoted part of his energies to politics, 'I could never have acquired the technical and aesthetic power I developed,' and that therefore, 'I never made speeches, nor propaganda, nor did I try to convert people'. Moreover, as a naturalized citizen he felt unsure of his 'right to

[2] Schoenberg, 'My Attitude toward Politics', in *Style and Idea*, 505.
[3] Ulrich Dibelius (ed.), *Herausforderung Schönberg* (Munich, 1974), covers a wide range of neo-Marxist views on the subject. As usual, Schoenberg was way ahead of his time when, as early as 1923, he predicted the 'Bourgeoisification of the Proletariat' (Rufer F 26). Throughout this chapter unpublished items are identified, whenever possible, by their listing in Josef Rufer's *The Works of Arnold Schoenberg* (London, 1962), which remains an indispensable, though necessarily incomplete, bibliographical tool.

participate in the politics of the natives'.[4] He could have added that, confident of the natives' ability to take care of themselves, he had devoted his considerable powers of persuasion to ways and means of forestalling the European holocaust, his personal nightmare throughout the violent years of Hitler's rise to power. In all likelihood, however, Schoenberg never even thought of the many pertinent proposals, speeches, and letters he produced over a period of nearly a quarter of a century as political activity in the usual sense of that term, but rather as intrinsic functions of the holy mission with which the 'supreme commander' had entrusted him—'one chosen', in the nomenclature of *Die Jakobsleiter*.

That he could not have disassociated himself completely from the political realities of the day, had he wanted to do so, goes without saying, if only because the pernicious spread of anti-Semitism as a political weapon affected the fortunes and misfortunes of every Central European of Jewish descent. A full decade before the Third Reich was officially established, prodded as much by Alma Mahler's reports of bigotry in the Bauhaus as by lingering memories of the racist restrictions that had prevented him and his family from spending the summer of 1921 at Mattsee, Schoenberg had not only warned his long-time friend Kandinsky of selective anti-Semitism; he also foresaw the decimation of German Jewry, victimized by an essentially mindless form of prejudice: 'What is anti-semitism to lead to,' he asked, 'if not to acts of violence? Is it so difficult to imagine that? You are perhaps satisfied with depriving Jews of their civil rights. Then certainly Einstein, Mahler, I and many others would have been got rid of. But one thing is certain: they will not be able to exterminate those much tougher elements thanks to whose endurance Jewry has maintained itself unaided against the whole of mankind for 20 centuries. For these are evidently so constituted that they can accomplish the task that their God has imposed on them: to survive in exile, uncorrupted and unbroken, until the hour of salvation comes!'[5]

Thus, months before Hitler's Beer Hall *Putsch* and the official beginning of the 'national revolution', Schoenberg appraised the political predicament of European Jewry with deadly accuracy, while asserting his unshakable belief in the ultimate redemption of those chosen to carry on the historical task. Two weeks earlier he had rejected Kandinsky's invitation to join the staff of the Weimar Hochschule and the newly founded Bauhaus. According to widely circulating rumours, the Bauhaus

---

[4] Schoenberg, *Style and Idea*, 505–6.
[5] Letter of 4 May 1923 to Wassily Kandinsky, in *Arnold Schoenberg Letters*, 93.

had its share of anti-Semites, and Schoenberg felt constrained to declare unequivocally that: 'I have at last learned the lesson that has been forced upon me during this year, and I shall not ever forget it. It is that I am not a German, not a European, indeed perhaps scarcely a human being (at least the Europeans prefer the worst of their race to me), but I am a Jew.'[6]

Just prior to his suicide in December 1935 the great satirist Kurt Tucholsky is said to have admitted: 'I abandoned Judaism in the year 1911, now I know that such a thing cannot be done.'[7] Apparently it also took Schoenberg a quarter of a century fully to acknowledge the fact that, hard as one may try, one cannot wash off one's Jewish origins. Yet that quarter of a century had not been lacking in pertinent reminders. On the contrary, anti-Semitism had become so integral an aspect of social and political life in pre-First World War Austria that it was virtually taken for granted by many Jews, who, as a condition for psychological survival, somehow managed to ignore it. As a political force, anti-Semitism had received an unprecedented boost from both Pan-Germanism and Pan-Slavism even before the Dreyfus affair turned a seemingly internal French matter into a broadly-based confrontation, with international ramifications. An international congress of Europe's anti-Semitic parties had taken place as early as 1882, when Schoenberg was eight years old, and in 1885 Georg Ritter von Schönerer amended the so-called Linz Programme of his nationalistic party to call for 'the elimination of Jewish influence from all areas of public life, as indispensable for the realization of the desired reforms'.[8] By 1902 the Christian Socialists, under Karl Lueger's leadership, managed to seat fifty-one anti-Semitically committed members in the lower Austrian Diet. In 1907, the year Adolf Hitler arrived in Vienna to study art, their representation increased to sixty-seven members, who, together with a number of conservatives, quickly formed a permanent anti-Semitic caucus.

Just prior to the full deployment of the anti-Semitic forces in 1881, twelve Jews had entered the Reichsrat, representing mostly the Constitutional or Liberal Party, at a time when Jews made up slightly over 10 per cent of Vienna's 704,000 inhabitants.[9] After the merger of several

[6] Letter of 20 Apr. 1923 to Wassily Kandinsky, ibid. 88.

[7] David Bronsen, 'Austrian versus Jew: The Torn Identity of Joseph Roth', *Leo Baeck Institute Yearbook*, 18 (1973), 220.

[8] Menachem Z. Rosensaft, 'Jews and Antisemites in Austria at the End of the 19th Cent.', *Leo Baeck Institute Yearbook*, 21 (1976), 79.

[9] Ibid., 49.

suburbs into metropolitan Vienna, the total population nearly doubled, but the Jewish component declined to 8.68 per cent, which comprised, however, well over half of the city's lawyers and physicians.[10] Barred, by and large, from the army, the government, and the established prestige careers generally, Jews characteristically seized any opportunity to leave their traditional preserve of trade and commerce, not only for the so-called liberal professions but increasingly also for the arts. Jakob Wassermann found not only that Jews constituted the vast majority of his intellectual and purely social contacts but also that in the capital of the Dual Monarchy the dynamic Jewish segment 'kept all the others in perpetual motion'.[11] Even Karl Lueger, the perennial mayor who had come to power on an openly anti-Semitic platform, felt constrained to acknowledge: 'I like Hungarian Jews even less than Hungarians, but I am no enemy of our Vienna Jews; they aren't really that terrible, and we certainly can't do without them. My Viennese are ready to take a rest anytime, the Jews are the only ones who like nothing better than to keep busy.'[12]

As guardians of an essentially Old Testamentary work-ethic, both Mahler and Schoenberg inevitably incurred the lasting wrath of their more easygoing fellow musicians. And this fundamental incompatibility was, for all we know, at least a secondary consideration in Schoenberg's decision to embrace Protestantism rather than the Roman Catholic faith of the Austrian majority. Victor Adler, the leader of the Social Democrats, had taken that road, as did Weininger, the eccentric psychologist. But those who retained their formal ties with Judaism were virtually indistinguishable in their basic intellectual attitudes from those who converted. What has been said of Arthur Schnitzler in this respect undoubtedly goes for others as well: 'a spiritually liberated Jew, the equivalent of the free-thinking Protestant of those days who had separated himself completely from his church.'[13] Sigmund Mayer, the author of a standard history of the Jews in Vienna, later confessed that he was hardly any longer aware of his Jewishness when 'the antisemites brought me to this unpleasant discovery'.[14] Indeed the emancipation of

[10] Rosensaft, 'Jews and Antisemites in Austria', 63–4.

[11] Ibid., 65.

[12] Sigmund Mayer, *Die Wiener Juden, 1700–1900* (Vienna and Berlin, 1917), 475.

[13] Hans Kohn, *Karl Kraus, Arthur Schnitzler, Otto Weininger: Aus dem jüdischen Wien der Jahrhundertwende* (Tübingen, 1962), 33–4.

[14] Rosensaft, 'Jews and Antisemites in Austria', 68.

Austrian Jewry was wellnigh complete when xenophobic nationalists began to cry for the containment, if not total elimination, of the 'alien intruders', whose regional roots often went considerably deeper than those of their 'aryan' detractors.

Ironically, conversion proved anything but a reliable shield at a time when racist theories furnished welcome 'scientific' rationalizations for anti-Semitic excesses. The so-called Waidhofen Manifesto, terminating Jewish membership in the German-Austrian student organizations, for example, explicitly stated that 'everyone of a Jewish mother, every human being in whose veins flows Jewish blood, is from the day of his birth without honor and void of all the refined emotions. He cannot differentiate between what is dirty and what is clean. He is ethically sub-human. Free intercourse with a Jew is therefore dishonorable; any association with him is to be avoided.'[15] In 1912 Arthur Schnitzler, who cites this decree in his autobiographical account *My Youth in Vienna*, jotted down a note to himself that would seem to apply to the substance and psychological motivation of Arnold Schoenberg's Jewish politics no less than to the tribulations of the great physician-dramatist, his senior by a dozen years:

In these pages a lot will be said about Judaism and antisemitism, more than may at times seem in good taste, or necessary, or just. But when these pages may be read, it will perhaps no longer be possible to gain a correct impression (at least I hope so), of the importance, spiritually almost more than politically and socially, that was assigned to the so-called Jewish question when these lines were written. It was not possible, especially not for a Jew in public life, to ignore the fact that he was a Jew; nobody else was doing so, not the Gentiles and even less the Jews. You had the choice of being counted as insensitive, obtrusive and fresh; or of being oversensitive, shy and suffering from feelings of persecution. And even if you managed somehow to conduct yourself so that nothing showed, it was impossible to remain completely untouched.[16]

By the turn of the century anti-Semitism had in fact become intellectually fashionable, thanks in no small measure to Richard Wagner's son-in-law, Houston Chamberlain, whose *Foundations of the Nineteenth Century* was 'the literary fad of 1900 and maintained its tremendous appeal over many years'.[17] Not only for the devout Wagnerians who

[15] Arthur Schnitzler, *My Youth in Vienna*, 128.

[16] Ibid., 6–7.

[17] Geoffrey G. Field, 'Antisemitism and Weltpolitik', *Leo Baeck Institute Yearbook*, 18 (1973), 82.

met regularly in Chamberlain's apartment, but for hundreds of others frustrated in their intellectual ambitions, which were unmatched by commensurate abilities, 'antisemitism was the anvil on which they hammered out their self-image'.[18] Occasionally, even men of Jewish ancestry, like Otto Weininger, fell under the spell of German racial theories, while many a socialist remained impressed with the argument, first made by Friedrich Engels and August Bebel, that social democracy could only benefit from anti-Semitism, since sooner or later the most phlegmatic and uncritical among the labouring classes would realize that the true enemy was capitalism, not the Jews, and that only socialism, not anti-Semitism, offered a viable solution to their problems. Strange and dangerous though it may appear today, this grotesque idea was 'shared by nearly all prominent socialists in the late nineteenth century'.[19]

Among Vienna's artists, it is true, ideology was of relatively little import. Perhaps because, paradoxically, so much of the quality of Viennese life was determined by individuals of Jewish descent anxious to escape a plainly hostile social environment, political reality entered the aesthetic realm far less than, say, in Berlin, where progressive art and politics seemed at times indistinguishable. While artists of Jewish descent were prominent in both cities, in Vienna they tended to eschew naturalism and/or social realism in favour of psychological probings into the individual condition of man confronting events quite beyond his control. Not only did the earlier Schoenberg typify this pervasive trend; he was also one of the principals in the supreme cultural effort to which the Jews of pre-First World War Vienna devoted virtually all their resources, not unlike their Spanish brethren centuries earlier, 'before the equally tragic decline', as Stefan Zweig so astutely observed. Needless to say, Viennese Jewry made its epochal contributions 'not in a specifically Jewish way; rather through a miracle of understanding they gave to what was Austrian and Viennese its most intensive expression'.[20]

And yet there were inevitable stirrings in the opposite direction as well. Schoenberg had not even conceived Verklärte Nacht when Theodor Herzl, Vienna's leading literary journalist, published Der Judenstaat, under the traumatic impact of the Dreyfus affair. And he had barely begun work on his Gurrelieder when Benno Staucher made his way to the Austrian Parliament as a representative of the Jewish Popular Party,

---

[18] Field, 'Antisemitism and Weltpolitik', 85.

[19] Hans Helmuth Knülter, Die Juden und die deutsche Linke in der Weimarer Republik 1918–1933 (Düsseldorf, 1971), 127.

[20] Stefan Zweig, The World of Yesterday (New York, 1943), 23.

which advocated Jewish peoplehood within the multinational context of the Austrian Empire. Soon the pros and cons of political Zionism were hotly debated in the coffee-houses frequented by Vienna's intelligentsia. That Schoenberg kept abreast of all such developments is attested by many a subsequent remark, especially with reference to the so-called Uganda affair, which caused Herzl's dramatic defeat at the Zionist Congress of 1903. Though by no means actively involved in Zionist politics at this early stage, Schoenberg held those who had rejected the Uganda proposal directly accountable not only for Herzl's early death but also for the ultimate lack of an adequate land of refuge at a time when the Christian world closed its doors to the victims of Nazi persecution.

Once the First World War turned into the protracted tragedy of a civilization at odds with itself, even the most assimilated of Austrian Jews could no longer deny that they were, in the words of Ernst Simon, 'alien, stood at the periphery, hence had to be specially classified and counted, registered and treated, the dream of our communality was gone'.[21] It took a most humiliating event, indeed, the so-called *Judenzählung*, to bring the painful truth home to all and sundry. On 11 October 1916 the Austrian government ordered a precise count of all Jews in the armed forces, supposedly to counteract popular rumours that Jews were trying to avoid the draft through a variety of subterfuges. The government's protestation notwithstanding, the affront was a deliberate one engineered by anti-Semitic forces, and it outraged in particular the many thousands of Jewish volunteers who had rallied to the patriotic cause. Schoenberg, after his initial rejection on medical grounds, had been inducted in December 1915. Admitted soon thereafter to the officer's training/school in Bruck an der Leitha, he returned to Vienna in May 1916 for a brief duty-assignment prior to the extended leave he was granted a month later. By the time he was recalled in the autumn of 1917, the groundswell of indignation over the *Judenzählung* had engulfed not only the Austrian Jewish community but politically progressive circles throughout Central Europe. Yet Schoenberg, following the advice of Gabriel in *Die Jakobs-leiter*, looked as yet neither right nor left. Upon his final release from the army he plunged into a spate of organizational and compositional activities, laying the groundwork for his association for private perform-ances of twentieth-century music as well as for the compositional innovations that culminated in the method of composing with twelve

[21] Cited in Hans Tramer, 'Der Beitrag der Juden zu Geist und Kultur', in Werner E. Mosse (ed.), *Deutsches Judentum in Krieg und Revolution 1916–1923* (Tübingen, 1971), 321.

tones related only to each other. Meanwhile the socio-political instability of the immediate post-war era did anything but relieve the unofficial pressure upon Austrian Jewry. When, three years after the war, in what was ostensibly a liberal republic, Schoenberg and his family found that Jews could no longer holiday in an Austrian resort of their choice, the composer, struck to the heart, divested himself of whatever illusions he had left about any possible benefits of assimilation and conversion and, with typical vigour and determination, plunged headlong into his personal search for constructive answers to the Jewish question.

The autumn of 1923 brought not only Hitler's abortive *Putsch* but also the League of Nations' ratification of the British mandate in Palestine in terms hardly compatible with the original intent of the Balfour Declaration in favour of a Jewish national home in the area. Shortly thereafter Hitler was arrested, brought to trial, and eventually given a farcically mild sentence. He used his brief house-arrest in the Landsberg fortress to write *Mein Kampf*, that brazen programme for world domination and the destruction of 'inferior' races. In the meantime the runaway tide of inflation had been stemmed and the German economy stabilized, affording the Jews a welcome reprieve at least until the next economic disaster—the Great Depression. As journalists, politicians, and social scientists everywhere debated the merits and alleged iniquities of Jewish emigration to Palestine, Schoenberg was asked for his views on Zionism by the editor of *Pro Zion*, a broadly based collection of pertinent statements by prominent statesmen, intellectuals, and artists. For all we know, it was this fortuitous challenge which reactivated his plans for a spoken drama exploring the complexities of Jewish nationhood. In his brief printed reply, at any rate, he expressed profound scepticism about the willingness and ability of any outside power to protect the Jews in Palestine 'against the many enemies that surround them'. History, he argued, shows the Jews no more capable than others of maintaining their independence without victorious wars. And he therefore concluded that the 're-establishment of a Jewish state can come about only in the manner that has characterized similar events throughout history: not through words and moralizing but through the success of arms and a happy combination of interests'.[22]

Pro Zion had barely appeared when, in 1925, Jabotinsky, invoking the

[22] Rudolf Seiden (ed.), *Pro Zion* (Vienna, 1924), 34. Seiden also sent Schoenberg his *Judentum, Judenvolk, Judenland*, a collection of essays by non-Jews on the cultural values of Judaism.

biblical mandate as opposed to that of Britain, broke with the Zionist majority in a dramatic act of defiance and pride which in all probability precipitated the completion of Schoenberg's own drama of national liberation, whose chief protagonist 'has seized upon the idea that the liberation of the Jews must be sought in accordance with the biblical example through the appropriate use of power. (He has recognized as a fallacy the attempt to rely on the goodwill of other nations) . . . Once this idea has taken hold, all else flows forth from it.'[23]

How 'the idea' took hold of Schoenberg is not difficult to assess, given the historical circumstances. The summer of 1925 saw Jewish delegates from all over the world gathered in Vienna for the fourteenth Zionist Congress. While the conference-rooms vibrated with the often intemperate sounds of the most vigorous debates about the respective merits of militant and diplomatic steps designed to secure the Jewish homeland, the streets outside were filled with anti-Semitic terror. 'Last night', one American wrote to his wife, 'was the first genuine feeling I had of what is meant by a pogrom although it was far removed from such. Jews running, stores closing, streets darkened, police chasing and chasing . . .' By the same token, he added with a mixture of sadness and hope, 'these *Hakenkreuzler* will be making many Jews Zionists'.[24] One as conscious of the Jewish problem as Schoenberg could hardly fail to take notice, even from the relative distance and quiet of his summer retreat in Traunkirchen. And so the prospect of a speedy move to Berlin, Europe's liberal musical metropolis, seemed more attractive than ever.

The decision to accept 'the Great Call' to Berlin was not an easy one, even though after months of contractual negotiations, an offer was made that Schoenberg could not possibly refuse since it amounted to a complete vindication of his ideals and of the steadfastness with which he had defended these against so much post-war cynicism. Still, he had no taste for victory celebrations, let alone for self-congratulation. As he told one Viennese journalist eager to elicit some kind of statement from him: 'I want no accusations, no attacks, no defence, no publicity, no triumph! Only: quiet!'[25] Berlin, of course promised not merely the relative quiet of a stable and well-paid position but also some much needed relief from the stifling atmosphere of a nominally republican, democratic Vienna that continued to behave as if nothing had changed since the pre-war days of

[23] Variants of this sentence appear in a number of places, including 'Zum Drama' [*Der biblische Weg*] 5 July 1923, *I. Niederschrift*, and 'Sprich zu dem Felsen' (Rufer E 14).

[24] Meyer Weisgal, . . . *So Far* (London and Jerusalem, 1971), 75.

[25] Cf. Stuckenschmidt, *Schoenberg*, 280.

Karl Lueger. And for several years Schoenberg, secure in his new compositional technique, completing in quick succession his Third Quartet, the Variations for Orchestra, and the one-act opera *Von heute auf morgen*, flourished in the German capital, which was now fully recovered from the great inflation, materially if not quite spiritually, and teeming with musical and literary talent of the highest order. Nowhere was creative originality more warmly welcomed by performers and audiences alike, and he was determined to take full advantage of such wellnigh ideal conditions. Yet, sensitive as always to the rough reality so often hiding below a shining surface, Schoenberg understood, vaguely at first but with increasing certainty as the years progressed, that he had merely exchanged 'death in Vienna' for a frenzied 'dance on a volcano', edging inexorably to the fiery abyss.[26] In the end life in Berlin during the merciless political and intellectual crisis that turned Germany into the nemesis of all mankind merely deepened his concern over the moral decadence of Christian Europe. Having arrived, as it were, under the motto 'Thou shall not, thou must', he left seven years later, with *Moses und Aron*—the dramatic exemplification of that very idea—uncompleted, and *Der biblische Weg*, on which he worked a great deal during his early Berlin years, still unperformed.

Reflecting on the doctrine 'love thy neighbour as thyself' in July 1926, Schoenberg concluded that a long evolution was needed before mankind could be expected to function under its aegis. So far, mothers alone seemed to have overcome the inherent contradictions between self-love and love of one's neighbour.[27] Six years later, struggling to come to terms with 'The Decline of the West', he rejected heroism in favour of martyrdom, because only idiots live in order to fight: 'Deprive the hero of his enemy and there is no hero left . . . As a Jew, as a member of a nation, yes, an entire race of martyrs, I place the martyr above the hero.'[28] In an oft-cited anecdote, Schoenberg's idol Gustav Mahler, asked as a boy what he would like to be in adult life, replied: 'A martyr.' However, various romantically inclined interpreters notwithstanding, neither Mahler nor Schoenberg harboured any unusual longing for death. Historical evidence suggests rather that both regarded martyrdom at the behest of a worthy cause as the only justifiable form of heroism, not the conventional heroism directed against an enemy but the compelling heroism of those who must fulfil their calling.

For the notion of collective martyrdom as a historical form of Jewish

---

[26] See Chapter 7.   [27] Rufer K 6.   [28] Rufer K 2.

heroism Schoenberg may have been indebted to Jakob Klatzkin, the
Jewish philosopher whom he consulted repeatedly after his move to
Berlin, especially in connection with *Moses und Aron*. Schoenberg was
clearly impressed with Klatzkin's argument that Jewish heroism was
nothing but 'the martyrdom of a small people resisting a world of
enemies for two thousand years'. In short, martyrdom had provided a
historical guarantee of survival for the people of the Bible, who, though
deprived of political statehood for nearly two thousand years, never lost
their national constitution.[29] By the same token, Klatzkin reasoned, such
a unique concept of spiritual peoplehood precluded individual loyalty to
a host-nation. Schoenberg, who was rapidly losing his patience with Jews
professing to fight for national regeneration while subscribing to various
internationalist ideologies, whether socialist, pacifist, or capitalist, wholeheartedly agreed. In principle he also shared Klatzkin's conviction that
the Jewish 'national liberation, if it is not to deteriorate into chauvinism,
can mean nothing else but liberation for the sake of humanization and
international cultural development at the highest level'.[30] By the early
thirties, however, Nazi storm-troopers were spreading daily terror
through the streets of Berlin, throttling free expression and overthrowing
what was left of democratic institutions in Weimar Germany. Realizing
that if the Jews were ever to fulfil their historical mission their survival
had first to be ensured Schoenberg turned his immediate attention to
practical ways and means of 'averting the evil decree' or at least its most
devastating consequences. The very idea of completing a work like *Moses
und Aron*, which epitomized Israel's struggle for national freedom at the
behest of all mankind, seemed ludicrous under the circumstances.

The strong showing of the Nazis in the successive parliamentary
elections in the spring of 1932 raised the spectre of impending tragedy for
all with the psychological fortitude to face it. Schoenberg, on a working
holiday in Spain, hated the very thought of having to 'go back to
Germany at this juncture'.[31] Unfortunately the prevailing currency
restrictions made it impossible for him to get money out of Germany, and
he was forced to return 'among the swastika swaggerists and pogromers'.
When the July elections strengthened the Fascist grip even further, he
jettisoned the last vestiges of ethnic ambivalence and confessed:

---

[29] Jakob Klatzkin, *Probleme des modernen Judentums*, 173.
[30] Ibid., 208.
[31] Letter of 24 May 1932 to Joseph Asch, in *Arnold Schoenberg Letters*, 167.

I've had it hammered into me so loudly and so long that only by being deaf to begin with could I have failed to understand it. And it's a long time now since it wrung any regrets from me. Today I'm proud to call myself a Jew; but I know the difficulties of really being one. But that's enough about that. The whole thing's certainly working up to a decision, and one of quite a different kind.[32]

Following Hitler's elevation to the chancellorship, the president of the Prussian Academy of the Arts, the conservative composer Max von Schillings, announced that, on behalf of the Prussian Minister of Education, he was going to cleanse his institution of all 'Jewish influence'. Schoenberg chose not to await his official dismissal and left Berlin on 13 May 1933, never to return. He had hardly found temporary quarters in Paris when he began to organize the rescue-mission that was to occupy him so completely and intensely during the years to come. Haunted by the vision of an impending holocaust, he noted: 'We don't have time like the Zionists' because, he added in French, 'the settlement of fourteen million Jews, at the rate of fifteen thousand a year would take two hundred and eighty years.'[33] As Schoenberg saw it, the strongest possible measures were called for then and there. And so, from his room at the Hotel Régina on the Place de Rivoli, he embarked on an extensive letter-writing campaign designed to inform prospective collaborators, including Dr Klatzkin, of his plans for a Jewish Unity Party embracing Jews of all backgrounds and modes of thought, a movement permitting the most varied convictions to exist side by side and to develop independently, provided such diversity did not interfere with the 'unity of action'.[34] Schoenberg made no secret of his preference for a 'new party, a new sect ... nationalistic-chauvinistic to the highest degree, in the religious sense, based on the notion of the chosen people, militant, aggressive, against all pacifism, against all internationalism'. But these were his personal inclinations, and, while he would obviously try to convert others 'to these methods (for I'm looking for battle methods)', he had no intention of imposing himself, as long as the interests of the Jewish people were safeguarded, and as long as the needs of the hour were promptly met:

That much we learned as soldiers ... and none about to shape his people's fate may dismiss such ancient popular wisdom. The timid will never be able to make

[32] Letter of 25 Sept. 1932 to Alban Berg, in *Arnold Schoenberg Letters*, 167.

[33] Rufer H 40. Note Schoenberg's miscalculation: the correct figure is 933 years. He may have meant 'four million Jews', but in that case 267 years would have been more accurate.

[34] For this and the quotations immediately following see the typewritten copy of his letter of 13 June 1933 to Jakob Klatzkin, JEW 8 in Schoenberg's own classification.

the sacrifices required by courage and self-denial. Those unwilling to risk life and property won't be able to participate in our struggle for liberation. We must succeed in persuading Jewish youth of the necessity of this struggle completely and without qualifications.

Adamant in his demand for individual sacrifice, if need be, in the collective interest, he had no use for a western system of values that emphasized material well-being:

We are Asians and nothing of real substance connects us with the West. We have our destiny and no other temptation can honour us ... our essence is not occidental; that is merely an exterior appearance. We must return to our origins, to the source of our strength, there where our toughness has its roots and where we will recover our old fighting spirit.

Heinrich Berl had something very similar in mind when, as early as 1926, he suggested that the historical mission of composers of Jewish descent— Mahler and Schoenberg in particular—could be properly understood only in terms of a characteristically 'Oriental' disposition in favour of unfettered melodic-rhythmic impulses opposed to the European harmonic tradition in which they too had been raised.[35] Had Berl's admittedly novel yet persuasive arguments found more willing ears than they did at the time among Schoenberg's devoted pupils, their master's later highly emotional affirmation of his Middle Eastern roots might have come as considerably less of a shock to them. Whatever the case, the political philosophy, as outlined in the letter to Klatzkin and a number of contemporaneous writings, was without precedent or counterpart in the intricated European party web, since at the behest of its sole goal, the creation of a Jewish state and the contingent liberation of the Jews, it welcomed socialists and capitalists, authoritarians and democrats, republicans and monarchists, without preference or distinction. Whether a man enjoyed full civil rights or suffered political deprivation, whether he was permitted to defend his country in war or not, 'the movement into which I wish to recruit him will think of him only as a Jew, and he may think only of the Jewish struggle for liberation'.

Schoenberg's was, of course, not the only prominent voice calling for the closing of Jewish ranks in the face of the Nazi threat. John Dewey's friend and disciple, the American philosopher Horace M. Kallen, also urged 'Jewish unity in freedom for self-fulfillment, for service, and for

---

[35] Berl, *Das Judentum in der Musik*, 172.

self-defense'.[36] According to Kallen, Jewish survival demanded an 'associative relationship' accommodating

Albert Einstein as well as the Gerer Rebbe; Benny Leonard as well as Stephen Wise; Leon Trotsky as well as Horace Kallen. It must even have a place for Cyrus Adler. It must provide a common platform for all persons who are called Jews, regardless of class, creed, or country.

But for Kallen

the least common denominator of such a platform is defense. It is the unity of laboring together against the false and the cowardly attacks of antisemitism in every walk of life. Beyond defense, there is always the constructive program which so many Jews share—the upkeep and development of Hebraic culture and ideals as the Jewish contribution to the substance and purpose of our civilization. And there is the upbuilding of the Jewish homeland.

As the avalanche of hatred and unreason descended upon Germany's Jews with ever-increasing speed and intensity, men and women across the entire spectrum of Jewish opinion unwittingly moved closer to Jabotinsky's 'monism', his refusal to tie the concept of Jewish nationhood to any extraneous ideology, whether socialism, capitalism, or Fascism. In the name of history, past and present, Jabotinsky claimed 'a Jewish state on both sides of the Jordan and social justice without class war within Palestine Jewry'.[37] Early in life Jabotinsky, like Schoenberg, had flirted with socialism. But then he discovered Mazzini and henceforth remained an uncompromising nineteenth-century-style democrat, ready to go to any lengths in order to preserve the spiritual and physical integrity of his people. Schoenberg, for his part, applauded Jabotinsky's ultimate willingness to seek redress through armed resistance. But at times he displayed considerably less patience with the more cumbersome aspects of democracy, and correspondingly greater affinity with behaviour patterns typical of the old-style monarchy rather than of democratic Europe between the wars. While he never failed to stress the historical significance of democracy, especially in the field of human rights—to which he was totally committed—he deplored its endemic inability to react swiftly and effectively to patently dangerous or otherwise intolerable situations. 'We face fantastic necessities,' he noted on 3 November

[36] Horace M. Kallen, 'Jewish Unity', as reprinted in Arthur Hertzberg (ed.), *The Zionist Idea* (New York, 1966), 531.

[37] Cf. Erich and Rael Isaac, 'The Impact of Jabotinsky on Likud's Policies', *Middle East Review*, 10/1 (autumn, 1977), 33.

1933, 'hence must make decisions that would seem fantastic under normal circumstances.'[38] And in the very document that was to bring his Jewish politics to their ultimate theoretical fruition, his *Four-Point Program*, he refers to himself as a one-time 'kind of dictator' who did not hesitate to take the most drastic measures when 'political extremists' persisted in opposing him on fundamental issues affecting the musical society he had founded after the First World War. Having tried every other means, he finally had to do 'something which under other circumstances could be called illegal: I dissolved the whole society, built a new one, accepted only such members who were in perfect agreement with my artistic principles and excluded the entire opposition . . . right or wrong . . . these principles were my country'.[39] Now that the issue was not one of artistic principles but of the very survival of an entire people, his people, how could he be expected to tolerate procedures that were not only sluggish almost by definition but also prone to advance various vested interests and thus likely to endanger the very unity that was so essential at a time when emergencies had to be met head-on and often ruthlessly?

Ironically, Schoenberg's authoritarian propensities were reinforced by the same Spenglerian philosophy that had contributed so substantially to the intellectual undermining of the Weimar Republic.[40] Nor did Schoenberg miss many opportunities to denounce 'Jewish internationalism' and 'Jewish intellectualism', which, he contended, had given the false impression of constructive cultural involvement while actually promoting a kind of Jewish enslavement to alien civilizations. Such reasoning dangerously paralleled that of the enemy, and if there was a tragic flaw in Schoenberg's political activities on behalf of the Jewish people it was precisely his tendency to castigate both the Nazis bent on genocide and their stunned victims with figures of speech adopted from the totalitarian idiom.

The immediate cause of Schoenberg's profound dissatisfaction with the Jewish response, or rather the lack thereof—the basic irritant, as it were, that sparked his relentless agitation for a Jewish United Party—was the world-wide drive for economic sanctions against Germany—the boycott, which he abhorred as mere tokenism, apt to forestall truly

[38] 'Notizen zur jüdischen Politik', Rufer H 41 (JEW 5 in Schoenberg's classification).

[39] Rufer H 39. See app. C, p. 235.

[40] Playing on the title of Spengler's *magnum opus*, *The Decline of the West*, Schoenberg facetiously called him 'Untergängler des Abendlandes' (Decliner of the West).

effective countermeasures. While accounts of the Nazi era as a rule
mention the notorious Nazi boycott *Aktion* of 1 April 1933, which led to
such dastardly public scenes all over Germany, the original boycott-
declaration had come eleven days earlier from the other side, when the
Jews of Vilna, then under Polish sovereignty, pledged to abstain from
purchases of goods made in Germany. The ensuing formation of a Polish
United Boycott Committee stimulated similar efforts throughout Western Europe and the United States. And at first the Nazis were sufficiently
worried about the effects on their shaky economy to insist on an anti-
boycott clause in their ten-year 'non-aggression' treaty with Poland,
signed on 1 January 1934. As long as Marshal Pilsudski was alive, the
Poles ignored the anti-boycott provisions for all practical intents and
purposes. But after his death in 1935 the Polish boycott-movement was
quickly liquidated. By then, however, it had taken firm root in England;
at least one lively form of British–German trade, that of furs, ceased
almost completely. In France, where Schoenberg repeatedly expressed
such an intense dislike for the boycott-concept, the refugees themselves
were the main sponsors. Both the Comité de Défense des Juifs Persécutés
en Allemagne and the International League against Antisemitism had
their headquarters in Paris. As in Britain, where the Board of Deputies of
British Jews voiced strong objections, the official representatives of
French Jewry associated with the Alliance Israélite Universelle remained
opposed to the boycott. In the United States support came primarily
from the labour movement, first through the non-sectarian Anti-Nazi
League to Champion Human Rights, later through the so-called Joint
Boycott Council. While the boycott may well have been a contributory
factor in the rapid transformation of the German economy from peace-
time production to all-out war-production, Arnold Schoenberg feared
above all that the Germans would in retaliation further aggravate the
already precarious condition of their Jewish hostages. Morally he objected
because, as he noted on 2 September 1933, among various anti-
boycott considerations, it seemed a cheap way to deal with a complex and
dangerous situation, a way involving little, if any risk, and one from
which some unscrupulous individuals might even derive profit.[41] Instead
of relying on their own strength, the Jews were once again turning
elsewhere for help. And that to him betrayed a lack of dignity which he
identified with RACHMONES, a pejorative Hebrew-Yiddish term for hand-
outs that appears prominently in capital letters at the end of this
particular anti-boycott harangue in his collected *Notes Concerning Jewish*

---

[41] Rufer H 41, p. 27.

Politics, written during the Paris days and replete with historical, psychological, and economic arguments against the boycott. The clincher for Schoenberg was the Soviet experience, which he cited as proof that 'once a people surrenders enthusiastically to such simplistic thought-patterns, it will rather see everything in ruins than give in'.[42] At the very least the boycott involved a waste of precious energy, and that was the last thing needed. 'No waste of energy! Nothing against Germany! Instead: *Everything* for Jewry!'[43]

As early as May 1933 Schoenberg sought support for his political plans from fellow artists whose sensitivity and good judgement he respected. The first to receive a substantial personal communication was Max Reinhardt, scheduled to stage *Die Fledermaus* at the Théâtre Pigalle later that year.[44] After reviewing his long-standing devotion to the welfare of the Jewish people in some detail, Schoenberg breaks the news of his decision to provide the initial leadership of a unified movement seeking political autonomy for Jews of all backgrounds and religious orientations. In an obvious allusion to Hitler's ubiquitous invocation of fourteen years of struggle, he recalls how he himself had needed fourteen years to arrive at a full understanding of his ultimate task. While *Der biblische Weg* had always been intended as a dramatic opener for an intensive propaganda campaign, in the mid-1920s, 'unsure and discouraged by the lack of interest', he had shelved his production-plans time and again. Now, however, with the urgency of the matter unfortunately no longer in question, 'I'm ready to begin.' And what could make for a better beginning than this dramatization of concerns harking back to *Die Jakobsleiter*, staged by a man of Reinhardt's unmatched talents, if possible simultaneously in German, English, and French? Even if it failed on literary grounds, its message would not go unheard. There was no reason to fear any kind of controversy, since 'it deals only with matters with which all the world is likely to agree'. In a Reinhardt production the play was sure to move audiences everywhere, and 'let us not forget wherever there are Jews, the non-Jews must also be informed about what we have in mind'.[45]

[42] Ibid., 28.

[43] 'Die Judenfrage', Rufer H 40, p., 8.

[44] Typed copy, not in Rufer.

[45] Nothing came of the proposed Schoenberg–Reinhardt collaboration. But long after he received Schoenberg's letter Reinhardt involved himself with a project that may well have been inspired in some measure by Schoenberg's reference to his propagandistic play: Franz Werfel's *Eternal Road*, with music by Kurt Weill, produced by Meyer Weisgal and directed by Reinhardt, the spectacular historical pageant that was the theatrical sensation of the 1937 New York theatrical season.

After Reinhardt, he approached the composer Ernst Toch, a fellow Viennese who had left Berlin about the same time and was eventually to rejoin him in California. His sole aim, Schoenberg explained, was to see the Jews living politically united in their own land, pursuing the unique ways of a people 'destined to guard one idea, the idea of the unimaginable Lord'.[46] But if that historical goal was to be reached strong leadership was needed, leadership ready and able to get around the perennial debaters and protesters, not to speak of alleged supporters who, because they usually recoil from decisive action, do more harm than good. Since he had a great deal of experience hitting his head against stone walls without much perceptible damage, 'let people follow me until someone else turns up. In the meantime, no one is going to stop me.'

Schoenberg's resolve to seize upon one of the most dangerous moments in Jewish history as an opportunity for national regeneration was, of course, in the grand manner of the prophets from Moses in Egypt to Isaiah in Babylon, who would have agreed with him that, as he noted on 2 September 1933, 'a people defined as such by its religion can once more become, be, and remain a people only as a people of religion'.[47] By the same token, his symbolic reconversion in mid-summer 1933 (see Fig. 1) merely dramatized in a highly personal way the prophetic insight that 'in the diaspora the idol worship of our host nations has uprooted us and deprived us of our own faith . . . we must surrender once again to our faith . . . it alone ensures our viability and justifies our existence'. In other words his plans, though designed to avert imminent disaster, would, if properly executed, also safeguard the future. (See Fig. 2.)

In retrospect, the sheer numerical weight of the articles and speeches, calculations, aphorisms, and miscellaneous notes from those hectic initial months in exile appears staggering. Nor did Schoenberg's impending departure for the United States lessen this boundless activity. On the contrary, during the last week of October 1933, just before he and his family embarked on the Ile de France, he spelled out the organizational details of his proposed political campaign in a remarkable document that deserves to be read *in extenso*:[49]

---

[46] Typed copy, undated, not in Rufer. In a handwritten rejoinder at the bottom of the page Schoenberg repeats his favourite anti-boycott slogan with the following slight changes in direction and emphasis: 'Nothing *against* anyone; everything *for* the Jews.'

[47] 'Jewish Religion', Rufer H 41, p. 7.

[48] 'My Plans', ibid., 13.

[49] Typed copy marked 'G 4'.

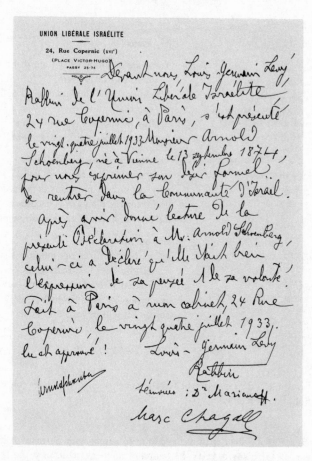

FIG. 1 Schoenberg's 'Re-entry into the Community of Israel', 24 July 1933

I intend to engage in large scale propaganda among all of Jewry in the United States and also later in other countries, designed first of all to get them to produce the financial means sufficient to pay for the gradual emigration of the Jews from Germany. I propose to move the Jewish community to its very depths by a graphic demonstration of what lies in store for the German Jews unless they receive help within the next two or three months. The immediate goal of my efforts is the commitment of all Jews in all countries to a monthly contribution of two marks per head for several months. As soon as the proceeds of this collection

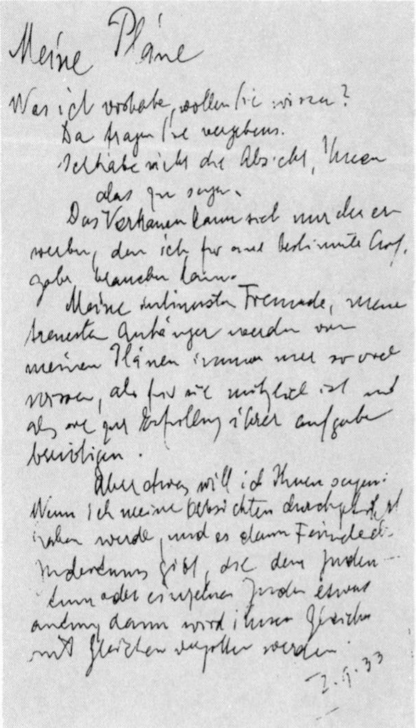

My Plans

You want to know what I am planning?
  There you ask in vain.
  I do not have the intention of telling
  you that.
  Only he can win my trust whom
I can use for a specific assignment.

My most intimate friends, my
most faithful associates will know
only as much of my plans as is
useful for them and as is necessary
for the fulfilment of their assignment.

But one thing I must tell you:
once I have realized my intentions, and
should the Jews find themselves
confronted with enemies out to hurt them
as a group, or as individuals, every
hostile act will be repaid in kind.

[2.9.33]

FIG. 2 Facsimile and Translation of a Section of Schoenberg's 'Notes concerning Jewish Politics', 2 October 1933

have been secured, I shall attempt to open negotiations with Germany, with the aim of getting Germany to relax the tempo of its measures against the Jews to the point where emigration can be distributed over several years so as to avoid the loss of countless human lives simply because of the precipitation of events (four- or five-year plan). My idea is that this agreement with Germany be put on an economic base offering Germany sufficient advantages in exchange for its co-operation, so that ethical considerations can be dropped once and for all. As far as the settlement of the emigrants is concerned, I have discussed various plans with many wise and non-orthodox minds, plans whose realization, given a measure of realistic thought—i.e. provided one has understood that the events are of a war-like nature—should not pose insurmountable difficulties if properly approached. But details don't have to be dealt with until the first steps have been taken and the collection has proved successful.

  I would prefer to open my campaign with a speech broadcast on radio. But then I would like to travel—if need be to the smallest places—in order to inflame

Jews everywhere. It would be most desirable if I had ample means at my disposal for this purpose. For none aware of the impression which such propaganda, properly staged, makes in Germany and upon the Germans will want to do without such support. I don't think I am completely out of line if I propose:

1. to lease an airplane permitting me to complete as quickly as possible the travels which it would enable me to undertake;
2. if at all possible, also a mobile home;
3. a special broadcasting staff and, possibly, assuming that the project is generously conceived—
4. disc recordings of my important speeches (which I would compose accordingly);
5. sound films.

In addition, some assistants would have to be engaged, and I would have to have at my disposal people able to brief me in every instance and in good time concerning special local conditions as well as the prevailing mentality regarding specific points.

Should it be possible to conduct propaganda through the press, then thought might be given to some journalistic assistance (but perhaps only at the later stages—even though I am of the opinion that one cannot begin early enough to shoot sparrows with cannon if one wants to prevent their growing in number and size to the point of invincibility).

And now in conclusion I must add the following personal observations:

I offer the sacrifice of my art to the Jewish cause. And I bring my offer enthusiastically, because for me nothing stands above my people.

However: my art has not made me a rich man, and I cannot finance this movement out of my empty pocket.

For the moment I have been placed on leave and until further notice receive no salary from the Prussian Academy. I shall have to relinquish my position and my contractual claims as soon as I initiate this movement. For, not only would it be unseemly to negotiate with Germany as an 'employee' but I would certainly have to count on unconditional dismissal as an act of revenge.

This is why I must ask that I be given enough security for the duration of my propaganda campaign, so that my family too, to the extent to which it receives my support and sustenance, is taken care of in a manner no worse than were I to devote my activities to them as before. I leave it to those who greet my plans with enthusiasm to find a dignified way: one which would enable nobody ever to say that I had undertaken this task 'in order to enrich myself'.

Whatever else might be said about this astonishing proposal, Schoenberg's grasp of the nature and importance of modern propaganda clearly matched that of the enemy, some of whose most effective procedures he actually anticipated. The same, of course, could be said of his oft-stated preference for military solutions, indeed the essentially nineteenth-century racial conceptions which induced him at a given point to claim Jewish priority for racial pride: 'except for its specifically German exaggeration, racism is an imitation (good imitation is always a bad imitation) of the faith of the Jews in their own destiny. We Jews call ourselves God's chosen people and are the guardians of the divine promise.'[50] But, he added, while the Jews were 'chosen to think the thought of the One and Only, the Eternal, the Unimaginable, the Invisible God, to its ultimate conclusion, to preserve its essence,' German racism, devoid of any transcendent goal, inevitably remained 'mired in mere phrases,' condemned to 'measuring noses, ears, legs, stomachs, because the thought is missing'. And therein lies the all-important difference: whatever methods, whether adopted or newly invented, circumstances may impose, the moral imperatives inherent in the Jews' spiritual peoplehood must prevail.

Schoenberg and his family arrived in the United States on 31 October 1933. Barely installed, rather precariously at that, in Brookline, Massachusetts, the composer redoubled his effort on behalf of the Jewish Unity Party, making personal contacts and, above all, drafting and redrafting in his budding English the manifesto which, in its ultimate form, was to become *A Four-Point Program*. The sketch dated 1 December 1933 bears the proud inscription 'reworked, for the time being without any help'. Schoenberg soon realized, of course, that few Americans paid much attention to the issues that moved his pen so relentlessly. But relative isolation, far from deterring Arnold Schoenberg, had always tended rather to intensify his pursuit of a given goal. Accordingly, on 28 December 1933 he proceeded to calculate the capital needs of his projected movement. Sixteen million Jews, he figured, ought to produce four million members in the long run. Even if at first no more than one and a half million members contributed one mark a month, the projected total of a million marks over a quarter of a century would suffice to repay in no more than thirty years at least the capital spent on land-purchases. Should the membership reach the expected four million within ten to fifteen years, on the other hand, all interest could be paid off as well, and plenty of money would remain for the cultural development of the new country.[51]

---

[50] Quoted in German in Eberhard Freitag, *Schönberg*, 133.

[51] 'Berechnung eines Landes', in *Jewish Unity Party* (PUJ), 2–3, Rufer H 42.

But money was not all that concerned him that day. To President Rosenfeld of the Jewish Swim Club Hakoah in Vienna he pledged his moral and material aid not merely because for too many centuries 'our power was rooted exclusively in knowledge' but also because he preferred the demonstrable, objective feat of 'one hundred metres in thirty-five seconds' to a mirror canon whose aesthetic validity was always open to doubt. Above all, as far as he was concerned, sports stood for the universal truth that 'one individual must always excel, since in so doing he advances everybody's cause'.[52] Years earlier, in his Frankfurt radio lecture, he had used the simile of a group of cave-explorers reaching a narrow impasse permitting only one of their lot to squeeze through. In such a situation all concerned may suggest a solution, but in the end 'only one will get to do the job, and the others will have to rely on his judgment'.[53]

Characteristically, Schoenberg eventually filed a whole set of 'Aphorisms for Dr Rosenfeld' among the materials for his 'Program for Assistance and Promotion of the Party', the direct predecessor of *A Four-Point Program*, which dramatically documents how he, who was trying to create a political party essentially in his own image, was beset by the problem of leadership, its nature and initial determination. On 16 January 1934 he finally concluded that the party should be led by men who:

1. had occupied important positions in Jewish politics before,
2. had distinguished themselves in the sciences, arts, business or athletics,
3. had demonstrated competence as organizers, instructors or propagandists,
4. had shown enough valuable character traits to justify faith in their judgment.[54]

Confident that the party leadership would automatically be self-generated, because reasonable men were likely to select the most suitable individuals, he had nevertheless no doubt that the burden would be his, at least at first. But it was to youth that he looked primarily as guarantors of the future. Not only had he just recently become a father again, he had always communicated most easily with his students and disciples, whose basic idealism he admired and respected. Then, too, he foresaw the need for soldiers 'To lay the foundation of a new Jewish life in HONOUR

---

[52] PUJ, 4, Rufer H 43.

[53] Cf. Christian Martin Schmidt, 'Über Schönbergs Geschichtsbewußtsein', in Rudolf Stephan (ed.), *Zwischen Tradition und Fortschritt* (Mainz, 1973), 94.

[54] Rufer H 48.

AND POWER'.[55] In the section entitled 'Lessons for the Young', Schoenberg, at his most aggressive, dismisses the very notion of effective defence as belated by definition, stating bluntly that while one can always find reasons to attack, 'if need be one can do without reasons'.[56] No friend of 'smartness and caution' he asked not merely for ordinary courage but for outright foolhardiness, 'even if it results in failure'.

The unqualified preference for action over thought expressed here and on numerous other occasions was matched by a general suspicion of intellectuals devoted to knowledge *per se*. For Schoenberg the relative value of knowledge was a direct function of the contingent ability to act. Certainly at this point he seriously questioned any moral justification for the kind of intellectual incest typically practised by alienated men and women anxious to avoid social and political responsibilities. He was therefore anything but inconsistent in foreseeing important roles for informed, action-oriented intellectuals in the top echelons of his Jewish United Party, if only because he assumed that the Jewish retreat into the house of intellect had originally been a most effective means of cultural self-defence.

Schoenberg's political testament *A Four-Point Program for Jewry*, was essentially completed in 1938, after an incubation period of five years, as an all-encompassing last-minute call to action, covering thirty-seven double-spaced pages in its final typed version.[57] It begins and ends with the same inviolable postulates:

I.   THE FIGHT AGAINST ANTI-SEMITISM MUST BE STOPPED.

II. A UNITED JEWISH PARTY MUST BE CREATED.

III. UNANIMITY IN JEWRY MUST BE ENFORCED WITH ALL MEANS.

IV. WAYS MUST BE PREPARED TO OBTAIN A PLACE TO ERECT AN INDEPENDENT
     JEWISH STATE.

At first Schoenberg's attention had been fully absorbed by the Jewish plight in Germany and Austria. But now that war appeared inevitable, he turned to Europe at large, praying that 'there will not be an additional 3,500,000 from Poland, 900,000 from Romania, 240,000 from Lithuania and 100,000 from Letland [Latvia] ... Is there room in the world for

---

[55] 'Forward to a New Jewish Unitary Party', Rufer B 12, p. 4. Schoenberg's typescript is inscribed 'Brookline, December 1, 1933'.

[56] 'Lehren für die Jugend' 7 and 8, Rufer H 48, p. 30.

[57] Rufer H 39. In view of the nature and substance of 'A Four-Point Program', most of the preceding documents must be regarded as mere preparatory sketches. For the complete document, see Appendix C.

almost 7,000,000 people? Are they condemned to doom? Will they
become extinct? Famished? Butchered?' If the dreadful visions that had
pursued him since the early twenties were turning into reality, the blame
must be shared by a Jewish establishment which, after first misinterpret-
ing every danger-signal, subsequently lost precious time and energy on
the 'war on antisemitism' and 'emigration to Palestine'. Having
renounced the relative ease of European exile in the conviction that
America 'is in many respects the promised land, especially in what
concerns the hopes of Jewry', he had been appalled to find American
Jews 'hypnotized by the boycott ... the cheapest way to give the
impression that something was being done'.[58] And, even though the
boycott had failed precisely as he had anticipated, the fight against anti-
Semitism continued in complete disregard of the Jewish people's 'duty of
self-preservation'. Since anti-Semitism is not a rational phenomenon, it
cannot and should not be fought with appeals to reason. That entire
nations owed their wealth and power to Jewish traders, or that Jews
'brought medicine, culture, music and literature to barbarian countries'
was politically as irrelevant as the undeniable fact that 'the Bible in its
legal and moral viewpoints is the backbone of the civilization of almost
half of the people of the world'. History has shown that nothing is apt to
mitigate the hostility provoked by a people arrogant enough to believe in
its own chosenness. Because one may as well 'try to fight against rain and
snow, against lightning and blizzard, against hurricane and earthquake;
try and fight against death and destiny', the fight against anti-Semitism
'has brought us rather close to doom. It has lulled into sleep every manly
attitude, every energetic and intelligent action. And it has hindered us in
doing what intelligence and honor ask us to do'. Irrespective of errors
made during a relatively calm past, however, the current emergency calls
for a United Jewish Party comprising Jews of all backgrounds and
persuasions, recognizing the need for concerted political action as well as
the truism that it is one thing to behave like a gentleman, another to act
like a statesman: 'He who wants to work for his nation cannot be a
sentimentalist but must be—if necessary—unscrupulous, faithful only to
his goal.'

Like Herzl before him, Schoenberg never flagged in his commitment
to 'Palestine as the ultimate Jewish homeland', an idea which to him was

[58] 'No Jewish leader foresaw the impending danger in its full dimensions. At best a
passing sense of foreboding struck a conversation or a speech like a flash of lightning,
impressing people as prophetic without being taken quite seriously at the time, not even by
those who uttered the warnings.' Alex Bein, *Die Judenfrage*, i (Stuttgart, 1980), 381.

'self-evident without any question, a matter of fact which needs no special mention and is not dependent on voting. No true Jew could ever forget that Palestine is ours and that we have been deprived of it by mere force; that we will never consent to the claim of another nation upon our promised land.' (Cf. Fig. 3.) But such irreversible truths, perpetuated by deep spiritual attachments, must not blind us to the political realities of the day, as had happened early in the century when majority rule in the World Zionist Organization thwarted the establishment of an independent state outside Palestine. Were it not for that 'enormous mishap' European Jewry would now be in a position to act from strength rather than utter weakness. Unfortunately, the Jews had been so intoxicated with the ideals of democracy, which had given them their basic rights, they had sacrificed their leader Herzl, even though history usually vindicates 'great men, standing alone, persecuted, unsupported'. Clearly the fate of a nation is 'much too important a question to submit to a majority'. What kind of army would force superior officers to seek the approval of the majority of those under their command? The majority might actually reach the right decision, 'but in all probability it will have come too late'.[59]

Schoenberg felt that he had to explain 'what this little word "united" means', because, as he put it in an inverted paraphrase of Gabriel's charge to the Chosen One in Die Jakobsleiter, 'one knows from experience that people find in every concept a left and right side, a before and a behind, an and and an if, a but and an in spite of'.[60] He definitely did not have 'a union of the different Jewish organizations', with a proportionately representative board, in mind. Nor did he look for any of those 'social affairs, dinners, receptions, meetings to satisfy ambitions, vanities, and desires for publicity'. Instead, his united party would be comparable to 'an ideal matrimony', dedicated to the rearing of a healthy progeny, and where 'everything which promotes this common purpose is duty, is moral, is law'. But just as 'no husband and no wife may do anything

---

[59] On 3 Sept. 1933 Schoenberg had noted: 'To me democracy has always meant an environment in which *I* shall *never* succeed in making my will known, let alone enforce it.' And shortly thereafter, in the first systematic draft of his party program (PUJ), he observed that the party would have to renounce democracy because (*a*) democracy must lead to corruption, since those rising from below want the wealth without which there is no power; (*b*) in a democracy only the will of him who flatters the masses can exert itself. By the same token, democracy will never permit the ideas of the truly great to prevail.

[60] The underlying biblical idea recurs in one formulation or another no less than five times in Deut. alone.

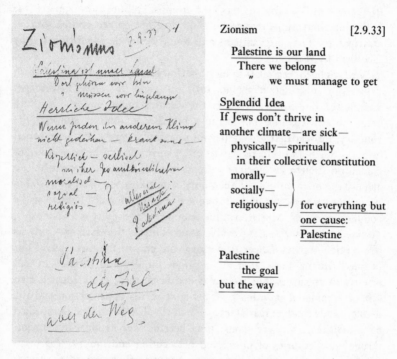

Zionism [2.9.33]

Palestine is our land
There we belong
  " we must manage to get

Splendid Idea
If Jews don't thrive in
another climate—are sick—
  physically—spiritually
   in their collective constitution
  morally—
  socially—   ⎫
  religiously— ⎭ for everything but
                  one cause:
                  Palestine

Palestine
   the goal
but the way

FIG. 3 Facsimile and Translation of a Section of Schoenberg's 'Notes concerning Jewish Politics', 2 October 1933

which is against the law, so, in every country, every member will have to avoid conflict with the laws of the respective countries even if that should force members of the Party to kill each other in case of war'. For in the end 'life and death of the individual are without influence on historical processes'.

In the third chapter of *A Four-Point Program* Schoenberg lays the philosophical groundwork for the two crucial constants in his national equation: unanimity and its effective enforcement. Quoting the familiar saying that 'doubt is the beginning of philosophy', he adds that 'skepticism is its shabby misshapen, vulgar little brother', a negative force that has 'done more harm to the world than optimism which is also a killer, but one of another kind'. The sceptic optimistically anticipates 'the failure of favorable matters'; the optimist sceptically anticipates 'the failure of unfavorable matters ... both live not on recognition, but on anticipation. They are gamblers and would better decide their stand by dice than by reasoning'.

Next, Schoenberg takes to task 'the Jewish sort of intelligence which delights in disputation for its own sake and therefore discourages unanimity. The iron rule, under the circumstances, must be never to enter into discussion, not because of ulterior motives but, on the contrary, for fear that 'the fighter for unanimity' might wax sentimental 'over so much and sincere conviction'. Conversely, to be sure, outright contempt, though an efficient weapon in some contexts, 'would fail to achieve the main purpose of unanimity, which is not to make every Jew a powerless yet resisting slave, but an active and convinced fighter for the common purpose'. Moreover, 'this astonishing mentality is a divine gift, destined to protect us, to enable us to outlast the diaspora with its persecution and its danger to personal life and to the existence of our people'. Among Jews, after all, religious inquiry and debates are not priestly prerogatives 'but recommended to all men: every learned man can be a rabbi, if only his zeal, his studies, his apperception and the dignity of his conduct mark him as a man who lives with God in the ideas of the faith'. Indeed, religious study became 'our national fundament' throughout centuries of unrelieved persecution and misery: 'the over-development of Jewish intelligence ... was our only way to cope with the weapons of others, it was our only way to project ourselves and our race.' The issue, therefore, is by no means its rejection—clearly a useless exercise to begin with—but its redirection 'so as to promote the understanding of the necessity of unity'. And similar considerations apply to 'Jewish internationalism', in Schoenberg's eyes a related cause of disunity. Had the thousands who joined various radical parties directed their 'real idealism, conviction, and enthusiasm' towards the promotion of Jewish self-interest, 'the Jewish situation today would be quite different'.

Schoenberg was, of course, not unaware that he was treading the borderline of political Utopia. Yet he remained convinced that practical questions such as how to get extremists of the Right and Left to act with perfect unanimity would and could 'be resolved without sentimentality'. In order to avoid 'difficulties in such numbers and of such measure that despair might reign among the members and the leaders, and it will very often appear as if everything was lost and as if the whole movement were to break down', he favoured slow initial growth: 'with some exaggeration one could say the party should at first consist of not much more than the future leaders. If they can preserve unanimity among themselves, they will succeed in unifying the members they have won.' And even this limited goal was not going to be attained without considerable disappointment on the part of many members who would have to learn the hard way that 'ancient military axiom' that 'one who cannot obey, cannot command'.

Schoenberg fully realized that the final chapter of *A Four-Point Program*, where the territorial question is broached in purely pragmatic terms, was liable to sow consternation and outrage among Zionists who had faced this emotional issue in the past: 'If it was difficult to discuss the first three points of this program, it is much more difficult to treat the fourth point publicly. It asks for an almost unreasonable amount of tact and discretion, and if the preceding many points could not be expressed directly, then here much more cannot be said—but only hinted at.' After several references to alleged missed opportunities to return to the ancient homeland in the more distant past, Schoenberg inevitably turns to modern Zionism, with its strongly Messianic overtones. At this point, ironically, his faith in the historical potential of a unique people, on which he bases so much of his reasoning elsewhere, appears to desert him. In fact, eager to prove the immediate impracticality of a Jewish state in Palestine, he comes up with the rather original theory that the British opposed Jewish colonization yet had nothing against Arab immigration to Palestine because, due to its strategic position, 'only a powerless nation can possess it, one which cannot deny others the right to cross it'. In the current emergency, though, it does not really matter where the Jews of Europe will be permitted to settle, since 'present technic makes life possible anywhere'. Nor did he feel that he needed to specify the methods through which the land would be acquired: 'as long as Jews possess money, they will be able to buy a land and perhaps even one which presents the best conditions for a modern state.' Since 'one can buy everything on installments today', and 'there are a number of states which need money, long-term contracts or leases could be signed' attractive enough to make it 'of the greatest interest to world bankers to finance such a program'. In fact, Schoenberg envisaged mutual benefits all the way down the line: 'might not such an enterprise solve, at least for a time, the present crisis in production and trade? Has one ever considered such an enterprise from the standpoint of the great business it is?' He, for one, could find no reason why 'the great financial non-Jewish powers' should not underwrite such a lucrative project. But 'at present it is not wise to go into details. All depends on the readiness of the Jewry to undertake decisive steps in his direction, and much depends on the non-Jews to resolve these problems in a lawful and dignified way.'

By 1939, within a few short months after the completion of *A Four-Point Program*, Central European Jewry, still numbering in the hundreds of thousands, had been reduced to the state of helpless, impoverished prisoners, first among the millions whose systematic extermination a callous world was to watch in morbid fascination from the sidelines of history. As the unprecedented drama unfolded, Schoenberg found his worst fears confirmed. While there was no dearth of public condemnations from the mouths of politicians capitalizing on the Jewish tragedy, and while the newspapers revelled in atrocity headlines, the depression-ridden democracies did not feel constrained to save lives. The abortive conference called by the Western powers at Evian in July 1938 had not merely dashed all hopes for an agreement as to how to deal with the refugee problem, its dismal failure had reinforced the resolve of the German government, which proceeded to intensify its anti-Jewish measures. Beginning in October 1938, Jewish passports were marked 'J'. Then, during the notorious *Kristallnacht* of 9 to 10 November, the remaining Jewish businesses were destroyed, and thousands wound up in concentration camps. Jewish children were expelled from all state schools, and the 'aryanization' decree finalized the expropriation of all Jewish assets. When, a few months later, the steamship *St Louis* attempted to unload its human cargo anywhere in the Western hemisphere, the captain of this 'voyage of the damned' found the borders of the so-called free world hermetically closed to Jews. Schoenberg and the few Zionist stalwarts craving for action were condemned to standing idly by. Soon the Nazi invasion of Poland shut the last escape-hatch and left millions of East European Jews in the clutches of a ruthless conqueror determined to do away with them.

As the German war-machine rolled across the Continent, Schoenberg, realizing the utter futility of his political effort, turned increasingly inward. As if to give symbolic expression to his deep sense of frustration, he combined, in the reordering of his papers 'Notes on *Kol Nidrey* and a 4 point program'.[61] The composition of *Kol Nidre* in 1938 had not only

---

[61] Rufer C 60. The utterly practical spirit in which Schoenberg conceived such proposals emerges also from a curious note at the bottom of p. 12 of this document, which lists suitable business-enterprises for the new nation. Thinking no doubt of both prior expertise and the possible dearth of national resources in the as yet undetermined territory, he mentions entertainment, health and recreation, film and chemical industries.

drawn his attention to theological-liturgical problems of which he had
been but dimly aware, it also provided an opportunity for reflection,
confession, and rededication at a moment of near-mortal despair.
Meanwhile, his growing family received his full loving attention, as did,
though to a much lesser degree, the substantial intellectual and artistic
refugee colonies in Hollywood, Pacific Palisades, and the other little
Berlins, Viennas, and Parises of the American West. But the activist in
Schoenberg did not remain dormant for long. Impressed with the
intermittent press reports of the significant contributions to the war-
effort made by various governments-in-exile, he began to ask himself
whether the time had not come for a Jewish government-in-exile, to
safeguard whatever rights the international community might be willing
to accord Jews under the impact of cataclysmic events that left none
untouched. If any group deserved such official representation, it seemed
to him, then it was surely that which actually lived in exile.

Precisely how his ideas evolved along these lines is difficult to ascertain.
Their ultimate gist, however, has come down to us in the manuscript
copy of a projected speech announcing the formation of such a government, drafted toward the end of the war in the oversize letters typical of
that period, when his eyesight rapidly deterioriated.[62] The less charitable
may look upon this final link in the long chain of pertinent documents as
the *ne plus ultra* of personal ambition, if not outright arrogance. But those
conscious and appreciative of the traditionally Jewish interpretation of
'chosenness' as readiness to choose a higher calling, irrespective of the
consequences for the one choosing, will sense both courage and humility
in Schoenberg's message, kept in unmistakably biblical tones and
intended for broadcast at the appropriate moment 'to all countries where
Jews are living':

I'll speak to you saying:
Here I am, Arn. Sch., the president of the government in exile of the Jewish
nation on a ship which we have received through the generosity of Pr. Tr.
[President Truman] the Am. government and the Am. people . . .

After outlining various steps to be taken without delay, Schoenberg
places the mandate of history squarely on the shoulders of both Western
Jewry and the world at large:

Jews of all countries! for 2000 years we live in exile and never has the idea been
conceived to erect a Government in exile of the Jewish nation, capable of guiding

[62] Rufer H 46, *The Jewish Government in Exile*.

such activities as would render us a nation again capable and powerful enough to give orders on this behalf, and powerful enough to see that these orders will be obeyed, and carried out precisely in the manner as requested by a world strong enough to take on the responsibility of shaping the destiny of our nation.

Schoenberg's vision was of a phoenix rising from the rabble of the ghettos and the stench of the concentration camps, like the divine order created out of chaos, which he evoked in his virtually contemporaneous *Genesis Prelude*. There was no doubt in his mind that the material and spiritual failure of the survivors was inexorably predicated on their political and religious autonomy. The immediate post-war events not only proved him correct, they also quickly overtook him. Turning their backs on Europe's dungeons, the pitiful yet proud remnants of his people took their destiny into their own hands and almost to a man chose 'the Path of the Bible' to the promised land. The stampede of the condemned, depicted in *A Survivor from Warsaw* turned into the survivors' rush towards freedom and dignity in the ancient land of their forefathers. When the victorious nations, hard pressed by their own guilt, mandated Jewish sovereignty in partitioned Palestine, the Arabs unleashed their combined might on the barely established state. Once again Schoenberg hovered on the brink of despair, until finally he could rejoice that 'Israel has returned and will see the Lord again'. Moreover, no longer torn between the conflicting demands of musical creativity and political action, he felt the time had come to pass on to the musicians of modern Israel the lofty ideal that animated all his works on behalf of his people: 'to set the world an example of the old kind that can make our souls function again as they must if mankind is to evolve any higher.'[63]

Arnold Schoenberg's passionate involvement in the politics of Jewish survival ended thus for all practical intents and purposes with the emergence of the State of Israel from the ashes to which, in the course of a dozen years, Hitler had reduced so much of Europe generally, its Jewish population in particular. Its philosophical-theoretical roots reached back nearly half a century, to the very beginning of political Zionism, a historical development which, perhaps more than any other, affected not only Schoenberg's socio-political attitudes but inevitably also the aesthetic orientation of one so totally dedicated to the truth as he

---

[63] Letter of 26 Apr. 1951 to Frank Pelleg and O. Partosh in Jerusalem, *Arnold Schoenberg Letters*, 287. For an unexpurgated version of the complete letter, based on the German original as published in *Tatzlil* 2 (1962), 62–3, see app. D.

saw it. Unlike Richard Wagner, who, in the wake of nineteenth-century Romanticism, viewed music essentially in mythical terms, on a par with traditional religion, Schoenberg never thought of it as a moral force *per se*. Whereas Wagner readily embraced the essentially static substance of Teutonic lore, Schoenberg acknowledged above all the centrality of history and the contingent spiritual values of the Old Testament. It was this deep-seated sense of history as a dynamic force in life which enabled him to proceed unerringly on an often rocky artistic path. That path, reinforced by the Messianic message of modern Zionism, eventually caused him to assume politically the same prophetic stance which, in the realm of art, had exposed him to so much ideologically motivated criticism on the part of men of little understanding, anxious to avert any threat to their smug psychological comfort.

Like his ancient models, Schoenberg inveighed no less mightily against fellow Jews who, unwilling to face reality, persisted in the wishful thought that the anti-Semitic monster would somehow pass, and leave them miraculously unharmed. A true prophet, to be sure, has no choice but to attack false prophets with all the persuasive vigour at his disposal. And if the strident tone of Schoenberg's relentless attacks, the uncompromising quality of his ideals, appear surprising at times, it is because, an established purveyor of romantic illusion, music had no previous prophetic tradition to speak of. Even Gustav Mahler, who was fundamentally in sympathy with the forces of social change and identified with the Dreyfusards through his friend Colonel Picquart, scorned sociopolitical controversy at the verbal, and of course, at the operational, level. Among nineteenth-century artists generally, only Leo Tolstoy seemed similarly inclined to seize the political animal by the horns. Indeed, the warm words of personal gratitude which the great Russian novelist's selfless devotion to the ideal of a society founded on Christian humility and brotherhood elicited from his Jewish biographer Stefan Zweig, perfectly convey the ultimate import of Arnold Schoenberg's extensive pleading and planning on behalf of his people as well:

It is always a rare privilege to experience a supreme artist also as a moral example, as a man who, instead of using his personal fame to dominate others, chooses to become a servant of humanity, rejecting all earthly authority except one: his own incorruptible conscience.[64]

[64] Stefan Zweig, *Zeit and Welt* (Berlin and Frankfurt am Main, 1946), 88.

8

The Composer and the Rabbi

IN the autumn of 1933, when Arnold Schoenberg and his family reached the shores of the United States, few voices inveighed more powerfully against the Nazi menace than that of Rabbi Stephen S. Wise, Schoenberg's exact contemporary—born in 1874 in Budapest, the native city of Theodor Herzl and a whole host of prominent Austrian Jews. Brought to the United States as an infant, following his father's appointment as rabbi of a leading New York congregation, he graduated from Columbia University at the age of eighteen, then returned to Europe for further studies in Oxford and in Vienna, where he was ordained by the city's Chief Rabbi, Adolph Jellinek, in 1893. That same year he secured a position as assistant rabbi in New York City and re-entered Columbia University as a doctoral student of Richard Gottheil, the renowned Orientalist and first president of the Federation of American Zionists, who was so impressed with the young man's vigorous intelligence that he made him Honorary Secretary of the organization. It was in this capacity that he attended the Second Zionist Congress in Basle in 1898, where Herzl personally asked him to serve as American Secretary of the World Zionist movement. From that moment on, Stephen S. Wise assumed major roles in Jewish as well as general American politics, an ardent Zionist who defended the cause of the poor and helpless of every race and creed with unflagging dedication until his death in 1949.

Wise advised American presidents from Woodrow Wilson, in whose election he took an important part, to Franklin Delano Roosevelt, whom he endorsed wholeheartedly in 1936, although at the height of the Great Depression in 1932 he had favoured Norman Thomas, the Socialist candidate. Among the leading pioneers of the budding ecumenical movement in America Wise also worked closely with Protestant and Roman Catholic clergy. Above all, as one of the pillars of Reform Judaism, he established the Free Synagogue of New York as early as 1907 and, in 1922, the Jewish Institute of Religion. His powerful oratory and political courage were legendary by the time Hitler seized power in Germany, and Wise tirelessly called for ways and means of saving German Jewry, indeed the Jews of all Europe. For, like Schoenberg, he

understood from the outset that Hitler's true aim was the destruction of
Jews wherever he could lay his hands on them. If for no other reason, a
second world war seemed a foregone conclusion unless everything was
done to stem the Nazi tide in its early phases.

As a long-time Zionist who was among the first followers of Herzl in
the United States, Wise had worried about the future of Continental
Jewry long before a private trip to Poland shocked him into the
realization that there were millions of Jews in Eastern Europe eking out a
meagre existence or living literally from hand to mouth. He was, in fact, a
co-framer of that crucial war-time document known as the Balfour
Declaration, and he fought relentlessly for its judicious implementation.
In so doing, however, he also placed himself squarely among those
Jewish leaders whom Arnold Schoenberg later accused of having wasted
valuable time when, in the face of Britain's mounting opposition to large-
scale settlement in its mandatory territory, alternative solutions should
have been explored with all possible energy and dispatch. In 1933,
moreover, Wise gave his support, albeit reluctantly, to the very boycott of
German goods which Schoenberg, with a good deal of justification,
regarded as ineffective, costly, and humiliating to boot. Still, the rapid
and ominous turn of events inevitably led the composer and the Rabbi to
common ground, not only in terms of their basic temperaments but in
specific matters as well, including their mutual disdain for 'pussy
footing', that is, the tendency of their more 'circumspect' fellows in
religion to try and placate the foe, for fear that forceful action might only
make things worse for those whom they wished to assist. As the Rabbi
confessed to one of his erstwhile congregants in April 1933, his was 'a
hideous job ... with timid and fearful German Jews at my heels to
desist'.[1] Yet, like Schoenberg, he felt he could not even afford a moment's
breather, for he too was convinced that 'it is a war of extermination that
Hitler is waging: and it is a deliberate thing planned since the 25th of
February 1920, when the Hitler program was first issued'. The day after
he wrote this to a friend, he reminded an adversary, who had publicly
declared that 'Dr. Wise will kill the Jews of Germany': 'if counsels of
expediency and timidity such as yours had not prevailed in Jewish life in
Germany during the last ten years, this great disaster might have been
averted.'[2] Arnold Schoenberg could hardly have agreed more, and one

[1] Stephen S. Wise, *Servant of the People: Selected Letters*, ed. Carl Hermann Voss
(Philadelphia, 1970), 185.
[2] Ibid., 186.

wonders whether it was not he who impressed upon Wise the need for
immediate action, without regard for possible repercussions, since in a
Paris meeting attended also by Schoenberg in the summer of 1933, the
Rabbi was told in no uncertain terms: 'You cannot hurt the Jews of
Germany. They are finished. You may help them. You cannot hurt
them.'[3]

Rabbi Wise and his wife went on to Geneva to attend the World
Jewish Congress which Schoenberg had to miss for 'a comic reason', as
he explained to his cousin Hans Nachod in a letter dated 18 September
1933: 'my bank did not manage to return my passport in time.'[4] Had he
gone as intended, he most likely would have spoken out against the
declaration of a world boycott of Germany. Then again, in the end he
might have gone along with Wise, for whom a boycott remained 'the last
and not the first weapon of the Jewish people',[5] and who yielded to the
majority only because he 'thought and said that moral and economic
boycott ultimately would develop into political action'.[6] At Wise's urging,
the Geneva conference led to the creation of the World Jewish Congress,
the international counterpart of the American Jewish Congress he
himself had founded in 1916. Whether the proposals for a Jewish Unity
Party, which Schoenberg had evidently submitted to him at least
informally in Paris a short time before, encouraged him further along
these lines, is difficult to say. The letter Schoenberg addressed to him
half a year after his own arrival in the United States implies, if nothing
else, that there was a definite meeting of minds in Paris, if only because
Dr Wise had spoken in terms Schoenberg appreciated, as when he
referred to the wealthy American Jews as 'grand dukes'. This letter, at
any rate, has all the earmarks of an extensive summary of Schoenberg's
side of their Paris conversation. The Rabbi—not surprisingly, given his
background and general attitude—valued the composer's intentions and
reasoning but, as an experienced politician, saw no possible way of
implementing such a Utopian scheme. Deeply affected by the plight of
the refugees he met that summer in Europe, he apparently did not reject
Schoenberg's ideas outright, and the latter therefore felt free to approach
him again, as soon as he himself was half-way settled in the New World.
Aware of the Rabbi's Viennese associations, he did not hesitate to write to

---

[3] Wise, *Servant of the People: Selected Letters*, 190.
[4] John A. Kimmen (ed.), *The Arnold Schoenberg-Hans Nachod Collection*, 25.
[5] Wise, *Servant of the People*, 183.
[6] Stephen S. Wise, *Challenging Years: An Autobiography* (New York, 1949), 257.

him in German and at considerable length. So comprehensively, in fact, did he state his case that his letter of 12 May 1934, written on stationery of the Hotel Ansonia in New York, serves admirably to illustrate his overriding concern for the safety of his fellow Jews at a moment when he was hard pressed to feed and house his own family, commuting between Boston and New York as a teacher of relative beginners and at serious danger to his fragile health.[7] 'Most Reverend Dr. Wise,' Schoenberg began,

In 1916, when I was an Austrian soldier who had joined the military with enthusiasm, I suddenly realized that the war was being conducted not merely against enemies from abroad but at least as vigorously against those at home. And the latter comprised, besides all others interested in liberal and socialist causes, the Jews. A few years later I had a nice experience in the Salzkammergut, not far from Salzburg: I was possibly one of the first Jews in Central Europe to become the victim of an actual expulsion.

Those two experiences shook me awake and led me to the realization that internationalism (something that was admittedly always alien to me) was nothing but a vain fantasy and that all the theories produced by liberal attitudes were ultimately futile: pacifism, democracy (which I had opposed for some time already) but in particular those untenable assimilation attempts. From there it was but an easy step to define assimilation as undesirable and to move on to a healthy as well as vigorous Jewish nationalism based on our national and religious belief in our chosenness. It was at that time that I resolved to devote myself to Jewish propaganda.

But then, you know yourself how difficult it is to persuade an intelligent Jew (and which Jew is not—unfortunately!—intelligent?) of anything whatsoever. Although I could point to the fact that even before 1921, long before Mussolini, I had predicted the end of democracy; although earlier (at the end of 1918)—when democracy erupted all over the place—I had founded an artistic organization in which, fully aware of the symbolic implications, I was the dictator (I called myself the first dictator in Europe at that time!); although during the same period I told Viennese communists—Jews—that the Jews would have to bleed for their communist propaganda; although I wrote to Einstein in 1925 that I was less interested in the discovery of a Jewish music (without ignoring the publicity—

[7] The author is greatly indebted to Rabbi Clifford Kulwin of Rio de Janeiro, who brought this precious item to his attention in 1983, soon after he located it in the Jewish Historical Archives on the campus of his *alma mater*, the Hebrew Union College in Cincinnati, Ohio. The Archives' director, Dr Abraham Peck, graciously granted the permission for its publication in the present context. The author himself takes full responsibility for the English translation. Shortly after this volume went to press the composer's grandson Randol Schoenberg offered the same letter in a somewhat different translation in his 'Arnold Schoenberg and Albert Einstein', *JASI* 10/2 (Nov. 1987), 165–8.

value of such endeavours) than in militant ways of forcing a solution of the Jewish question, and asked for an opportunity to discuss the matter with him in person, whereupon I had to undergo a very earthly treatment from this astronomer, whose eye ranges much too far to catch what lies closest—he neglected to reply. A pity: for, were he possessed of the requisite fire and clarity, or if I looked as beautiful and captivating as he, perhaps either of us would have sufficed. (Things being what they are, the two of us should have worked together.)[8] 1925! After this and many another failure, I came up with the idea of writing a propaganda piece with the intent of restoring Jewish self-confidence to a level commensurate with that of this 'stiff-necked' people in historical times when it consisted of fighters who prized national and religious independence over their own lives. I made several attempts to get one of the two pieces (the other, an opera 'Moses and Aaron', has remained three-fourths complete for over two years, as I told you), 'The Path of the Bible' (that is the path to freedom) published or performed, but I gave up when I began to feel that the selflessness of my intention was deliberately being misconstrued.

I am telling you all this because I believe that it proves a certain degree of political insight, something that, unfortunately and un-understandably, the leaders of the Jews do not seem to possess in any large measure. Amazingly so; for their ability to deal with diverging concerns is revealed not only in business life but also on the chess-board, and I would almost believe that it is not that they are incapable of applying historical facts to the present but that the erstwhile sense of community that once existed, and the character and courage required to activate it, have disappeared. There is a shortage of people ready to give their life for a purely Jewish ideal; but there is an abundance of people hoping to save themselves from the catastrophe. To make clear to the latter that *fate has tied them to the Jewish people* as a whole, to ensure an *awareness* and, where necessary, a *feeling* for it, would seem to be the first task of a Jewish-national politician—an educator, a renewer, such as Jewish history has, after all, known in numerous instances.

I believe, as I already suggested, that I have shown considerable political foresight. But please don't misunderstand me: I have no political ambitions; my ambitions could have found complete fulfilment on music paper, had I had any ambitions at all. I only insist on the quiet honour to be permitted to sacrifice my life for the existence of the Jewish people. And then only in case none more suitable could be found, especially one younger and healthier than me, only then, lest I withdraw from a duty fully recognized as such, would I put my own person forward. For in the lead belongs a person *worth seeing* and *worth hearing*, like you or Einstein.

I have long been of the opinion (which in Paris I hid behind more appealing

[8] The composer's animosity against Albert Einstein, whose pacifist tendencies greatly irked him, never abated. The scientist's famous head, it appears, offended his vanity (see below).

ideas) that a man of strong will and devoid of fear, who has all of Jewry behind him (in so far as that is possible: I count on life!), could come forward and *negotiate* as well as *conclude agreements*: the only thing in the life of peoples that is within reach of the weak and enables him possibly even to become strong.[9] Don't regard these perhaps somewhat clouded words (in political matters one should never become too explicit: there must always be room for retreat) as mere manners of speaking, behind which there is nothing. But as an indication that in my view the Jewish people can pursue *no other path than that taken by other peoples*; if it wants to ensure its survival!

I mentioned to you a speech in which I called for the creation of a Jewish Unity Party. The creation of such a party is no easy task and there is really no reason why it should be: in our situation none has the right to look for easy tasks. But today, when even the least of the Jews has been frightened to his bones, or will be before long, it is actually going to be much less difficult than at a time when they imagined themselves completely secure. Our time confronts us with a fantastic problem, so fantastic our imagination could never have conjured it up. At a time like this one can only survive, save, if one has the courage to consider something even more fantastic not only possible but achievable.

The creation of a Unity Party is less difficult today because the helplessness of all other parties in the face of the catastrophe is horrifyingly evident. Who would dispute it, who assert that one of the other parties might be able to act in a more appropriate fashion: who, above all, could deny that the Unity Party is apt to accomplish (at the very least) more than any other party?

The Unity Party would in no way threaten the existence of any of the other parties and viewpoints and insist on unity only for the sake of warding off the catastrophe.

Who except the Unity Party could be so bold as to speak in the name of all Jewry? Who else would have credibility in foreign affairs?

But needless to say: national unity resulted *never* from a people's *voluntary* decision but rather has always come about *under duress*. What courageous man, who loves his nation, would be afraid to exert such benevolent force? In war, storm-troops are given rum to drink and when that does not help machine guns are placed in their backs. WE ARE AT WAR![10]

I have been told that the Jews of America (didn't you refer to them as 'grand dukes' while in Paris?) have no intention of abandoning the boycott, since Germany, they say, is about to collapse (apparently enconomically: that would be for the third time in the last twenty years), and it is only a question of a short time

[9] As is obvious from statements made elsewhere, for example in *A Four-Point Program*, the reference here is not to negotiations with Nazi Germany but with countries amenable to refugee settlement, conceivably even the British.

[10] Schoenberg's early recognition of the seemingly absurd fact that the war had already begun and that it was indeed 'The War against the Jews', as Lucy Dawidowicz called it decades after the fact, was truly unique.

... etc., etc. ... During the war we were consoled the same way. But: how do these gentlemen imagine the collapse? Do they perhaps think there will be a vote in the German Parliament? Or do they really believe in the possibility of a rebellion or mutiny against a dictatorship? Those gentlemen who have such ideas surely were never soldiers and have no notion of the degree of certainty with which one may count on the proper execution of orders in any well-disciplined army. But in this instance the additional factor that this army consists of a fanaticized crowd must be taken into consideration. And anyone in the least sensitive to mass-psychology and aware how difficult it is to get a mass to embrace a given cause, also knows that, once it has become aroused, a long, long time passes before it becomes possible to detract them from that cause. And don't forget: Germans never give up! And they would not have abandoned the war, had it not been hopelessly lost thanks to Mr Ludendorff. They would still be at it.

I don't feel I have a right to mix into American affairs, only Jewish ones. Nor am I, therefore, in a position to speak out publicly against the boycott. The more so as it is quite clear to me that the damage it is doing will have to be endured by Jews in all countries not only in America: but its benefits, it seems to me, are of very special interest also to non-Jews. And that is one of the reasons why I can understand the Jewish position only from one perspective: they are accustomed to being turned into scapegoats; and they are so accustomed to it that they have loudly announced to the world, long before it might be necessary, that they are ready to be the scapegoats. And that they are ready to do that without regard to themselves, but also without regard to the *hostages in the hands of the enemy!*

I hope you will not take the free expression of my viewpoint as arrogance. I am only a musician, but as a Jew I have nevertheless some experience and have lived through some things that give me the right to speak.

I would be overjoyed, if we could find an opportunity soon to talk about such and related matters, provided, as I hope, that this would not bore you too much.

In the meantime I am with many respectful and humble greetings, also to your wife,

Yours,

/s/ Arnold Schoenberg

The Rabbi's reply, if there was one, remains unknown. He rarely kept carbon copies of his letters, and there is no trace of any such communication in the vast documentation now housed in the Arnold Schoenberg Institute in Los Angeles.[11] Even so, it is by no means unlikely that the

---

[11] The Institute's archivist, R. Wayne Shoaf, was kind enough to do the necessary checking. The author also owes him thanks for a copy of Schoenberg's original English text of his lecture of 29 Apr. 1934 on 'The Jewish Situation', in which the Jews are chided for their 'discord', which prevents them from doing jointly what has to be done: 'It is the tragicomedy of the democracy in our people: our aim to [sic] freedom in spiritual things has caused a new babylonian captivity.'

requested interview did take place. And if so, a remarkable meeting of
two superior sets of hearts and minds regrettably and unaccountably
disappeared into the darker recesses of history. Nor do we know whether
Wise was by chance in the audience when, two weeks earlier, Schoenberg
had spoken on the Jewish situation as he perceived it.[12] Stressing once
more the inevitability of anti-Semitism as an intrinsic psychological
function of Israel's chosenness, he had warned his distinguished listeners
of the world-wide disaster which he and Rabbi Wise foresaw unless some
drastic measures were taken without delay. Since he viewed anti-
Semitism as 'a result' rather than 'a cause', he was convinced of the
futility of any attempt to fight it. Instead he called upon the men and
women present, no doubt to their astonishment (most were colleagues),
to rally behind him in his Jewish Unity Party, with a single goal in mind:
to snatch as many from the Nazi clutches as time permitted before the
deluge descended upon European Jewry. Non-feasance in this grave and
urgent matter, he told them, was sure to result in countless innocent
victims and saddle all who procrastinated until it was too late with a
heavy burden of guilt.

Rabbi Wise's repeated appeals to President Roosevelt merely appeared
to prove that little help was to be expected from non-Jews, including
those who truly abhorred Hitler and his ilk. The Jews, for their part,
were already so thoroughly Americanized, that they too encountered
great difficulty in trying to understand Europe and its many unsolved
problems. Those of German origin, in particular, could not conceive of a
Germany reverting to medieval barbarisms. That the unrelenting pleas of
Rabbi Wise fell largely on deaf ears merely confirmed what Schoenberg
had to say about the sad condition of a Judaism devoid of prophecy.
Meanwhile, with the outbreak of the Second World War, the situation of
European Jewry became desperate. By the end of 1941 the United States
was engaged mostly in rearguard actions against the Japanese, while
Hitler was master of Europe from the British Channel to the Urals. But
even though virtually all of Europe's Jews were now in imminent danger,
Britain refused to lower the barriers to Palestinian immigration, and
America, soon badly in need of manpower, also refused to open its gates.
In August 1941 Wise wrote: 'I am really sick over what is happening to
the refugees, the utter denial to them of the right to come in. I shall urge
vigorous action of the President...'[13] To little avail, of course, for the US

[12] Cf. 'Die jüdische Situation', in Schönberg, *Gesammelte Schriften*, ed. I. Vojtech
(Frankfurt am Main, 1976), 328–32.

[13] Wise, *Servant of the People*, 244.

State Department employed every possible means of obstruction, its own chiefs, Undersecretary Sumner Welles in particular, notwithstanding. Wise later spoke of 'death by bureaucracy', as he recalled how official Washington had refused to give credence to the authentic reports of massive exterminations in Eastern Europe that reached the World Jewish Congress in the summer of 1942, when the Jewish communities of a shrinking free world were still in shock over the tragedy of the *Struma*.[14] That small refugee-laden boat sank off the Turkish coast shortly after being denied further harbour privileges in Istanbul. British landing-permits for Palestine had not been forthcoming, and 768 persons, including numerous children, perished. One survived. To the President's deeply concerned wife Wise wrote: 'If Palestine is to be ruled out, the situation of the unhappy refugees indeed becomes hopeless. Assuming Mr. Welles is right in saying that refuge cannot be found for these people in South American countries or in Africa, is not the obvious answer that they should be admitted to the one country which they can call home, to which they could go—in the words of Mr. Churchill—"not on suffrance, but out of right"?'[15]

Confronted with a disaster of unprecedented proportions, even the ardent Zionist Wise had to come to accept the idea of alternative, if only temporary, solutions which Schoenberg had promoted so forcefully for so many years. The problem, of course, was that no such solutions were ever seriously in the offing, not then and not before. Field Marshal Rommel stood not far from the gates of Palestine, yet the British proved unwilling to grant Jewish settlers even minimal means of self-defence. Many in America were outraged, and more and more voices were heard in support of a Jewish Army to fight the Nazis on the battlefield and to secure Palestine once and for all for the Jewish people. In California it was the playwright and screen-writer Ben Hecht who promoted this cause most forcefully, and in early spring 1943 both Schoenberg and Kurt Weill, now united in their hatred of Nazi Germany, joined his 'Committee for a Jewish Army'. The Committee's public appeal in the *New York Times* and other leading American newspapers so outraged Edgar Hoover, the head of the Federal Bureau of Investigation, that he denounced Arnold Schoenberg, Lion Feuchtwanger, William Zorach, and the rest of the distinguished group of signatories as 'thoroughly

---

[14] Wise, *Challenging Years*, 274.
[15] Wise, *Servant of the People*, 247.

disreputable Communist Zionists'.[16] As his authority he cited an unnamed member of the executive board of the American Jewish Congress. Assuming that such was his source, and that the fanatical anti-communist Hoover did not embellish his outrageous story in order to make it more believable, who could have spread such a grotesque falsehood? Some unfortunate internecine warfare among Jewish organizations did exist. And the fact is that Stephen Wise had scant regard for the 'radicals' of the Emergency Conference to Save the Jews of Europe, sponsored by the same group around Ben Hecht that hoped to enlist hundreds of thousands of stateless and Palestinian Jews in the proposed Jewish Army, thus saving large numbers, from Rumania and Hungary in particular, who faced certain death because the allied nations, though locked in battle with the same merciless foe, refused to shelter them. Wise, however, was a truly honourable man, contemptuous of vilifications of any kind. And it is doubtful that he tolerated such behaviour on the part of his associates. Still, he did go as far as to insist that Hillel Kook, the most dynamic of the 'radicals', be barred from a high-level unity meeting of the American Jewish leadership in 1943.[17] As for the British, they eventually relented at least to the point of equipping a Jewish Brigade that saw action during the closing stages of the European campaign and then devoted itself to the ingathering of the remnant and its transportation to Palestine by any legal or 'illegal' means available.

The Second World Jewish Congress finally convened in 1948, once again in neutral Switzerland. It was, Rabbi Wise recalled, 'a congress of saddest memories, because of the ever-present shadow of the mass slaughter of millions of our fellow Jews . . . barely one hundred thousand Jews remained in Poland'.[18] The composer whose urgent pleas on behalf of the helpless millions had gone unheeded when there was still time was left to set the victims a lasting memorial, that shattering *Yiskor* entitled *A Survivor from Warsaw*. It was heard for the first time in remote Albuquerque, New Mexico, the same year the Rabbi, presiding in Lausanne, recited the tragic balance-sheet. Less than a year later, barely consoled by the rise of a proud Jewish state from Europe's ashes, he died,

---

[16] Cf. Yitshaq Ben-Ami, *Years of Wrath, Days of Glory* (New York, 1982), 325.

[17] Cf. Monty Noam Penkower, *The Jews were Expendable* (Urbana and Chicago, 1983), 138.

[18] Wise, *Challenging Years*, 320–1.

a broken man. Arnold Schoenberg followed on 13 July 1951, disenchanted with the 'liberalized' religion of American Reform Judaism. 'One thing is sure,' he observed just nine weeks before his death, 'only the strict believers among the Israelites could be counted on, in case of need, to warn the world of a second Sodom and Gomorrah and to lead it back to the serene modesty of Paradise.'[19]

[19] Thus concludes the penultimate completed 'Psalm' from Schoenberg's pen.

9

Prague and Jerusalem

THE Eastern territories of the Austrian Empire, in particular Galicia, Hungary, and the provinces consolidated after the First World War into the Republic of Czechoslovakia, were among the principal reservoirs of Jewish culture not only throughout the nineteenth century but right up to the destruction of European Jewry at the hands of the Nazis during the Second World War. Arnold Schoenberg's mother, Pauline Nachod, was born in Prague during the year of the revolution, 1848, into a family that had been there for generations. His father, a native of Szécheny in Hungary, had lived and worked in Preßburg, the later Slovak capital of Bratislava, before moving on to Vienna. Alexander von Zemlinsky, Schoenberg's early mentor, friend, and brother-in-law, was the principal conductor of Prague's German Theatre from 1911 to 1927. In the course of that period too, Mozart's favourite city offered Schoenberg's Verein für musikalische Privataufführungen at least temporarily a new lease of life. Most importantly, it was his Czech background which at the moment of gravest danger enabled the composer and his family to reach safety abroad, thanks to a co-operative Czechoslovakian consul willing to issue urgently needed passports. Those Nachods and other relatives who stayed behind in the city that harboured one of the oldest and most fully integrated Jewish communities in Europe perished virtually without exception in Hitler's death camps.

Under the circumstances, a believer in ultimate historical justice like Schoenberg might well have seen more than sheer accident in the curious twists of fate that ultimately landed the bulk of the documentation of his prolonged and vital Prague connections in the Jewish National and University Library in Jerusalem, the final destination, as he made clear less than three months before his death, of all relevant materials in his musical and literary estate.[1] This quite unequivocal resolve on his part was subsequently thwarted—the pertinent passage was in fact dropped

---

[1] The pertinent letter of 26 April 1951 was published in its entirety first by M. Taldor in his 'A Shortened and Falsified Schoenberg', *Tatzlil* 2 (1962), 62–3; English summary, 130. For an expurgated version see *Arnold Schoenberg Letters*, 286–7.

from the letter as printed in Erwin Stein's collection. If some important autograph and printed materials are now nevertheless exactly where Schoenberg wanted them to be, it is largely thanks to the prescience and generosity of Georg Alter, the instigator and permanent secretary of the Prager Verein für musikalische Privataufführungen, who somehow miraculously managed to preserve the organization's archive intact—not only as a refugee in London under the *Blitz*, and on his return to post-war Prague, but also through several wars in beleaguered Israel, where he spent the final decade of his life.[2]

Dr Alter, later a noted astronomer, was in his younger years a dedicated amateur violinist who made a living, much like Schoenberg, as a commercial clerk. A guest-appearance of Schoenberg's Viennese Verein in 1920 so fascinated Alter that he immediately looked for ways and means to make sure that such concerts would be heard in his native city on a regular basis. His initial approach to Alexander Zemlinsky, among others, met with little enthusiasm. But a sensational return-engagement of the Viennese musicians with *Pierrot Lunaire*, meticulously coached by Schoenberg himself, rapidly led to the realization of his dream. At the charter meeting of the Prague Verein in the spring of 1922 Zemlinsky was elected president and Alter, who had done most of the negotiating with Schoenberg, secretary. Schoenberg himself was offered, and subsequently accepted, the honorary presidency.

Since the charter of the Prague Verein was essentially an adaptation of its Viennese model, modified to accommodate specific local conditions, it may be worth recalling some of the principal guide-lines set forth in the last Vienna prospectus as drafted by Alban Berg in 1921. The organization's prime objective was the promotion of contemporary music in all its stylistic variety through carefully prepared programmes designed to inform broadly rather than to further the parochial interests of any particular 'school' or aesthetic orientation. Schoenberg was firmly convinced that the blurring of aesthetic issues was due largely to a fundamental lack of knowledge even on the part of experts and that it was a basic insecurity of judgement which had caused the retreats into so many doctrinaire positions. Obligatory repeat performances were, therefore, an intrinsic feature of his elaborate scheme to familiarize a more or less permanent audience of subscribers with new idioms and structural

---

[2] Unless otherwise identified, the quotations below are from unpublished material in the Jerusalem collection. The gracious donor, Georg Alter, died in 1972. This author, for one, will always remember him for his personal kindness and selfless dedication to everything Arnold Schoenberg stood for.

procedures. Success of a given work or composer was regarded at most as a tolerable by-product: 'the organization thus exists by no means for the sake of the composers but exclusively for the sake of the public.'[3] The charter prohibits public performances and critical reviews. Members were not allowed to applaud nor, conversely, to manifest their misgivings; only moderate acknowledgements of understanding had Schoenberg's reluctant approval. The most outstanding characteristic of these private concerts, however, was the unprecedented perfection—attained in countless hours of study and rehearsal—with which a select group of young musicians rendered a host of difficult works ranging over the entire contemporary spectrum. Amongst those fully represented were not only Bartók and Stravinsky but also Milhaud and Honegger, and Willem Pijper, the gifted Dutchman. More intriguingly still, the two hundred and twenty-six performances presented under the auspices of the Vienna Verein during the 1920–1 season included forty-two of music by Max Reger.

The archives of the Prague Verein, now housed in Jerusalem, shed light on a number of questions pertaining to Arnold Schoenberg and his circle during the crucial years 1921–4. The widely held view, for example, that the Vienna Verein was forced to terminate its activities after three ostensibly successful years because it did not manage to survive the financial crisis that had gripped Central Europe in 1921–2 receives little support from the letters Erwin Stein addressed to Georg Alter at Schoenberg's behest. On the contrary, these confirm that the organization did in fact maintain its identity for several more years but succumbed in the end to Schoenberg's personal decision to limit himself henceforth to teaching and composition. Schoenberg's published correspondence alone should have sufficed to establish the real reason for the gradual demise of the Verein, just as it testifies to the utter devotion with which Stein assumed most of the responsibility, first during the winter of 1920–1, while Schoenberg lectured and conducted in the Netherlands, then from 1922 on, when the composer relinquished his leadership altogether. However, the Jerusalem documents also provide important evidence to the effect that the creation of the Prague Verein opened up much-needed opportunities for similar programmes, in many instances with the very same artists, for a further two years. The Vienna prospectus

---

[3] A copy of the prospectus is among the many printed items in the Jerusalem collection. See also Bryan R. Simms, 'The Society for Private Musical Performances', *JASI* 3/2 (Oct. 1979), 127–49, for additional documentation on the Vienna Verein.

of 1921 may have failed to produce the expected results at home; by inspiring the Prague charter it ensured at least the short-term survival of one of Schoenberg's most cherished projects. It would seem, at any rate, that for all practical intents and purposes the Verein functioned uninterruptedly from 1918 to 1924, albeit with a change of venue from Vienna to Prague in 1922. Operating as it did at the height of a period of runaway inflation, the Prague group could never hope to attain anything like the scope or level of intensity of the parent organization. Even so, beginning with the opening event of 25 May 1922, which once again featured *Pierrot Lunaire* under the composer's direction, Zemlinsky and Alter maintained a steady flow of concerts, provided in the main, though by no means exclusively, by Viennese performers, under Stein's capable management and Anton Webern's superb coaching.[4]

If only because it hails from the few short years that yielded the method of composing with twelve tones, the Jerusalem collection retains considerable historical value. In addition, however, a number of the items illuminate some characteristic trait of the complex, overpowering personality that was Arnold Schoenberg. Even his hastily pencilled draft of the proposed agreement between the two organizations, its rather prosaic content notwithstanding, assumes significance far beyond that of a mere curiosity. As is only to be expected, Schoenberg's detailed business proposal is filled with figures: figures covering the number of yearly concerts as well as first and repeat performances, figures relating to various types of pieces and their distribution among the programmes envisaged, figures pertaining to fees and expenses, indeed to every possible aspect of such an ambitious artistic enterprise run on the proverbial shoe-string. The surprising feature is Schoenberg's final reduction of all these material issues to a series of mathematical equations making use of simple abbreviations of the principal terms: *Konzertzahl* (Kz), *Teures Konzert* (TK), *Vorschuss* (V_1, V_2, etc.). A formula like

$$TK = Kr_1 + V_1 \text{ (expensive concert} = \text{fee} + \text{advance) or } Kr = Kr_1 - \frac{V_1}{rKz_1},$$

offers anything but trivial corroborative evidence that the composer's intense preoccupation with the 'objective', logical representation of creative musical processes was rooted in a basic mental attitude covering every aspect of his thought and behaviour, material existence not excluded. In all probability the draft agreement was put together in 1922,

---

[4] Acting on behalf of the Vienna Verein, Schoenberg signed the typescript of the final agreement on the day of the concert, 25 May 1922.

little more than half a year after Schoenberg received Josef Rufer at his summer home in Traunkirchen and revealed his 'discovery', which, he was confident, spelled German pre-eminence in musical composition for another hundred years.

The extent to which the Schoenbergian method of composing with twelve tones reflects the strictly cerebral system of Josef Matthias Hauer has long been a subject of partisan debate. Schoenberg's pupil Egon Wellesz has intimated that he acted as an intermediary between the two rivals after Hauer came to see him in the early days of the First World War. According to Wellesz, 'Schoenberg, who had already worked *de facto* with rows of six or seven tones, adopted Hauer's twelve-tone music and created a system based on fugue and variation technique'.[5] Schoenberg himself later admitted his fear that the publication of Hauer's theories might make him appear a plagiarist even though he had entertained similar notions over a long period of time.[6] In order to put their relationship on a proper footing, he was looking for some form of public clarification of their essential agreements and differences. Thus on 1 December 1923, having rejected as impractical his initial idea of a joint publication, he approached Hauer about a possible partnership in a school devoted to the exploration of theoretical issues posed by the music of their time. Such an institution he felt would shield them from the ever-present danger of misinterpretation and deliberate distortion. Hauer must have accepted Schoenberg's invitation to a face-to-face meeting at his home without delay, for Schoenberg's next letter, written on 7 December 1923, confirms the date (three days later) and offers for discussion the additional alternative of a regular exchange of views in print. It also sets the general mood of the forthcoming encounter by suggesting that 'we approach our conversation like former belligerents looking for peace'.[7]

Exactly what, if anything, was resolved in the course of that historic meeting may never be known, except that Hauer committed himself to Schoenberg's last alternative—a series of expository publications. The fact that Hauer dedicated the first of his theoretical pamphlets, *Vom Melos zur Pauke*, to Schoenberg and subtitled it 'An Introduction to Twelve-Tone-Music' has long pointed in that direction. But we now

[5] Egon Wellesz, 'Erinnerungen an Gustav Mahler und Arnold Schönberg', *Orbis Musicae* 1 (summer, 1971), 80.

[6] Cf. the letter addressed to Hauer on 1 December 1923, *Arnold Schoenberg Letters*, 107.

[7] Translated here from Schoenberg's original German as printed in Arnold Schönberg, *Briefe*, ed. Erwin Stein, 110.

have proof positive in the form of a letter, unquestionably the most extraordinary item in the Jerusalem collection. Dated 16 December 1923, six days after the meeting at Schoenberg's home, it started out as a programme-proposal by Erwin Stein, acting in Schoenberg's name as executive secretary of the Vienna Verein. But before Stein could finish his first sentence, Schoenberg impulsively seized his pen and did not release it until he had made his point imperiously and with typical dramatic flair. Even though no translation can do Schoenberg's characteristic style proper justice, this unique document (Pls. 5, 6) is offered here, for what it may be worth, in English.

[Stein:] Dear Mr Alter, For the next presentation of the Prague Verein we would like to

[Schoenberg:] Rather I propose that Mr Josef Mathiass [*sic*] Hauer, who has published writings on 'atonal music' for several years, give a lecture on his theories. For that will be *very interesting*!!! because in certain respects, though in a different way, he has arrived at results similar to, in part even identical with, my own. We will shortly publish a pertinent exchange of letters, and it would seem desirable that the public of an 'Association for Private Performances' be somewhat prepared. Mr Stein will write about the rest, while I send you in the meantime best regards. Your Arnold Schönberg

[Stein:] So, dear Mr Alter, please let me know when this evening can take place. Soon if possible—Hauer is in dire material straits. The evening can, of course, be a one-time event.

Please send your reply to Donaustadt where I shall be until 3 January.

With best regards

Your Erwin Stein

Nothing came of the planned public exchange of letters, but Schoenberg paid Hauer generous homage in the fourth edition of his *Harmonielehre*, praising his rival's theoretical prowess in well-chosen words, even though he had no use for Hauer's notion of 'atonality'. As for the proposed lecture in Prague, Zemlinsky, claiming lack of interest even among the select crowd of his Verein, quickly vetoed the idea, and Schoenberg was forced to turn elsewhere for material support of this somewhat abstruse colleague who found himself in dire straits due to circumstances largely beyond his control. As early as 24 April 1923 he had written to Paul Stefan requesting Hauer's current address for submission to the Friends Relief Mission. In his letter of acceptance to Professor Klatte in Berlin, who had asked him to join the honorary committee of the American Fund for the Relief of German and Austrian

Musicians, he emphatically proposed Hauer and Alban Berg as immediate recipients of its aid.[8]

Concern for the material welfare of a respected adversary is matched in the Jerusalem letters by new evidence of Schoenberg's tireless efforts on behalf of his pupils and, for that matter, of anyone bound to him by a sense of artistic-spiritual community. Informed of the misfortunes of his former pupil Travnicek, who was struggling desperately to survive on the meagre income of a minor Prague theatre coach, he wondered whether Georg Alter could not get him at least one decent meal a day with some private family. Within a few days Alter secured not only a daily meal but also, and more importantly, an additional position for Travnicek as conductor of a local men's glee club. Schoenberg sent a warm note of thanks by return. Over four decades later, informed that Travnicek, after many years in South Africa, had returned to Europe, Dr Alter sent him copies of the pertinent letters in his archive, and Travnicek, who had known nothing of Schoenberg's characteristic move, replied: 'Today I feel ashamed that I even mentioned the matter to him at the time. But that he addressed himself to you immediately is proof of his touching concern for his pupils.'

While there is no direct documentary evidence that Schoenberg undertook similar steps on behalf of Hanns Eisler, the latter's communications to Georg Alter, dating from the beginning of 1923, point strongly in that direction. Eisler's Piano Sonata had met with considerable success at a concert of the Prague Verein, and the moment seemed propitious for the enlisting of aid for this promising young musician, who, like most of the Schoenberg disciples, suffered greatly at a time when the price of bread could triple from one hour to the next. Alter, with his proven inventiveness and efficiency, got Eisler a commission for the orchestration of an operetta. But, whereas earlier in the century Schoenberg himself had managed to survive on precisely this kind of work, Eisler felt constrained to decline. The budding socialist first drew up a detailed list of his estimated expenses, including the—admittedly exorbitant—price of good music paper, then rejected the suggested fee of 500,000 kroner as 'a ridiculous compensation for at least four weeks' work, . . . even though the knife sits at my throat and won't leave'. Among the followers of Schoenberg, it may well have been Eisler who identified most closely with some of the master's more negative attitudes. But perhaps it would be fairer to the memory of both men to assume that Eisler was the one who least understood Schoenberg's paradoxical personality at that time

[8] Schoenberg, *Briefe*, 87, 89.

because he shared only one of his principal character traits—his stubborn single-mindedness.

In the early 1920s *Pierrot Lunaire* was the focus of many a reactionary, if not outright anti-Semitic attack on Schoenberg, possibly because, more than any other work, it pushed the Wagnerian aesthetic well beyond the point of no return. By the same token, this uncanny evocation of unreality rarely failed to make its point with sophisticated progressive audiences. In Prague it not only determined the artistic direction of the Verein in its formative stages; it was also the featured event on its final programme. The rest of that historic concert of 2 May 1924 was given over to the first performance of the piece in which Pierrot assumed the post-war garb of neo-Classicism: the Serenade, Op. 24. The pairing of Schoenberg's pre-war masterpiece and its natural progeny of course made eminent stylistic sense. At the same time it offered the composer a double opportunity to test his abilities as coach and conductor of intimate yet highly intricate chamber works. Schoenberg's wish to conduct *Pierrot Lunaire* in particular, the only piece eventually recorded under his direction, was noted by Erwin Stein in a letter he addressed to Georg Alter on 20 February 1922. Even so, as Stein explains in another communication, Schoenberg did not like the idea of appearing on the programmes of the Prague Verein, in person or otherwise, if Zemlinsky was not equally represented. Zemlinsky, for his part, merely followed the example of Schoenberg, who had withheld his own music throughout the entire first season of the Vienna Verein to avoid any possible suspicion that he had formed the organization for purposes of self-promotion. The result of Zemlinsky's caution and Schoenberg's policy of even-handedness was a virtual stalemate that caused Erwin Stein considerable anguish, especially after the Prague Verein refused to accept many of the Reger works offered as alternatives. As Stein eventually put it to Alter in utter despair: 'If one is not allowed to perform Zemlinsky, Schoenberg, or Reger, with what is one to produce modern programmes??!!' On 26 October 1922, Schoenberg tried to break the deadlock by writing to Zemlinsky at length. He repeated his conviction that Reger, a prolific composer still largely unknown, was 'a genius', and took issue with Zemlinsky's characterization of Darius Milhaud as 'insignificant'. Quite in line with the slightly earlier prospectus, this programmatic letter represents in fact a forceful restatement of Schoenberg's genuine commitment to all truly creative talent, irrespective of stylistic direction.[9]

For Christmas 1922 the Schoenberg circle pooled its meagre resources

---

[9] Schoenberg, *Briefe*, 80–1.

and offered the master a typewriter. The single published item from the Jerusalem collection figures among the first tangible results of this historic purchase, which enabled Schoenberg to increase substantially the volume of his correspondence and of other forms of verbal communication. In this typewritten letter, dated 14 January 1923, the composer apologizes for the neglect of his presidential duties, both in Vienna and in Prague, pleading priority for several works in progress, presumably the piano pieces Op. 23 and Op. 25, the Serenade, and the Wind Quintet.[10] In 1923 he was nevertheless more prominently in evidence on the Prague musical scene than at any previous time. Thus in February the Verein arranged for a reading of the text of *Die Jakobsleiter* by Wilhelm Klitsch, and Webern brought his Viennese performers for two concerts of novelties, including Eduard Steuermann's ingenious piano transcription of the Chamber Symphony, Op. 9. In April Zemlinsky performed the Five Orchestral Pieces, and on 10 October 1923 the Verein presented Marya Freund, who had come over specially from Paris, with Eduard Steuermann in a programme that offered songs from Op. 6, the new piano works, Op. 23 and Op. 25, and the complete *Buch der hängenden Gärten*. Only the first performance of the fourteen-year-old monodrama *Erwartung*, planned by Zemlinsky for 1923 as well, had to be postponed once again to the following season.

Such a spate of activities required much communication, and the archives of the Prague Verein have preserved most of it, including early correspondence with the newly formed Wiener Streichquartett. After rehearsing at first mostly Reger trios (in the absence of Felix Khuner, the second violinist), Rudolf Kolisch was finally in a position to propose a choice of works, including Berg's Op. 3 (first performance!), Schoenberg's Op. 7 or 10, Webern's Op. 5, Zemlinsky's Second Quartet, Suk's Second, and all five Reger quartets. In his next letter he became more specific, settling on Berg, Webern, and—Pfitzner. When the Quartet eventually made its way to Prague, Schoenberg took the precaution of sending a telegram insisting on free meals for the four members 'because honorarium insufficient'. Zemlinsky in turn wanted Alter to find out whether the reading of the text of a musical work was subject to entertainment-tax before confirming the arrangements for Wilhelm Klitsch's recitation of the *Jakobsleiter* text.

More precious than any of these and numerous other historically valuable items, however, are the five letters written by Anton Webern in preparation for his Prague concerts. They not only testify to the

[10] Ibid., 83–4.

meticulous care with which Schoenberg's favourite *Vortragsmeister* attended to every detail; they also underscore the breadth of his artistic interests, particularly on the French side of the post-war ledger. It is certainly not without interest, in view of more recent developments, that the bulk of Webern's programmes was of French inspiration, if not always musically, then at least textually. Financially, Webern's condition was, of course, no better than that of the Schoenberg circle in general, and Schoenberg was greatly worried about his star pupil. Hence, while on holiday in Traunkirchen in the summer of 1923, he addressed eloquent appeals for material aid for Webern to a number of foreign benefactors, unfortunately with only moderate success.[11]

On 18 October 1923, a few months after the Schoenbergs returned to their Mödling home, Mathilde Schoenberg, born Zemlinsky, quite unexpectedly died. In response to the expressions of sympathy that reached him from all over the world, the composer sent out printed notes of thanks; Georg Alter received a personally signed copy and ten months later the printed announcement of Schoenberg's subsequent marriage to Gertrud Kolisch.

In 1922 Alter had joined the composer and his family for a while at their Traunkirchen retreat and returned from that visit, which was devoted to business as well as pleasure, with important additions to the Schoenberg iconography. Among other pictures, he took one of the entire family on a relaxed boat-ride (Pl. 7). He also caught a number of candid glimpses of the composer, who, while thinking about *Die Jakobsleiter* once again, was eagerly looking forward to his next visit to Prague. Just before leaving for his holiday, Schoenberg had written to Zemlinsky not to worry about the dismal fee he was to receive for *Pierrot*, since it was, after all, not money that attracted him to Prague.[12] And it is indeed a proud man secure in himself who speaks from Alter's portrait of the composer on the porch of his summer home (Pl. 8): the mature man, unyielding on artistic principle yet eclectic in his taste and interests, seemingly arrogant in human relations yet so genuinely modest and affectionate in his contacts with those he loved and respected; the nominal Christian proud to be a Jew, the prophet little honoured by his own people, let alone by others, who was, in the eyes of most, not unlike Franz Kafka's anti-hero in *The Trial*: guilty by definition.

The general turmoil that characterized the immediate post-war years

---

[11] Cf. letters to Boissevain in Holland, and to Reinhart and Mme Hensch in Switzerland, Schoenberg, *Briefe*, 102–5.

[12] Ibid., 67.

in Central and Eastern Europe reached its climax in Prague with 'a three-day orgy of anti-Jewish and anti-German riots':[13] in November 1920 Czech nationalist mobs 'sacked the offices of German-language news-papers, attacked "Jewish-looking" victims in the streets, broke into the German National Theatre, and the Jewish Town Hall, destroyed the archives and burned ancient Hebrew manuscripts in front of the Old-New Synagogue, an act which the city's mayor hailed as a manifestation of national consciousness'. It was a devastated Kafka who wrote to his friend Milena that he had been 'bathing in Jew-hatred—*prasive plem-cho*—filthy brood—is what I heard them call the Jews. Isn't it only natural to leave a place where one is so bitterly hated? (That doesn't even take Zionism or feelings of national pride).'[14] Four years later the situation had improved to the point where at least the German runaway inflation was coming to an end, and a period of relative stability seemed in the offing. Still, among the Jews in particular, who furnished the bulk of Schoenberg's patrons in Prague no less than in Vienna, the psychologi-cal consequences persisted unabated. The pervasive sense of crisis adversely affected virtually all institutions, including some of the most venerable, not to speak of one as fragile as that which Georg Alter had built from scratch and guided with such personal devotion in the wake of some of the worst episodes in the entire long history of Jewish settlement in the Bohemian capital. And so the memorable concert of 2 May 1924 proved in every sense both the culmination of, and the beginning of a speedy end for, the Prague Verein.

That its *spiritus rector* should have been a budding astronomer is one of those curious twists of fate which Arnold Schoenberg, with his mystical tendencies bordering on superstition, steadfastly refused to dismiss as mere coincidences. For the fact is that Prague occupies a secure place in the history of astronomy, thanks largely to the Habsburg Emperor Rudolph II, a highly intelligent if tormented would-be scientist and philosopher who in the late sixteenth century hired first Tycho Brahe and then Johannes Kepler to his court. Around 1600 Prague was that rare place where Christian and Jew, Protestant and Catholic, believer and unbeliever, lived in relative peace with each other, in an atmosphere of tolerance and quest for knowledge. Thus in 1592 it came to pass that the Emperor did something no other ruler in Christendom would have considered. Intrigued by the fame and spotless reputation of the great Rabbi Yehuda Loew, then living in his city, he personally took the

[13] Ernst Pawel, *The Nightmare of Reason: A Life of Franz Kafka* (New York, 1985), 408.
[14] Ibid.

initiative for a private discussion of matters of mutual interest. By then Rabbi Loew was eighty years old; not only had he published profusely in Hebrew but he was also widely known for his far-reaching concerns in virtually all fields of human endeavour. Not surprisingly, it is he whom tradition credits with the creation of the golem, the homunculus who developed a will of his own and nearly succeeded in destroying everything sacred to his master.

Yehuda Loew, better known in Jewish scholarly circles by the acronym Maharal, was certainly unusual for his time: a Jewish humanist who enjoyed the respect and admiration of his rabbinical colleagues for his learned comments on the Law yet at the same time was shrouded in mystery as a master of the cabbala, the secret knowledge accessible only to those who had attained the highest steps on the ladder of spirituality. His disciple David Gans, moreover, worked with Tycho Brahe until the great astronomer's death in 1601, then assisted Johann Kepler, Tycho's successor in Prague and himself an avid student of the cabbala. As the late André Néher has shown in a brilliant study, there existed in fact a whole network of intellectual connections between Johannes Faustus, Brahe, Kepler, and the Maharal, whose influence left repeated traces in Kepler's *Harmonice Mundi* ('The Harmony of the World') where scientific observation, astrology, cabbalistic reasoning, and Pythagorean conceptions of the nature of music join in a dramatic effort to demonstrate the divine harmony of the cosmos to a world increasingly loath to abandon its God-given faculty of reason at the behest of blind faith.[15]

When Arnold Schoenberg came to Prague in March 1912 to deliver his famous Mahler memorial lecture, which revealed at least as much about himself as about the lamented composer he eulogized, the city was in the process of commemorating the fourth centenary of the birth of its most illustrious Jewish son. A long series of pertinent cultural events culminated in the placement of an oversize statue of Rabbi Yehuda Loew at the entrance of city hall, a symbolic acknowledgement of the Maharal's lasting impact on Prague's intellectual and spiritual life. By a curious coincidence, it was also the three hundredth anniversary of the death of Rudolph II and of the hurried departure of Johann Kepler upon his enlightened patron's passing, when the forces of reaction were lying in wait for him. In short, in 1912 Prague was awash with stories about

---

[15] André Néher, *Faust et le Maharal de Prague* (Paris, 1987). See also the same author's *David Gans: Disciple du Maharal de Prague* (Paris, 1974).

Kepler and the Maharal, about seventeenth-century science and science fiction, about astronomy and the golem and, of course, about *Harmonice Mundi*.

In that celebrated treatise—no doubt conceived, though not written, in Prague—the much set-upon astronomer-musician reached the conclusion that 'the heavenly bodies are nothing if not a perennial polyphony (rationally rather than aurally perceived), a music employing dissonant tensions much like syncopations and cadences (of the sort used by humans in imitation of those natural dissonances) to achieve momentum in the direction of specific predetermined, always sixfold (as it were, in six parts) resolutions and thus insert distinct punctuation marks into the immeasurable course of time'.[16] Given nature's model and the history of man as 'the imitator of his Creator', Kepler regarded the invention of polyphony of the human variety as a foregone conclusion, since it represented an accurate reflection of order in the cosmos at the level of human creativity and understanding. What made it so attractive was not merely that it enabled man to experience 'the continuity of cosmic time within the span of an hour'; perhaps even more important is the fact that it places us in a position to 'savour as much as possible of the pleasure the Divine Master takes in his works, with that sweet sense of delight one derives from this imitation of God'.

Cosmic six-part harmony Kepler believed to be so rare that in all probability it occurred only once—at the creation of the world itself.[17] But man has no difficulty recreating it in music. Kepler was, of course, thoroughly acquainted with the music of Philippe de Monte, Rudolph II's senior musician until his death in 1603. De Monte, of Flemish origin, was a past master of multi-part music, cultivating full sonorities in both sacred and secular compositions. Indeed, the last book of madrigals from his pen to see publication in his lifetime was conceived 'a 6'. Not surprisingly, de Monte presided over one of the largest musical establishments of the day, comprising four discant singers, fifteen altos, no fewer than twenty-two tenor voices, and fifteen basses.[18] These numbers alone suggest that *divisi* performances were regularly called for, and it so happens that in discussing the planetary choir, as he thought of it, Kepler

[16] Cf. Michael Diekreiter, *Der Musiktheoretiker Johannes Kepler* (Berne, 1973), 58.

[17] Johann Kepler, *Die Zusammenklänge der Welten*, ed. and transl. Otto J. Birk (Jena, 1918), 99.

[18] Diekreiter, *Der Musiktheoretiker Johannes Kepler*, 134.

speaks of two planets 'corresponding to the alto, two like the bass, just as in certain compositions one part is treated simply, whereas other parts are divided'.[19] And if Mercury can be said to move in soprano fashion, it is because, like the highest voice, it behaves 'far more freely as well as faster'. No doubt de Monte's discant singers were among the most agile anywhere, first-rate solo voices that made up in quality what they lacked in numerical strength. As for Kepler, he wondered, 'perhaps all this is but coincidence', only to warn the reader at the end of the pertinent chapter that he was about to demonstrate why this could not possibly be the case. Evidently the 'supreme commander' had exercised his prerogatives in 'all this'.

Three centuries later Arnold Schoenberg chose Gustav Mahler's Sixth Symphony to demonstrate to his Prague audience the structural ramifications of his lamented mentor's thematic ideas. Was it sheer coincidence that he assigned such prominence to Mahler's Sixth? Did he merely wish to show that its relative inaccessibility was an inevitable function of its subtle sophistications? Was there no other work apt to reveal the roots of his own melodic thinking? What associations, if any, moved him to insist on the number six, the *numerus perfectus* of old, in this, his Prague attempt to extol the creative miracles wrought by the composer who on his death-bed had worried about what would become of his protégé without his guidance and protection? Schoenberg furnished the answer at least by implication when, after several references to the Faust excerpts of Mahler's Eighth Symphony, he arrived at the incomparable Ninth. Virtually at a loss for words to describe it, he could only speak in the end of what it was that caused him to identify so completely with Mahler, the man and his work. 'It seems', he told his audience of fellow Mahlerians, 'as though this work must have a concealed author who used Mahler merely as his spokesman, his mouthpiece'.[20]

Mahler's swan-song was by the same token also the clarion-call for an inexorable future: 'we must follow, for we must. Whether we want or not. It draws us upward.'[21] Mahler, not unlike the biblical Moses, had been 'allowed to reveal just so much of this future; when he wanted to say more, he was called away . . . But we must fight on.' Thus spoke Mahler's Joshua in 1912 in Prague, where Johann Kepler had been Tycho Brahe's

Joshua, and David Gans the Maharal's prize pupil. By 1925 'you must' had become Schoenberg's credo.[22] In the words of the first of the choral pieces Op. 27, echoing Franz Kafka, who had passed away the year before but may well have heard him speak in 1912: those who chose to be chosen no longer have a choice. Their fate is *unentrinnbar*.[23]

[22] Cf. Peter Gradenwitz, 'Gustav Mahler and Arnold Schoenberg', *Leo Baeck Institute Yearbook* 5 (1960), 283. The year given by Gradenwitz—1926—is incorrect. It should be noted, however, that his article represents one of the first and one of the few attempts to deal with Schoenberg's historical achievement from a specifically Jewish, indeed Zionist, perspective. The pivotal importance of *Der biblische Weg* is exemplified by excerpts in Gradenwitz's own English translation, and connections with other works, *Moses und Aron* in particular, are at least briefly explored. See also the same author's 'The Religious Works of Arnold Schoenberg', *The Music Review*, 21/1 (1960), 19–29.

[23] As early as 1923, a few short months after his dramatic exchange with Wassily Kandinsky, Schoenberg had written in an album belonging to his son Georg that, all things being equal, 'there is no such thing as aimless escape'. Cf. Ena Steiner, 'Schoenberg on Holiday', *Musical Quarterly*, 72/1 (1986), 48.

10

Faith and Symbol

DURING the last two years of his life Arnold Schoenberg was almost totally preoccupied with religious subject-matter, in both the literary and the musical field. After completing his contribution to Chemjo Vinaver's *Anthology of Jewish Music*, Psalm 130 for six-part a cappella chorus, he embarked, in the early autumn of 1950, on what may be regarded as nothing less than his literary last will and testament: 'Psalms, Prayers and Other Conversations With and About God'. It was from this remarkable collection that he drew the text of his last composition, 'A Modern Psalm', Op. 50c, begun on 2 October 1950 but still incomplete at the time of his death.

Arnold Schoenberg's manifest inability to complete any of his large-scale religious works is a striking aspect of his creative legacy that may well hold the ultimate key to its unique nature and motivation. Significantly, the composer decided, upon further reflection, to gather his setting of Dagobert Runes's *Jordanlied—Dreimal tausend Jahre*, Psalm 130, and 'A Modern Psalm', into a single opus, thus strongly suggesting that he regarded this, his last numbered work, as a major unit, on a par, though certainly not comparable in sheer size and weight, with his oratorio *Die Jakobsleiter*, left unfinished some three decades earlier, and with *Moses und Aron*, the opera that had lain in limbo since the early 1930s. Each of these breaks off with the protagonist in a prayer-stance, manifestly unable to find fulfilment through prayer. In all three, moreover, a single melodic strain endures to the last, as if such solitary prayer obviated the necessity for any harmonic or polyphonic enhancement. In the last completed measures of the oratorio, in an inconclusive two-dimensional soprano solo, the soul dissolves almost physically into the heavens, ascending ever higher on the ladder of prayer. In the opera, the last completed act ends with a rising string melody that settles on a sustained middle F♯ only as Moses sinks to the ground, destroyed by his inability to make verbal sense of the prophetic visions that had shaken him to his innermost depths: *O Wort, du Wort, das mir fehlt*. And the last scored phrase of 'A Modern Psalm' remains hauntingly suspended in musical time and space on the words 'and yet I pray', a choral soprano line lost, as it were, in eternity.

The ascent of the soul on the ladder of prayer is a concept deeply rooted in Jewish mystical lore, where it is, moreover, closely tied to numerological considerations. In Hasidic literature

the number of words which constituted a prayer and the numerical values of words, parts of sentences, and whole sentences, were linked not only with Biblical passages of equal numerical value, but also with certain designations of God and the angels, and other formulas. Prayer is likened to Jacob's ladder extended from the earth to the sky; it is therefore conceived as a species of mystical ascent . . .[1]

Hardly by coincidence, the cabbalistic image of the ladder of prayer, so crucial to Schoenberg's work in the long run, first caught his imagination in the wake of his Prague sojourns of 1912. By all appearances he was quite removed from Judaic tenets when, intrigued by the teachings of Swedenborg as conveyed by Balzac, he drew up plans for that large-scale Symphony which, soon transformed into an oratorio, was to have dealt with the dilemma of modern man, who, after searching in vain for truth in secular ideologies, 'finally arrives at the point of finding God and becoming religious. How to learn to pray!'[2] Determined 'to begin with positive religiosity', he decided to rework the final chapter ('Journey to Heaven') of Balzac's *Seraphita* instead of Strindberg's *Jakob ringt*. Even so, he confessed to Richard Dehmel, 'I could not get rid of the idea of "The Prayer of the Man of Today" . . .' That was, of course, how *Die Jakobsleiter* eventually came about.

Richard Dehmel, whose poetry had proved so valuable to Schoenberg in the past, lost no time in offering his *Oratorium Natale*, 'Schöpfungs-feier', with the observation that it was 'rooted in, and culminated in, that new belief in God at which you have finally arrived'.[3] He also com-mented, however, that his concern had not been with 'the struggle for God but the triumphant "rest in God", which exalts us above human life-and-death struggles'. For all we know, it was this particular admis-sion which convinced Schoenberg that, given their manifest differences in background, attitude, and outlook, any collaboration between him and Dehmel, at least in the religious realm, was bound to be a stillborn event.

[1] Gershom G. Scholem, *Major Trends in Jewish Mysticism* (London, 1955), 100.
[2] Cf. his letter to Richard Dehmel dated 13 Dec. 1912, excerpted in Joseph Rufer, *The Works of Arnold Schoenberg*, 117.
[3] Ibid.

Henceforth, at any rate, composer and poet, many a shared theosophic notion notwithstanding, went their separate ways: the nominal Christian Schoenberg, an unreformed Jew at heart, unable to identify with the essentially Christian attitude of the nominally non-Christian Dehmel, resolved rather to rely on his own Balzac-inspired resources. Having finished a draft of the text of *Die Jakobsleiter* in January 1915, he revised it two years later, upon his release from military service, then proceeded rapidly to compose most of its extant seven hundred measures in a veritable rage of inspiration, stopped in his tracks only by the mysterious ascent of the soul carried aloft by two wordless sopranos. Incomplete though it may appear, *Die Jakobsleiter* literally rises slowly but inexorably from the low opening ostinato, six ominous tones heard six times in immediate succession, to that final treble passage in which the original pattern returns, luminously transformed, cleansed, as it were, of its earlier disturbingly dissonant skips (a descending and a rising major seventh, followed by a descending major ninth), and thus ready to settle peacefully onto a 'pure' high C (Exs. 4 and 5).

Those extraordinary last measures are permeated by a palpable sense of metaphysical reality that precluded any further act of 'completion' if truth was to be served. Subconsciously, this appears to have been a foregone conclusion for Schoenberg, despite his intermittent statements to the contrary. A curious document preserved among his papers, a clipping from the evening edition of the *Berliner Tageblatt* of 5 February 1926 entitled 'The Last Vision of Adolphe Willette', adds considerable strength to this supposition, which derives general support from the remarkably consistent record of non-completion that characterizes Schoenberg as a religious artist. According to the paper's Paris correspondent, the artist, whose anti-Semitic caricatures had evoked the admiration of Aristide Bruant during the Dreyfus affair, passed away under rather peculiar circumstances: ' "I am rising higher and higher," he said with an expression of profound happiness. "Now I am ascending straight up, always up, continuously without stopping, quick as an arrow—straight into Paradise." Then he sank to the ground and was silent. He was dead.' A marginal note in Schoenberg's own later hand explains: 'I kept this because it is so exactly death, as it occurs in the *Jakobsleiter*.'[4] And, as if to emphasize the virtual interchangeability of art

---

[4] The item in question is now in the collection of the Arnold Schoenberg Institute, Los Angeles, California.

Ex. 4

Ex. 5

and reality at the threshold of transcendence, he thickly underscored the title of the oratorio. Like many a symbolist before him, Schoenberg, who carefully avoided measure 13 in *Dreimal Tausend Jahre* by counting 12, 12a, and 14, regarded faith and superstition as essentially complementary manifestations of the same metaphysical attitude. As he put it so beautifully in the concluding lines of the sixth Modern Psalm, written at the very end of his life:

What truly moves us in superstition is
The faith of the superstitious, his faith in mysteries
His is a true and profound faith, and it is
So closely related to faith in all that is true and profound that
One is often accompanied by the other.
The learned Philistine abhors mysteries,
Because they reveal that which can never be proven.[5]

Although his old friend and mentor Oskar Adler had warned him on the occasion of his seventy-sixth birthday of the potential danger inherent in the sum (13) of the constituent digits (7 + 6), Schoenberg did not appear overly worried when he told friends that he felt confident of the future, once 'I can pull through this year'.[6] In the end, he failed to survive 13 July 1951 by all of fifteen minutes. But when his wife rushed to his bedside shortly before midnight his countenance, far from betraying any sign of horror, reflected the profound inner peace of one possessed to his last moment of an abiding faith in mysteries, in 'that which can never be proven'. His last whispered word was 'harmony'.[7]

While the more macabre implications of Schoenberg's numerological concerns have received at least passing attention—not surprisingly, given the nature of human nature—their fundamental importance for a considerable portion of his creative output has been virtually ignored. In all likelihood, the persistent stigma of a coldly calculating brain engaged in allegedly strictly cerebral exercises such as the formulation of the method of composing with twelve tones has discouraged numerological inquiries beyond those unfortunate note-counting procedures which the composer himself held in such utter contempt. That he, who was never reluctant to speak out on aesthetic and/or ethical matters of importance to him, left remarkably few direct numerological clues, proved of little help, to be sure, if only because the more recent Schoenberg literature relies heavily on his own voluminous writings. But then it hardly seems logical to expect open references to what is secret by definition, where meaning is hidden rather than overt, where what counts is the essence of life rather than its exterior manifestations, where music rules, rather than words,

[5] Translation by the author from Schoenberg, *Moderne Psalmen*, ed. Rudolf Kolisch (Mainz, 1956).

[6] Cf. Walter H. Rubsamen, 'Schoenberg in America', *Musical Quarterly*, 37/4 (Oct. 1951), 488.

[7] See the pertinent letter from Gertrud Schoenberg to her sister-in-law Ottillie Blumauer, dated 4 (?) August 1951, at the Arnold Schoenberg Institute, Los Angeles, California.

because words are bound to fail, as they failed Moses, and where music alone is capable of carrying the message with impunity, a message which, by the same token, is likely to be understood only by the initiated few. Indeed, not unlike Machaut, who fashioned his canonic procedures after the infinity of Him who has no beginning and no end, or Ockeghem, who praised the Lord in hexachords and perfect prolations, Arnold Schoenberg has but little to say to those who seek to enter his spiritual world at the surface of musical events, oblivious to the unbroken chain that links him to a universal tradition of music as a metaphorical language quite removed from the sound and fury of everyday life, a language in which numbers behave conceptually as well as arithmetically. As the anonymous author of the *Scholia enchiriadis*, mindful of St Augustine, put it over a thousand years ago: 'Sounds pass quickly away, but numbers, which are obscured by the corporeal element in sounds and movements, remain.'[8]

Within that perennial frame of life's untold mysteries where musical numerology holds sway, the number six occupies a very special place in the creative world of Schoenberg, matched in significance, as in cabbalistic lore, only by the mystical ramifications of prayer. Thus, well before *Die Jakobsleiter*, in that prophetically intense stage-work *Die glückliche Hand*, a six-part chorus hurls its reproach at those who 'have the divine in you, yet covet the worldly'. Early Christian authors like Boethius and Martianus Capella generally agreed with Plato that six was the perfect number because it embodied the sum of its divisions ($1 + 2 + 3$). It was St Augustine who first invoked biblical authority, quoting the opening chapter of Genesis as irrefutable proof. Not only did the Lord create the world in six days; according to Augustine the senarius is exemplified by the very structure of the act of creation, since it took one day to generate life as such, two to establish the firmament and the earth, and three to make the stars, birds, fish, and creatures of the land.[9] Gregory the Great merely went one step beyond Augustine when he insisted that six owed its perfection not to any immanent *ratio*, but solely to its biblical validation.[10] Philo of Alexandria, on the other hand, a Jew deeply steeped in Hellenistic thought, had argued precisely the opposite. Loath to measure the Lord of Creation with human eyes, Philo believed that the world was not really fashioned in six days nor, for that matter, within any

---

[8] As translated in Oliver Strunk (ed.), *Source Readings in Music History*, 137.

[9] Cf. Heinz Meyer, *Die Zahlenallegorese im Mittelalter* (Munich, 1975), 30–1.

[10] Ibid., 33.

limited time-span. Genesis, according to Philo, rather invoked the perfect number to indicate that the world as we know it owes its existence none the less to a logically consistent, orderly plan.[11]

This is clearly not the place to try and trace the *numerus perfectus* in Western music, let alone in intellectual history generally. One instance, however, bears mention because of its obvious ramifications for Schoenberg: Zarlino, the most authoritative among late Renaissance theorists regarded the senarius as representative of the six directions: up, down, forward, backward, right, and left.[12] In Swedenborg's heaven, it will be remembered, all directions are interchangeable: there is no up and down, right or left, as such. And, needless to say, dodecaphonic technique, with its mirrors and retrogrades, is predicated on the analogous interchangeability of all melodic directions. The ultimate 'miracle' of the hexachordal 'miracle row' that occurred to Schoenberg so miraculously as he set out on the composition of his unfinished Psalm, Op. 50c, is indeed the complete interchangeability of its motivic components. But in this regard, too, *Die Jakobsleiter* had planted the seed, since its opening sixfold six-tone pattern turns out to refer metaphorically to Gabriel's initial exhortation of the weary masses, the unsatisfied, the doubters, the jubilant, the indifferent, as well as those gently resigned to their fate: 'whether to the right, or to the left, forward or backward, uphill or downhill, one must go on without asking what lies ahead or behind. It must remain hidden: it should, must be forgotten, if you are to fulfil your task.' Six directions—six tones.

When, in 1937, Schoenberg revealed to Nicolas Slominsky that the thematic treatment of a specific arrangement of the twelve chromatic tones had occurred to him first in connection with the Scherzo of his abortive symphony project of 1912, he failed to mention that he had also sketched out its retrograde, mirror, and retrograde mirror forms. This for its time most unusual procedure would tend to suggest that interchangeability of direction was an integral feature of the twelve-tone idea even at that rudimentary stage of development. That this was indeed so follows at least indirectly from the explicit reference to Swedenborg's heaven (as described by Balzac) in the celebrated lecture on 'Composition with Twelve Tones' of 1941.[13]

---

[11] Cf. Harry Wolfson, *Philo*, i (Cambridge, Mass., 1947), 120. The six-pointed 'star of creation', better known as the Star of David, has, of course, similar implications.

[12] Cf. Martin Vogel, *Die Zahl Sieben in der spekulativen Musiktheorie* (Bonn, 1955), 33.

[13] Schoenberg, 'Composition with Twelve Tones (I)', *Style and Idea*, 223.

For Emanuel Swedenborg, whose theosophy had such a profound effect upon *Die Jakobsleiter*, numbers were literally the keys with which science and scholarship were sure to unlock the secrets of the universe. As a student in early eighteenth-century England he had sat at the feet of illustrious members of the Royal Society, and the impact of those youthful contacts with the Newtonian circle never left him, even though his later writings do not always readily betray those intellectual roots.[14] Swedenborg's commentary on the book of Genesis in *Arcana Coelestia*, while retaining the age-old identification of the number six with the perfect act of divine creation, specifically relates the six days to 'so many successive states of the *regeneration* of man', the sixth and final of which is attained

> when, from a principle of faith, and thence of love, he speaks what is true, and does what is good; the things which he then produces are called the living soul and from a principle of love, as well as of faith, he becomes a spiritual man, and is called an image. His spiritual life is delighted and sustained by such things as relate to knowledges respecting faith, and to works of charity, which are called his meat; and his natural life is delighted and sustained by such things as belong to the body and the senses; from whence a combat or struggle arises, until love gains the dominion, and he becomes a celestial man.[15]

As a rule, cabbalistic representations of the unity of the ten *Sefiroth* feature *Tifereth*, the principle of cosmic harmony or beauty, in sixth position. This holds for both graphic representations in the form of concentric circles and diagrams in the shape of a tree (see Fig. 4) where *Tifereth* is placed midway between the supreme crown (*Kether*) at the top and the universal kingdom (*Malkhuth*) at the bottom. In circular designs *Tifereth* occupies the centre point, the 'heart' of God, harmonizing and synthesizing all others (Fig. 3).[16]

It has been said that, in the eyes of Jewish mystics, 'a thing is beautiful and perfect when it manifests, in one harmonious mode or another, the fullness of the possibilities of its kind, and when that kind reveals, in one

---

[14] Ernest Benz, *Emanuel Swedenborg* (Munich, 1948), 30–1, also passim.

[15] Emanuel Swedenborg, *The Heavenly Arcana* (New York, 1873), 4–5.

[16] An additional cabbalistic element deserves mention in connection with the double-soprano ending of the 'unfinished' oratorio *Die Jakobsleiter*: according to the *Zohar*, 'the task of establishing blissful union and harmony between the *Sefirah* of *Malkhut* (kingdom of God) and that of *Tiferet* (beauty) is entrusted to the highest of three female (angel) choirs'. See Amnon Shiloah, 'The Symbolism of Music in the Kabbalistic Tradition', *The World of Music*, 20/3 (1978), 64.

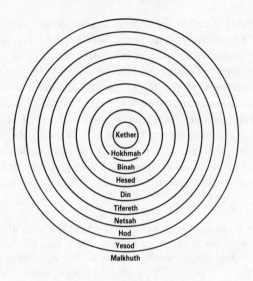

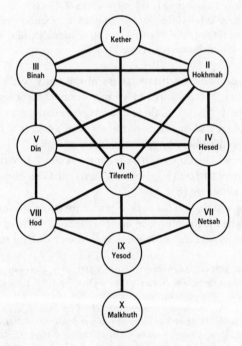

FIG. 4 The Ten *Sefiroth*, from Leo Schaya, *The Universal Meaning of the Kabbalah* (Secausus, NJ, 1971), p. 29

way or another, a spiritual archetype or divine aspect in all its purity'.[17] Surely, the 'miracle' hexachord that governs Schoenberg's last musical utterance demonstrates in more than 'one harmonious mode' the 'fullness of the possibilities of its kind'. And, if anything, this particular gathering of six notes embodies the *ne plus ultra* of the Schoenbergian musical ethos, Schoenberg's 'spiritual archetype ... in all its purity'. The composer's own explanation of his *Wunder-Reihe* as the pitch-arrangement offering the greatest number of possibilities for 'producing strongly related configurations which in sound are essentially different' merely confirms in a technical way the underlying truism that, where a stable arrangement of six pitches is the sole basis of an entire large-scale composition, the *numerus perfectus* has become the very essence of musical creativity.[18]

That the numerical symbol of divine perfection can be traced, up to a point, in seemingly secular works as well conforms entirely to a Jewish tradition that views the sanctification of human existence in an indivisible partnership with the divine as the ultimate test of man's humanity. From this traditional perspective the Christian dichotomy of the 'sacred' and 'profane' is not merely out of place; it falsifies the issues. Accordingly, in Schoenberg's output numerical references cut across such conventional lines of demarcation as early as *Verklärte Nacht*, the string sextet which truly exemplifies the spiritual unity of the Schoenbergian legacy, despite all conventional programmatic analyses to the contrary. For, as its six-part texture strongly implies, the composer, far from subjecting the superficial story of a man and a woman caught between sin and love to any literal treatment, approached it allegorically as an object-lesson pointing to man's inner divinity as his only hope of salvation.

The oft-repeated accusation that he was striving for the new at any cost never ceased to puzzle Schoenberg, who was wont to say, later in life, that he had persistently tried to attain the same ends, though in different ways and, if at all possible, with improving results. While this essentially classicistic attitude is certainly borne out by the nature and treatment of his thematic materials, which place him squarely in the company of Josquin des Prés, J. S. Bach, Beethoven, and others who endeavoured to build and rebuild manifold musical structures with bricks which, though not necessarily identical, were certainly limited in variety, it accounts no less for the remarkable continuity between *Die Jakobsleiter, Moses und*

---

[17] See Shiloah, *The World of Music*, 20/3 (1978), 53.

[18] The Miracle Row Chart with Schoenberg's own typed corrections in English and German is reproduced in Rufer, *The Works of Arnold Schoenberg*, opp. p. 113.

Aron, and the Three Psalms, a monumental triptych conceived in philosophical terms quite incompatible with conventional notions of completion. By the same token, the Schoenbergian aesthetic was remarkably in tune with that of his Jewish contemporary Marc Chagall, who often relied on mere variants of closely related symbolic figures and/or objects in scenes that similarly defy distinctions between 'sacred' and 'profane' at the behest of recurring transcendant ideas. Since music is free of inherent representational attributes and therefore functions metaphorically almost by definition, transcending spatial as well as temporal frames of reference as a matter of course, neither the oratorio nor the opera required 'completion' in purely musical terms. From a literary-rational point of view *Die Jakobsleiter* may indeed appear unfinished; musically, its conclusion, as it has come down to us, admirably underscores the sense as well as the letter of Balzac's words: 'Prayer will give you the key to Heaven! . . . the Universe belongs to him who will, who can, who knows how to pray . . .' The soul no longer complains; for it has, in the words of Gabriel, begun to understand what it must soon again forget. Its 'ego has been extinguished'—a last extended orchestral prayer yields the coveted 'key to Heaven . . . the Universe belongs to him'.

In a penetrating essay on *Moses und Aron* Dika Newlin once asked: 'Can we solve the riddle of the work's incompletion?' Whereupon she, the composer's devoted American disciple, went on to speculate that 'Schoenberg might have come to believe that the Supreme Commander would not grant him the completion of his greatest artistic testament— or, for that matter, of *Die Jakobsleiter* or of the *Modern Psalms*.'[19] Possibly so, but one may well wonder in the face of so many mutually re-enforcing circumstances, to what extent, if any, the ostensible unfinishedness of Schoenberg's religious-philosophical triptych corresponds to the cabbalistic notion of *En sof*, the infinite God, literally the One Without End. Consciously or not, a composer equating the 'faith of the superstitious' with the 'faith in mysteries that can never be proven' could hardly have missed the metaphorical implications of his own apparent inability to produce conventional endings. Rather than bow to convention, it would seem, the traditionalist who abhorred convention yielded to the inner dictates of his creative genius in an artistically unique manner truly commensurate with the incredible complexity of his mind. For it

¹⁹ Dika Newlin, 'Self Revelation and the Law: Arnold Schoenberg and His Religious Works', *Yuval* 1 (Jerusalem, 1968), 216.

was the oratorio which sparked the first systematic preoccupation with dodecaphonic procedures; the opera in turn proved crucial for their ultimate reduction to the hexachordal principle that was to govern so much of his work from then on.

If further proof were needed for the *numerus perfectus* as Schoenberg's central symbol for the divinity, the Psalm, Op. 50c, should do admirably, since here the six-part texture is pointedly limited to the initial phrase, 'Oh Thou, My Lord', yielding after a mere eight bars to four parts for the remainder. There is no lack of precedents in musical history for expansions of choral textures beyond the original number of voices for climactic or otherwise structural purposes, but precedents hardly exist for the opposite—a contraction after no more than eight bars of such a substantial, colourful composition.[20] Admittedly very little is known about Schoenberg's plans for the unfinished portion. But the pattern seems clear, and it should come as no surprise that the last passage committed to paper, 'and yet I pray', combines the minor seconds and thirds of the 'miracle row' with the symbolic minor sixth, employed here also for the earlier text-fragment 'when I say God' (Exs. 6 and 7), just as it highlights the name of the Lord in the concluding 'Sh'ma' of *A Survivor from Warsaw*. As if to counteract any remaining doubts, the extant sketches for a related choral project on the liturgical text 'Who is like unto Thee' offer a fascinating demonstration of the uncanny evolution of one fragment, 'unto Thee, oh Lord', towards its unmistakably final form: a rising minor sixth followed by a descending minor second and minor third. A contrapuntal draft of that very phrase, moreover, turns out to be virtually identical, rhythmically and texturally, with bars seven and eight of the piano piece, Op. 11, No. 1, thus closing the circle forty years after the first of the third–cum–second and, to a lesser degree, minor sixth compositions saw the light of day (Exs. 8 and 9).

One of Schoenberg's most distinguished commentators sees in what he calls Schoenberg's application of cosmic theory to musical form 'an act of

---

[20] The mass 'Sub Tuum Presidium' by Jacob Obrecht moves systematically from its Kyrie in three parts to the concluding seven-part Agnus Dei, no doubt for equally pertinent numerological reasons, given the initial acclamation to the Trinity on the one hand and, on the other, the final textual reference to the 'sins of the world', i.e. seven deadly sins of a world governed by seven planets. Coincidentally, this is also the first mass to have appeared in a modern edition from the hand of M. van Crevel, whose insistence on the numerological basis of Renaissance sacred polyphony aroused such a spirited scholarly controversy shortly after the Second World War. Cf. Jacobus Obrecht, *Opera Omnia: Missa VI 'Sub Tuum Presidium'*, ed. M. van Crevel (Amsterdam, 1955).

Ex. 6

creative intuition'.[21] But if creative artists of the first rank generally are poorly served by conventional distinctions between intuition and intellectual effort, between the subconscious and the conscious, how much more does this hold for Schoenberg, who was fond of quoting Balzac to the effect that 'the heart belongs to the realm of the head!'[22] While the exact nature, degree, and sources, whether christian or Jewish, of Schoenberg's actual acquaintance with the cosmic-numerological tradition, are not easily verified, Oskar Adler, the as yet little-known companion of his early Vienna years, may well have exerted a lasting influence in this respect. For their friendship not only survived the Second World War, it in fact intensified during the immediate post-war

[21] Stuckenschmidt, *Schoenberg: His Life, World and Work*, 131.
[22] Ibid.

Ex. 7

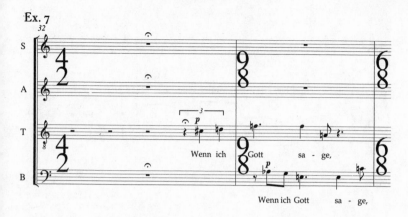

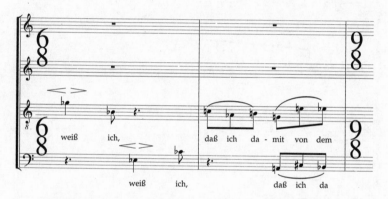

years. Adler, who in the spring of 1951 had sent Schoenberg a copy of the second edition of his 'Testament of Astrology', was among the first to be informed of his work on 'Psalms, Prayers and Other Conversations With and About God'.[23] In short, the bond of mutual concerns proved strong enough to resist the ravages of time as well as physical separation. But

---

[23] Ibid., 470; this was the original title of *Moderne Psalmen*. The second edition of Oskar Adler's book was published in 1950 as *Das Testament der Astrologie: Einführung in die Astrologie als Geheimwissenschaft*. Only the first volume, *Die allgemeine Grundlegung der Astrologie, Tierkreis und Mensch*, appeared. Meanwhile, Albert Einstein affirmed his readiness to assist Adler with his proposed emigration to the United States on condition that there was no implication of any involvement on his part with astrology. As for the number six, Adler joins Johann Kepler and others in pointing to its crucial importance to the geometry of the circle, the universal symbol of timeless perfection. After discussing its division into twelve parts, he writes: *die Zahl 6 aber bleibt des Kreises Grundmaß*.

Ex. 8

Ex. 9

leaving aside any such personal ties, Arnold Schoenberg figured prominently among the most alert residents of the European house of intellect
for nearly half a century, and Jewish mysticism held a curious attraction
for Central European writers and artists of the pre-First World War era
and beyond. The golem legend about the homunculus who did the
bidding of Rabbi Loew captured the imagination of Austrian and
German authors from Rudolph Lothar (1900) to Chayim Bloch (1917). A
'cabbalistic drama' by Johannes Hess, 'The Rabbi of Prague', was
produced in 1914, the year preceding Gustav Meyrink's widely read
golem novel which also inspired the famous post-war film. Schoenberg,
for his part, coined the term 'Art-Golem' in 1922.[24] By then, to be sure,

[24] Cf. Rufer, *The Works of Arnold Schoenberg*, 164.

the peculiar fascination with that passionate story of magic and possession had yielded to widespread admiration for Martin Buber's artful retellings of Hasidic stories, beginning with the tales of Rabbi Nachman in 1906. Buber's next volume, devoted to the legend of the Baal Shem, enjoyed at least five German editions in Schoenberg's lifetime, following its original publication in 1908, not to speak of translations into virtually every modern language. Meanwhile Martin Buber's friend Gershom Scholem, not yet having left Berlin for Jerusalem, was busily laying the scholarly foundations for his magisterial inquiries into the nature and history of Jewish mysticism.

Arnold Schoenberg could hardly remain untouched by these rapid developments, which inevitably reinforced his instinctive leanings toward a tradition represented no less by Philo of Alexandria than by Boethius of Rome, and sustained by musician-philosophers from Guido of Arezzo—whose hexachordal system became the foundation of half a millenium of structural thought in music—and Jacob Obrecht, the fifteenth-century Netherlander, to J. S. Bach in eighteenth-century Germany.[25] What differentiated Schoenberg from these and other illustrious predecessors was a Jewish heritage of which he was at first but vaguely aware but which, before long, he embraced with the fervour of one discovering an unsuspected treasure in his own backyard. Gustav Mahler, Schoenberg's mentor, insisted that the choristers puzzled by his Second Symphony forget all about pious submissiveness and remember instead Jacob wrestling with the angel. His disciple, who early on had considered setting Strindberg's 'Jakob ringt', was no less averse to quiet acquiescence at the expense of moral action. Unrelenting in his struggle for truth, and, like Jacob the patriarch, immune to the lures of the many false gods of his age, Schoenberg skilfully erected his own ladder to heaven on numerical foundations which, according to the ancients as much as to the Jewish Cabbalah, keep the universe in its eternal balance; step by step he proclaimed divine perfection in six parts, with sixths rising and descending, until harmony failed him altogether, and a single melody was left to affirm: 'And yet I Pray.'

---

[25] A well-known example of J. S. Bach's life-long preoccupation with numerology is the so-called St Anne Fugue (BWV 552). Its Trinitarian implications received renewed attention most recently in John Bertalot, 'Number Symbolism in Bach: Pt. I', *Musical Opinion*, 1246 (Aug. 1981), 413, 415.

Jewish Music and a Jew's Music

THE emancipation of European Jewry, which reached its high point in Arnold Schoenberg's lifetime, brought with it major changes in attitude regarding the Jewish cultural heritage on the part of both Jews and non-Jews. It caused many West and Central European Jews to think of themselves as a cultural species quite distinct in bearing and thought from the still largely ghettoized Jews of Eastern Europe; others envied the latter their separate, though anything but equal, existence among Gentiles, despite the fact that these continued to regard them at worst as contemptible Christ-killers and at best as an unavoidable resident evil. Meanwhile, modern Jewish scholarship, following in the footsteps of the 'Science of Judaism' (*Wissenschaft des Judentums*), proceeded to expand its influence from the realm of religion proper to Jewish culture in all its many-splendoured variety. In addition, the rise of musical ethnology around the turn of the century meant that it was but a matter of time before 'Jewish music' became a subject of serious investigation and often heated discussion. In Russia, the 'St Petersburg School', under Nicolai Rimsky-Korsakov's tutelage, had begun to take an interest in Yiddish song as early as the 1880s, and within two decades Abraham Zvi Idelsohn, who himself hailed from the Baltic region, embarked on his first comparative studies of Jewish liturgical melodies across the globe. By the beginning of the First World War the melodic treasures revealed by all this dedicated activity had attracted the attention of numerous musicians eager to capitalize on them with the sort of facile arrangements, paraphrases, and rhapsodies that Arnold Schoenberg condemned as incompatible with sound musicianship and, for that matter, good taste.

Idelsohn, the 'father of Jewish music research', felt much the same, even though Schoenberg appeared to epitomize those 'composers of Jewish origin' whose music in his estimation denied 'the Jewish spirit; they are renegades and assimilants, and detest all Jewish cultural values'.[1] Idelsohn, like Schoenberg, viewed Jewish song strictly as 'a folk art,

---

[1] A. J. Idelsohn, 'My Life', *Yuval 5, The Abraham Zvi Idelsohn Memorial Volume*, ed. Israel Adler, Bathja Bayer, and Eliyahu Schleifer (1986), 21.

created by the people'. The few composers who remained within the fold, he contended, 'have mostly corrupted the Jewish tradition with their attempts to modernize it, and have added very little toward genuine Jewish song'.

Schoenberg, though coming from the opposite direction, had very similar misgivings. Having previously tried his hand at folksong settings and being about to do so again, he ruminated in 1947 that 'folklore and artistic music . . . differ perhaps no more than petroleum and olive oil, or ordinary water and holy water, but they mix as poorly as oil and water'.[2] This was written no doubt with Ralph Vaughan Williams and all those in mind, who, intrigued by the modal characteristics of much of the folk-music they loved, forgot that those very qualities were functions of a purely melodic tradition fundamentally at odds with the harmonic requirements of extended musical structures in a post-nineteenth-century vein. Béla Bartók recognized the problem and, as the supremely gifted composer he was, formed the exception that confirmed the rule. Ernest Bloch, on the other hand, the 'Jewish composer' *par excellence*, fits the pattern at least in some instances. Schoenberg, for his part, valued 'real folk music' as something that comes into existence 'spontaneously, as an inspired improvisation'.[3] Attempts to turn it into 'artistic music' could only diminish it.

Some twenty years before he expressed these sentiments, he had broached the same subject from a socio-political perspective, observing that 'art can figure in the battle of nations as one way to achieve a place in the sun . . . there have been attempts to create national music on the part of certain people who up to now played no role in the development of art-music'.[4] Perhaps he was thinking of Bartók and of Zoltán Kodály, whose works his Vienna Verein had promoted and with whom he remained in friendly contact for many years. Then again, in context his remark does assume rather negative connotations. Whatever the case, in 1938 he complained bitterly to Jakob Klatzkin that 'the Jews have never shown any interest in my music', and now there are composers in Palestine 'out to develop, artificially, an authentically Jewish kind of music, which rejects what I have achieved'.[5] Yet Jews had formed the very core of his small band of devoted supporters, both among musicians and among the lay public, in Vienna and Berlin. The 'Mediterranean School' of

---

[2] Schoenberg, 'Folkloristic Symphonies', in *Style and Idea*, 162.
[3] Ibid., 166.
[4] 'Folk-Music and Art-Music', ibid., 168.
[5] *Arnold Schoenberg Letters*, 205.

Palestinian composers under Paul Ben Haim's leadership went consciously against its own Central European background in favour of more
transparent textures infused with the colouristic lyricism and rhythmic
vigour typical rather of a good deal of French music of the period. But
that crucial development, reflecting the spirit of the young pioneers of the
Jewish homeland, labouring, loving, and celebrating in the sun-drenched
Mediterranean landscape, was still several years away. In short, exactly
whom or what Schoenberg had in mind is somewhat of a mystery, unless
he meant fellow composers like Stefan Wolpe, Paul Dessau, and Kurt
Weill, who had in fact contributed a number of effective Palestinian folk-
song settings. The purely personal implications, on the other hand, are
obvious: 'what I have achieved' is being rejected, because it has not been
recognized for what it unquestionably is: the organic creative result of a
genuinely Jewish experience. When the founders of the World Centre for
Jewish Music in Jerusalem repeatedly asked for his co-operation in 1937
and early 1938, on the other hand, Schoenberg, in that paradoxical
manner he so often displayed, did not even bother to reply, unlike Weill,
Darius Milhaud, Ernest Bloch, Ernst Toch, and many other distinguished colleagues.[6] The Centre's stated purpose was to encourage
urgently needed unity in diversity, precisely the kind of thing Schoenberg advocated in the Jewish political arena. But unity requires a measure
of compromise under any circumstances, and in matters musical he
looked 'neither right nor left'.[7]

The debate about Jewish music touched on Schoenberg as early as
1923, when the appearance of the first four volumes of Idelsohn's
monumental *Thesaurus of Hebrew Melodies* prompted a lively scholarly
discussion. Arno Nadel, a versatile musician and critic, seized the
occasion to propose a set of basic stylistic criteria for Jewish music.
Idelsohn's collection suggested decided preferences for: 1) recitative, 2)
melodic diatonicism, 3) anapaestic rhythmic patterns, and 4) structural
parallelism. In addition, Nadel discerned three important secondary
characteristics: meditative tendencies, mixed tonalities, and unusual
rhythmic changes and irregularities. Nadel acknowledged that 'the new
music (especially Schoenberg!) attempts to free itself from the harmonic
basis and to proceed in new contexts in ways similar to what we assumed
of the ancients'.[8] But Schoenberg *cum suis* struck him as furnishing little

---

[6] For a complete listing of correspondents, see Philip V. Bohlman, 'The Archives of the
World Centre for Jewish Music in Palestine 1936–1940', *Yuval* 5 (1986), 241–9.

[7] For the original biblical passage see Deut. 5: 29.

[8] Arno Nadel, 'Jüdische Musik', *Der Jude*, 7 (1923), 235.

more than admittedly indispensable 'yeast'. Citing in particular the last
of Nadel's secondary characteristics, Heinrich Berl begged to differ.
Schoenberg's refusal to submit to the metric conventions of nineteenth-
century European music was, in his view, a typical manifestation of 'the
strong sense of time of the Jews and their motoric disposition'.[9] He could
have mentioned with equal justification Schoenberg's propensity for
rhetorical musical gestures, Nadel's first criterion (recitative). Schoenberg's 'bizarre' rhythmic practices certainly disturbed conventional
musical minds no less than his allegedly 'irrational' harmonic procedures.
That each of these manifest tendencies arose as an integral function of the
other goes without saying. By contrast, many a Jewish contemporary,
including Ernest Bloch, seemed resolved to 'civilize', with the help of
metric-harmonic straight-jackets, what had been conceived at the source
freely and 'spontaneously, as an inspired improvisation'.

   Schoenberg kept pointedly aloof from the scholarly debate and did not
show any particular interest in the musical results. But he was well aware
of what was going on. Indeed, long before he came to know and
appreciate Joseph Achron in Hollywood, he was in close contact with
Joachim Stutschewsky, another representative of the Russian school
dedicated to the cause of 'new Jewish music' and first cellist of the Vienna
String Quartet, Schoenberg's 'own'.[10] For all we know, Schoenberg's
disapproval of Stutschewsky's 'extracurricular' activities was at least a
contributory factor in the rapid deterioration of their mutual relationship, which soon caused the cellist to resign his position. Whatever the
exact circumstances in this particular case, however, in the mid-twenties
Arnold Schoenberg still thought of himself as one chosen to salvage
German music, even though it was abundantly clear by then that the
musical world, certainly in German-speaking countries, continued to
think of him as a Jew, despite his formal conversion thirty years earlier.
Heinrich Berl was among the very few who realized that, hidden behind
the new sounds and technical innovations, there lay a specifically Jewish
intonation which, unwittingly, might well offer German music an
unsuspected future.

   Not only did Berl's fundamental point that musicians of Jewish
descent tended to stress melodic-rhythmic features at the inevitable
expense of the German harmonic tradition betray a rare understanding of
the intrinsically musical roots of the controversies that surrounded first

---

[9] Berl, *Das Judentum in der Musik*, 318.

[10] Cf. Alexander L. Ringer, 'Joachim Stutschewsky und das Wiener Streichquartett',
Österreichische Musikzeitschrift, 39/6 (June, 1984), 307.

Mahler and then Arnold Schoenberg; historically it was also in keeping
with the position of the later Nietzsche, who regarded Felix Mendels-
sohn-Bartholdy as the last bastion of Europe's age-old Mediterranean
musical heritage against the barbaric incursions of Germanic harmony.
In castigating his erstwhile idol Richard Wagner for his neglect of the
kinetic attributes of music, Nietzsche had, perhaps unwittingly, put his
finger on a fundamental aesthetic issue that accounts for much of
Wagner's rabid anti-Semitism. For if it is true, as Berl and, by
implication, Nietzsche contended, that the Jewish musical temperament
is essentially Mediterranean in nature and hence, if not necessarily vocal,
primarily melodic-rhythmic in essence, then the man destined to carry
Central European harmony to its highest potential could hardly be
expected to favour those most likely to interfere with his artistic-national
mission, a mission he conceived and executed in an unremitting spirit of
historical inevitability and moral rectitude. This is not by any means to
say that Wagner's anti-Semitic tirades merit reconsideration just
because, from a purely musical point of view, he scored a point or two in
his predictions. But they ought to be read with an eye on musico-cultural
developments which before long turned Brahms, not Wagner, into 'the
progressive'.[11] Wagner especially objected to what he regarded as the
endemic tendency of Jews to mimic the gestures rather than enrich the
substance of German music. In all fairness, one who had come to think
of harmony as 'a sea into which man dives only to render himself
radiantly to the light of day',[12] could no longer condone the musico-
dramatic procedures of a Meyerbeer, let alone the Mediterranean vitality
of Bizet's Carmen, Nietzsche's favourite antidote to the Wagnerian
poison. Nor was it, in musical terms, anything but a matter of historical
consistency which eventually located some of Mahler's most violent
detractors in the Wagnerian camp. Mendelssohn and/or Offenbach fans
had few quarrels with the supposed banalities of a song-symphonist
whose only real failing was his lack of pretensions in the realm of
expressive harmony. Arnold Schoenberg, the ultimate scourge of functional harmony, not only admired Mahler's melodic-rhythmic mastery
but proudly yet humbly acceded to the direct succession of him who had
rejuvenated European music by restoring its ancient Mediterranean

[11] Schoenberg, 'Brahms, the Progressive', in *Style and Idea*, 401: 'It is the purpose of this
essay to prove that Brahms, the classicist, the academician, was a great innovator in the
realm of musical language, that, in fact, he was a great progressive.'

[12] Wagner, *The Art Work of the Future*, quoted here from Oliver Strunk (ed.), *Source
Readings in Music History*, 884.

birthright, at the same time rehabilitating the musico-physical energies of the dance, as embodied in particular in the march.

For centuries, only synagogue chant cultivated Mediterranean mono-phony in the very bosom of a Europe that had come to define itself musically along quite different lines. Wagner was thus but one of many late eighteenth- and nineteenth-century musicians of primarily har-monic, euphonic orientation who expressed their outrage at 'the travesty of a divine service in song' perpetuated by Jewish cantors of questionable learning and taste. 'Who has not been seized with a feeling of the greatest revulsion', he asked, 'or horror mingled with the absurd, at hearing that sense-and-sound confounding gurgle, yodel, and cackle which no inten-tional caricature can make more repugnant than as offered here in full, in naive seriousness?'[13] Wagner's observations, though obviously replete with cultural bias, were prompted by a state of affairs of considerable concern to knowledgeable Jewish critics as well. But the serious deterio-ration of musical conditions in many a European synagogue was in itself a symptom of the growing conflict between the Jewish monophonic tradition and the rapid development of functional harmony, which reached its expressive apogee precisely in the work of Wagner. Typically, it was the Hungarian-German Liszt who spoke in the most glowing terms of Salomon Sulzer's singing in the Vienna synagogue. Nor was it by accident that Liszt extolled the virtues of Sulzer's art in an essay ostensibly devoted to the music of the gypsies. Only the gypsies, equally, though more recently, non-European in origin, a nomadic people living on the margin of European society, had preserved similar pathogenic patterns in their essentially monophonic music and embraced dance-rhythms with even greater abandon, to the often undisguised horror of genteel critics. Indeed, as late as the eighteenth century the socio-artistic status of Jewish instrumentalists hardly differed from that of gypsy musicians. Franz Benda, the great Bohemian violinist-composer, grate-fully acknowledged that he learned his craft primarily from a blind Jewish fiddler whom he followed from village to village, absorbing as much as possible of his near-perfect phrasing, articulation, and purity of tone.[14] Needless to say, such itinerant musicians, reduced to little more than begging, played more often than not without any accompaniment whatsoever.

[13] Wagner, *Judaism in Music*, quoted here from *Wagner on Music and Drama*, ed. Albert Goldman and Evert Sprinchorn (New York, 1965), 55.

[14] Cf. 'Franz Benda's Autobiography', in Paul Nettl, *Forgotten Musicians* (New York, 1951), 212.

That the monophonic argument has so rarely been made is due in no small measure to the meta-harmonic practices of virtually all modern Jewish composers. Even as perceptive and thoughtful an analyst as Schoenberg unwittingly helped to obscure the issue when he employed such essentially Eurocentric terminology as 'the emancipation of dissonance', a catch-phrase readily seized upon and quoted out of context by friend and foe alike. That Schoenberg concluded, of all things, his *Harmonielehre* with the discussion of a type of absolute melody predicated on the dissolution of traditional harmonic thinking apparently struck his literal-minded commentators as no more significant than the fact that a contemporaneous piece like Op. 11, No. 1, eschewed the harmonically crucial relationships between consonance and dissonance in favour of chordal formations employed for purposes of accentuation and punctuation in a largely rhetorical context. Whether the early twentieth century realized it or not, dissonance *had* to become emancipated if strictly melodic-rhythmic forces were to prevail once again. As far as that goes, Darius Milhaud's polytonal practices, derived from the diatonic rather than the chromatic tradition, represented but a peculiarly Franco-Jewish approach to the same historical issues. Milhaud was also among the first successfully to explore substantive aspects of Afro-American jazz, which as a rule relegates harmony to purely supporting tasks, at the behest of melodic-rhythmic forces unfolding freely in a manner reminiscent of the figured-bass era which so fascinated Milhaud and his French fellow musicians.

Now if it is true that Jews did a great deal to expedite the creative obliteration of functional harmony at a crucial historical juncture when the structural potential of the harmonic tradition was already so sorely over-extended that it was liable to yield to any forceful assault on its chromatically weakened defences, how is one to view a composer like Ernest Bloch, that proud and informed Jew who held on to the European harmonic heritage with all his heart and all his soul? Bloch, to be sure, never attempted anything like the 'reconstruction of Hebrew music', wishing, as he put it, only 'to write good and sincere music'.[15] Hence, when San Francisco's Temple Emmanuel commissioned him to write a full-length service, rather than immerse himself in Ashkenazi liturgical melodies he decided to improve his vocal part-writing under the aegis of his Jewish friend Albert Elkus, a renowned teacher of modal counterpoint. The result was an impressive large-scale composition permeated

---

[15] Cf. Sam Morgenstern, *Composers on Music*, 41.

by modal harmony and which, in monophonic terms, figures among the least 'Jewish' of his works. Except for an occasional passage giving free rein to purely rhetoric-melodic impulses like the '*Sh'ma*', *Avodath Hakodesh* is an essentially contemplative, at times plodding, work quite lacking in the kind of dynamic forces that propel, say, the beginning of Mahler's Second Symphony, not to speak of the fervent cantorial intonations that pervade the Largo of Schoenberg's Fourth String Quartet. Indeed, in the light of the Schoenbergian heresy even the impassioned melodies of Bloch's *Shelomo* represent at best the inspired nostalgia of a Western Jew yearning for an exotic world irretrievably lost.

George Steiner has coined the term 'meta-rabbi' in an effort to characterize in a culturally meaningful fashion an entire category of modern Jews who, in the very process of shaping the foundations of modern life and thought, practised their 'Jewishness outside Judaism' and thus replaced the traditional 'expositors of the Law'.[16] These 'high masters of modernity' include not only Marx, Einstein, and Freud, Bergson, Durkheim, and Lévi-Strauss, but also Kafka and Arnold Schoenberg, all of them 'exiles twice over: from their Jewish past and, therefore, from a fundamental strain in their own being'. According to Steiner, the 'diaspora within the diaspora' proved 'one of the most creative but also tragic episodes in the history of the Jew and rational man'. Though prone to arouse a good deal of controversy even today, the idea that exceptional men have made specifically Jewish contributions to science, art, and politics thanks to their alienation from, rather than their commitment to, Judaism and the Jewish people is neither entirely new nor without merit. While a composer like Milhaud, who proudly pointed to his French birth and Jewish religion as the twin sources of his life's work, would not in Steiner's terms qualify for meta-rabbinical status, Gustav Mahler, the 'thrice alienated', virtually exemplified the concept when, for his Second Symphony, he waived Christian notions of salvation in favour of Jacob's struggle with the angel. Considering that Mahler's identification with the patriarchal figure of Jacob directly preceded Schoenberg's with Moses, the prophet; considering too that their respective meta-rabbinical accomplishments account for so much in twentieth-century music as we know it, and that metaphorically Jacob and Moses represent two distinct historical stages of the Jewish people's continuous interaction with its non-Jewish environments, it appears,

---

[16] George Steiner, 'Some "Meta-Rabbis"', in Douglas Villiers (ed.), *Next Year in Jerusalem* (New York, 1976), 76.

meta-rabbinically, that Mahler became the central figure in modern
music's Genesis, whereas Schoenberg in turning his back on the
fleshpots of Romantic harmony created its Law.

Romanticism cast the creative musician typically in the role of the
priest ordained by divine decree and intervention to enhance man's
spiritual welfare, to raise his soul to the most exalted realms of
experience. 'What love is to man', Carl Maria von Weber declared,
'music is to the arts and mankind. For it is actually love itself, the purest,
most ethereal language of the emotions, containing all their changing
colors in every variety of shading and in thousands of aspects; true only
once but to be understood simultaneously by thousands of differently
constituted listeners.'[17] Richard Wagner's ritualistic conception of music-
drama was but a sophisticated, logical extension of such Romantic tenets
in the context of a Christianity that institutionalized the highest form of
love. In this sense, Mendelssohn acted like a true priest of his art when he
insisted that, despite popular views to the contrary, instrumental music
communicated ideas 'too definite' to be put into words.[18] And there can
be no question but that the musician-priest committed to the absolute,
the certain, the undebatable, the ultimate, played a role of considerable
significance in the Romantic-Jewish symbiosis. But Romanticism was a
many-splendoured phenomenon almost by definition, capable of accommodating a Meyerbeer—who turned to historical legend in order to
imprint upon the bourgeois consciousness the destructive potential of
material wealth and power based on sheer greed, hypocrisy, and im-
morality—no less than an Offenbach—who wielded the even more
powerful weapon of parody and satire. In the wake of Jewish emancipation, at any rate, the issue was not Jewish music as such but rather Jewish
musicians, destined by fate, faith, or both, to reflect, each in his particular
way, at least some aspect of the Jewish experience, even where, on the
surface of it, that experience hardly appeared relevant.

Ever since Schopenhauer asserted that 'music never expresses the
phenomenon but only the inner nature, the will itself', the metaphysi-
cally inclined have tended to associate it with universals rather than
particulars. According to Schopenhauer, music cannot treat of 'this or
that particular and definite joy, this or that sorrow, or pain, or horror, or
delight, or merriment, or peace of mind; but joy, sorrow, horror, delight,
merriment, peace of mind themselves, to a certain extent in the abstract,

[17] Cf. Strunk (ed.), *Source Readings*, 804.
[18] Gertrude Norman and Miriam Lubell Schrifte (eds.), *Letters of Composers* (New York,
1946), 146.

their essential nature, without accessories, and therefore without their motives'.[19] Not only have thousands of pages been devoted to the thorny question of music as a universal language, but in the last century Wagnerians and promoters of so-called absolute music alike laid claim to the Schopenhauerian heritage, seemingly oblivious to the fact that its original inspiration had come from Rossini rather than Beethoven. Franz Grillparzer specified, and Felix Mendelssohn still agreed, that 'where words are insufficient, music takes their place ... whatever exceeds the power of words in depth or height belongs to music'.[20] In short, Romantic thought, however diverse in other ways, generally acknowledged music as the ultimate gauge of the subconscious, the most hidden realm of human experience, whether individual or collective, as represented in folk and national myth. From the nineteenth-century perspective, musical nationalism and the idea of a national music were thus by no means interchangeable, though they were interrelated. Unlike the former, the latter did not require recourse to specific folk traditions, which may explain why many, whether in Germany or in the world at large, looked upon Wagner, who had scant regard for folk-tunes, as the embodiment of German music, while others singled out Brahms. The national traits perceived in the music of both were of a textural, harmonic, and rhythmic nature; they pertained to universals rather than particulars. And it is precisely in terms such as these that the quest for meaningful 'Jewish' elements in a given music will have to proceed if it is to go beyond more or less obvious affinities with liturgical or folk-tunes, not to speak of mere textual references or the parochial effusions of composing chauvinists. For in art the ultimate test is rarely *what* but *how*, not the nature of the material but its treatment, its unique 'intonation'. And 'intonation' in that sense reflects not merely the individual psyche but the total historical experience of the community, physical and spiritual, to which the artist belongs, whether he identifies with it consciously or not.

Certainly no Jew can rid himself entirely of an affective inheritance handed down from generation to generation since the dawn of civilization. To put it in Schopenhauer's universalistic terms, where action supersedes faith, where love takes second place to justice, where the welfare of the individual is cherished as a function of the communal good, where history is not concealed merely in books but is a sacred personal

---

[19] Cf. Weisstein (ed.), *The Essence of Opera*, 183.
[20] Ibid., 165.

responsibility, where the majority is considered only as valid as its ethical commitment, where in fact free choice is practised as a divine mandate, there music inevitably differs not merely in degree but in principle from counterpart cultures which, however close physically and however well assimilated politically, do not share these tenets or have embraced them only in part, often in partnership with their ostensible opposites.

Ernest Bloch, in one of many attempts to fend off endless questions concerning his Jewish motivation, once observed that the most he could say of his *Shelomo* was that it reflected some of 'the holy fervour of the race which is latent in our sons'.[21] Bloch, of course, was mindful that music probes the total man at his deepest levels, as shaped by a plethora of conditioning factors from genes to historical memory and consciousness, from religious practices to secular ideology. Nor has anyone aspired more deliberately and at greater sacrifice to such completeness than the historical Jew, from Moses to Herzl to Ben Gurion. If Jakob Klatzkin was right in asserting that, though deprived of their nationhood a long time ago, the Jews never gave up their national constitution, then surely in the context of Jewish history the term 'constitution' applies not merely to the Bible but also to the cultural crystallization of psychological, sociological and economic experiences unprecedented in range and sheer agony. The fate of Jewish communities in the Diaspora, whether the East European *Shtetl*, the lower East Side in Manhattan, or a ghetto in the Maghreb, affected the psychological constitutions of countless generations and hence the constitutional history of all Jewry. Thus, when the opportunity finally arose, Jews quite naturally and willingly embraced a plethora of secular ideologies proclaiming collective welfare as a precondition for individual happiness. But characteristically, even though Jewish musicians were among the first to respond to the Utopian socialist stirrings of a Saint-Simon, the best among them sublimated their social concerns in purely artistic terms, in Gustav Mahler's choices and aggressive settings of outright pacifist texts no less than in the lean, 'non-culinary' styles of Kurt Weill, Paul Dessau, and Darius Milhaud, or indeed in the song-satires of the cabaret artist Rudolf Nelson—musical moralists all, worthy of at least honourable mention among the meta-rabbis of the twentieth century.

Scores of names could be cited to show that the era immediately preceding the Hitlerian onslaught on Western civilization generally and on the Jewish people in particular, produced some of Diaspora Jewry's

---

[21] Morgenstern, *Composers on Music*, 413.

finest musical hours. Nor was this powerful explosion of intrinsically melodic-rhythmic energies limited exclusively to Europe. Quite to the contrary. In the United States an uninterrupted flow of tunes emanated from the pens of Irving Berlin, George Gershwin, Jerome Kern, and all the other movers and shapers of a uniquely American tradition associated the world over with Tin Pan Alley. Needless to say, neither the sentimental lyricism of the earlier Broadway musical, so typical of America about to lose her innocence, nor the visionary Expressionism[22] of Europe on the threshold of apocalyptic disaster emerged unscathed from a world war that witnessed the destruction of a third of the Jewish people. Indeed, as soon as the emaciated but undaunted remnants served notice on a guilt-ridden world that henceforth their political fortunes would be of their own making, the meta-rabbi, dialectical symbol of the socio-intellectual alienation that haunted Europe's emancipated Jewry, made way for the fully integrated 'rabbi' speaking the biblical language of old to a people rebuilding its ancient homeland.

Once the focus of Jewish aspirations shifted from the Gentile world to an autonomous state of Israel, few Jewish artists persisted in swimming against the dramatic stream of history. But, by the same token, Jewish composers, saddled like most Jews with a self-image drawn as much by a hostile environment as by any indigenous cultural heritage, faced a dimly perceived musico-historical paradox: truly modern music had barely managed to transcend all remaining nationalistic barriers when fellow Jews were laying down their lives in a daily, unequal fight for their inalienable right to live in dignity in the Oriental setting that had given birth to Judaism well before the dawn of Western civilization.

At that historic juncture, unprecedented even in the axiomatically dramatic history of the Jews, Arnold Schoenberg poured all his sorrow and the full measure of his Jewish pride into a unique mini-drama, a relentless crescendo from beginning to end of unmitigated horror defeated by unyielding faith, that paean to Jewish suffering *A Survivor from Warsaw*, 'based partly upon reports which I have received directly or indirectly . . .'[23] Here, in the climactic *Sh'ma*, sung in unison by the condemned men as much in defiance of the enemy as in keeping with Jewish tradition, according to which the dying pronounce the unity of the Lord one last time, virtually all of Arno Nadel's criteria for a genuinely

---

[22] For Heinrich Berl Expressionism represented nothing less than European Jewry's moment of inner rebirth ('die Stunde seiner seelischen Wiedergeburt'). Cf. Heinrich Berl, 'Die Juden in der bildenden Kunst', *Der Jude*, 8 (1924), 337.

[23] Rufer, 73.

Jewish musical intonation combine in a dodecaphonic public exhortation that did not fail to make its unforgettable point, with the unconverted no less than with the rapidly growing community of twelve-tone devotees. In Schoenberg's last completed composition, Psalm 130, the stylistic consequences of modern Hebrew pronunciation are evident, especially in the careful treatment of the long vowels and characteristically sharp consonants, repeatedly in direct conflict with the Hasidic inflections of the melody used as a model. Hardly by accident, moreover, the composer told Chemjo Vinaver, who commissioned the piece for his comprehensive *Anthology of Jewish Music*, 'I have a plan for six voice chorus'.[24] And that plan involved from the outset 'every voice sometimes singing, sometimes speaking. And I started hearing what it would sound like'. But, he added apprehensively on 2 June 1950, 'if I only can write it'. Three weeks later he thanked Vinaver for 'furnishing me the translation and accentuation of every word, it seems to me that I might be able to finish the psalm in a not too distant time—if my health allows it. I also profited from the liturgical motif you sent me, in writing approximately a similar expression'.[25] Finally, a month and a half before his death, he solemnly declared: 'I plan to make this, together with two other pieces, a donation to Israel.'[26]

Did Schoenberg know that an orthodox reading of the psalms may entail both singing and speaking? Possibly so, from his own early synagogue experience. And, of course, there were friends and acquaintances whom he could have consulted, since it is doubtful that he ever entered an orthodox synagogue in Los Angeles or anywhere else in the United States. One such individual was Marc Chagall, who, at Vinaver's request, created the frontispiece for the *Anthology*. Chagall, at any rate, decided on an offering of truly symbolic significance, given the simple Hasidic tune that inspired Schoenberg's sophisticated composition. In the forefront he placed the crowned head of King David, the 'singer of Israel', slightly bent forward, listening intently, eyes closed, to his own music. But he is not alone, nor is this all of him, for from his back, just below the shoulders, protrudes the much smaller figure of a caftan-clad *Klezmer*, a Jewish street-musician, attached to the Psalmist like a Siamese twin, playing his humble fiddle as he gazes across the roof-top outlines of an East European *Shtetl*. Chagall had been one of only two

---

[24] Chemjo Vinaver (ed.), *Anthology of Jewish Music* (New York, 1953), 203.

[25] Ibid.

[26] The additional items are the chorus *Dreimal Tausend Jahre*, Op. 50a, and *Moderner Psalm* for chorus and orchestra, Op. 50c (see chapter 11).

witnesses when the refugee Arnold Schoenberg staged his demonstrative return to the Jewish fold in the office of a liberal Paris rabbi. An immensely tragic quarter of a century later, it seems, the same peerless master, deeply steeped in Jewish tradition, wished to pay homage to the ultimate creative consummation of that historic gesture. The miracle had come to pass; 'oil and water' had mixed after all, turning the music of the repentant Jew Arnold Schoenberg into genuinely Jewish music at its artistic best.

Postscript
Music, Race, and Purity

In the evening of 30 January 1933, when it became known that, in the wake of another by and large inconclusive election, an aged and ailing President Hindenburg had yielded, however reluctantly, to the urgings of his nationalistic supporters and appointed Adolf Hitler Chancellor of the German Reich, uniformed Nazis took to the streets *en masse*. Holding thousands of flaming torches high above their heads, they paraded, eight abreast, through the centre of Berlin. For hours their fear-inspiring riding-boots marked the beats of Hitler's favourite, the Badenweiler March, and the party's brutally effective anthem, the *Horst Wessel Lied*, which, hoarsely bellowed over and over again, signalled the onset of the 'new order', musically as well as politically. It was to take the Nazis less than a year to rid the premier musical city of Europe of 'alien' elements and transform it into a brazen showcase for 'Aryan' culture as defined by Alfred Rosenberg—Hitler's Court philosopher—and the pseudo-intellectuals in his retinue, not to mention their anti-intellectual rivals in the office of Joseph Goebbels, the Minister of Propaganda.

That the new rulers assigned the highest priority to the eradication of the Weimar Republic's chief claim to world fame was forcefully brought home to musicians and music-lovers alike a mere ten days after the 'seizure of power', when a regularly scheduled concert of new compositions by students from Professor Walter Gmeindl's class at the State Academy of Music became the scene of a carefully staged outburst of Nazi indignation. The next day the party's official newspaper, the *Völkischer Beobachter*, complained in self-righteous outrage that 'the wild sounds unleashed on a suffering mankind' had demonstrated in the most painful manner 'how badly things have deteriorated as a result of fourteen years of Marxist administration'. Fortunately, Paul Graener, the new head of the Academy's competitor, the Stern Conservatory of Music, had risen to the occasion by shouting at the top of his ageing lungs: 'Ladies and gentlemen, such pitiful stammering is presented to you by a German academy of music as German art. Against this I raise my voice in protest as a German artist.'[1]

[1] Cf. Joseph Wulf, *Musik im Dritten Reich* (Gütersloh, 1966), 15–16. Wulf's excellent selection of pertinent documents remains the only available survey of primary sources for

Most members of the audience knew, of course, that the underlying issues were not so much aesthetic as ideological in nature and to some extent purely personal, masked under the convenient cover of national politics. The Academy's director, the distinguished, racially unencumbered music-historian and educator, Georg Schünemann, was under suspicion simply because he had quite openly admitted his political neutrality. Professor Graener, by contrast, was a long-time fellow-traveller and recently installed party-member whose scandalous public behaviour, subsequently disavowed by his fellow Senators in the Prussian Academy of Arts, represented in fact a calculated move, the curtain-raiser, as it were, for a whole series of drastic manoeuvres designed to achieve the *Gleichschaltung* or ideological compliance of German music and musical life well ahead of other fields of artistic and scientific endeavour. That Graener's motivation was as much personal as political was certainly not lost on Schünemann. As the institution's director he felt honour-bound to come to the defence of the hapless student whose work sparked the first public musical scandal under the new regime. Still, he did so in pathetically meek terms, unwittingly revealing the growing impact of racist propaganda even on men of basically good will and of the most impeccable reputation. If anyone deserved to be regarded as 'a good German', he asserted, it was the young man in question; he was neither racially nor politically objectionable. This rather unprincipled attempt to stave off the party's evil decree for his school and himself at the expense of those with lesser credentials was, however, bound to backfire. As far as the party was concerned such naïve arguments actually raised the dreadful prospect of an outside world being misled into believing that what the Academy 'dares to teach in the name of German art . . .' was in some way representative of German culture. If the budding composer was indeed so unusually gifted, what monstrous conspiracy had confided a precious talent to thoroughly corrupt guidance? As the *Völkischer Beobachter* assured its readers, however, there was no reason to worry. Those entrusted with the country's artistic future were not inclined to perpetuate this manifestly intolerable state of affairs. And so it happened that Hans Hinkel had hardly taken office as the new Commissar for Culture when he served notice on the Academy that its polluted atmosphere was about to undergo a thorough cleansing.[2]

In accordance with established Nazi procedure, successive terror

---

the study of music as a political tool in Hitler's Germany. See, however, Fred K. Prieberg, *Musik im NS-Staat* (Frankfurt am Main, 1982), for a well-documented general account.

[2] *Deutsche Allgemeine Zeitung*, 19 Feb. 1933, as cited in Wulf, 16.

waves prepared the field for all-out attack. By the beginning of April the general student body had been so thoroughly intimidated by the storm-troopers in its midst that a desperate Schünemann, hoping to neutralize the worst of the rowdies, went as far as to request the appointment of a veteran member of the Nazi student-association, a certain Teschendorff, as president of the Academy's student government.[3] In so doing, however, he found himself unexpectedly caught in the intra-party struggles for power and position typical of the Nazi era, especially in the early stages, when numerous 'good' Germans attempted to collect rewards for past loyalties. In the end he lost his job, despite the protests—none too forceful—of the Senate of the Prussian Academy of Arts, his institution's parent organization. The affair concluded with a particularly ironic twist when, in response to the Senate's token appeal, the Minister of Science, Art, and Popular Education requested an 'objective' loyalty investigation that vindicated the dismissed director's political reliability on the following grounds:

1. He had the necessary documents to prove his Aryan descent.

2. Though never a member of any political party, he had joined the National-Socialist civil-service organization at the Academy as soon as it was formed.

3. While not a front-line soldier, he had volunteered for dangerous missions in the First World War and had contracted a chronic gall-bladder and liver affliction. He also rendered valuable services as a collector of German folk-songs among prisoners of war.

4. Most importantly, since his appointment as director of the Academy in July 1932 not a single non-Aryan had joined its faculty. In fact, all the party-affiliated teachers, including the notorious political syco-phant Gustav Havemann, had been hired at his suggestion.[4]

Under these circumstances, it was felt, a man of Schünemann's knowledge and talents deserved another chance. Even so, another two years elapsed before the combination of his 'irreproachable' credentials and his basically accommodating attitude, though insufficient for a position as visible as that of a university professor, got him the directorship of the Music Division in the Prussian State Library, safely out of the political limelight. His membership in the Senate of the

---

[3] Wulf, *Musik im Dritten Reich*, 18.
[4] For the complete document see ibid., 19–20.

Prussian Academy of Arts, which had been rescinded immediately after the Graener incident, was never reinstated.

The Schünemann affair remained at most a temporary *cause célèbre* in German professional circles. The so-called *Fall Hindemith*, on the other hand, focused the attention of the entire world of music on what was happening in Germany. For its protagonist was not a relatively obscure scholar-educator but Germany's only 'Aryan' composer of uncontested international stature. Since, moreover, Germany's leading non-Jewish German conductor chose to get involved, the Hindemith case served to dramatize, for all to behold, a number of fundamental issues at a time when the party leadership, its exterior bravado notwithstanding, was still feeling its way in matters of cultural policy.

Paul Hindemith, in the 1920s an avowed member of the German avant-garde, had long since turned to musical idioms and types of musical activity calculated to engage a broader public, youth in particular, at the highest aesthetic levels. Ostensibly this was a cause towards which the Nazi movement was well disposed. As one Nazi ideologist put it in the autumn of 1934, 'society is the rational, community the irrational form of social life'.[5] The concept of community (*Gemeinschaft*), with its Romantic devotion to 'the irrational form of social life', was at the heart not only of the *Wandervögel* mentality earlier in the century and the socialist youth movements of the Weimar Republic but also of the Nazi *Jungvolk* and Hitler Youth. Through the years, Hindemith had endeavoured to enrich the community repertoire with simple but by no means unsophisticated works for singing, playing, and listening. For Hindemith remained a Romantic at heart even while paying homage to an age of stylistic experimentation. For all we know, he actually agreed with the tenor of an article in the journal *Die Musik*, of late the party's official voice in musical matters, which deplored the materialism of a generation 'governed no longer by an image of man anchored in the cosmos but merely by his will to exist'.[6]

Like Thomas Mann, his literary counterpart in many ways, Hindemith was deeply rooted in nineteenth-century German idealism and hence by no means averse to the 'growth of irrational tendencies conducive to central concerns based not on utilitarian considerations but on the quest for ultimate and deep unity'.[7] What had saved him from falling into the philosophical trap laid by Nazi 'philosophers' like Alfred

[5] Ludwig Weber, 'Musik und Volksgemeinschaft', *Die Musik*, 27 (Oct. 1934), 81.
[6] Ibid.
[7] Ibid.

Rosenberg was not so much the living reminder of his wife's non-Aryan descent as a deep-seated ethical revulsion at the profusion of purely propagandistic versions of Wagnerian myths going back to Houston Chamberlain and his 'Foundations of the Nineteenth Century'. And it was this implicit heresy rather than the theatrical naturalism of an opera featuring a notorious bath-tub scene, which so riled the Nazi élite. As if to offer proof positive to that effect, the controversy centred on the composer of *Mathis der Maler*, with its unmistakable allusions to the book-burning orgy of 10 May 1933 that had signalled the end of what was left of free expression in Germany. 'Rome cannot tolerate resistance. The books must burn,' decrees the operatic inquisitor of heretic writings in early sixteenth-century Mainz: 'The only spirit is the spirit of obedience. A priest who disobeys must perish.'

The party leadership seized upon the Hindemith imbroglio (it mono-polized musical polemics in Nazi Germany throughout 1934) to clarify the issues and to develop positions and aesthetic guide-lines for the future. But the international renown of both the offending composer and his principal apologist, Wilhelm Furtwängler, also created a public-relations dilemma of global proportions, since the foreign press finally took notice of the outrages perpetrated in the name of German virtue and self-respect. The campaign against Hindemith, to be sure, had started well before 1933, as had the cry for racial purity in German music. But whereas in the 1920s ultra-conservative elements had condemned his opera *Sancta Susanna* as 'insufferable and frivolously against religious custom and the Christian faith',[8] in 1934 it was, typically, his trans-national outlook which incurred official and unofficial censure. He was accused of writing music fit for an 'atmosphere characterized by the names of Alban Berg, Arthur Honegger, Béla Bartók, and the quarter-tone mixer Alois Hába'.[9] None of these leading modernists of Austria, France, Hungary, or Czechoslovakia could in any way be considered 'racially' unacceptable, confirming rather that Hindemith's foes thought of him primarily as a 'cosmopolitan' composer, to borrow a well-known Soviet term, even though virtually all those listed vigorously embraced their respective national heritages in and outside music. Needless to say, precision of thought was not the real issue, as Furtwängler was to find out to his surprise and dismay when he published a long article in support of

[8] Cited in Wulf, *Musik im Dritten Reich*, 371.
[9] Paul Zschorlich in *Deutsche Zeitung*, 17 Mar. 1934; fac. in *Paul Hindemith: Zeugnis in Bildern* (Mainz, 1955), 46, with an intro. by Heinrich Strobel.

Hindemith in which he, the political innocent, attempted to show how his friend had become the guiltless victim of public persecution. Furtwängler admitted to 'matters of a purely political nature', referring in all probability to Hindemith's Jewish friends and his wife's Jewish relatives. But he maintained Hindemith had collaborated only with quite unimpeachable Jewish artists like Simon Goldberg, the Berlin Philharmonic's concert-master, and the renowned cellist Emanuel Feuermann. Granted that his early stage-works posed certain spiritual and political problems, but he had since then demonstrated a hundred times over his 'high ethos of modest craftsmanship, reminiscent of the old German masters'.[10] Surely, his prolonged didactic endeavours were fully in tune with the aspirations of 'the new National-Socialist Germany'. In short, Furtwängler, who on a previous occasion had pleaded the cases of several prominent Jewish musicians on the grounds that clear distinctions ought to be made between Jews as political and as aesthetic animals, again tried to have it both ways. Reichsminister Goebbels implied this much when, in a major policy speech ten days later, he called for the quick eradication of the Jewish-intellectual infection from the German body politic. In the meantime, Furtwängler had thrown in the towel.

Briefly, what had happened was this. A few hours after the newspapers with his defence of Hindemith hit the streets, Furtwängler, at a regularly scheduled public dress-rehearsal of the Berlin Philharmonic, received a standing ovation from a capacity audience. That same evening, as he entered the orchestra-pit of the State Opera House to conduct Wagner's *Tristan and Isolde*, his supporters behaved even more demonstratively, and Hermann Goering, Prussia's Prime Minister and Furtwängler's nominal boss, decided to inform the Führer himself of what he regarded with some justification as an act of outright political defiance.[11] Sensing the imminent danger, Furtwängler quickly resigned both his posts at the Philharmonic and the Opera, as well as the vice-presidency of the newly created Reich Music Chamber. With the matter thus temporarily laid to rest, Alfred Rosenberg wrote the official *post mortem*, with the characteristic title: 'Aesthetics or National Struggle?' Art for art's sake had no place in the Third Reich, the party's chief ideologist explained, if only because:

---

[10] Wulf, *Musik im Dritten Reich*, 375. For an abbreviated fac. of this article, which appeared in the centrist *Deutsche Allgemeine Zeitung* on 25 Nov. 1934, see *Paul Hindemith*, 48.

[11] Cf. Berta Geissmar, *Two Worlds of Music* (New York, 1946), 125.

an artist often represents political trends ... So, when a man like Hindemith, after a few German beginnings lives and works for fourteen years in Jewish company and feels himself at ease in that company; when he consorts almost exclusively with Jews and is loved by them, when he, following the trend of the November Republic, commits the foulest perversion of German music, we have a right to reject him and his environment. The accomplishments of such an artist within the November Republic, and the laurels reaped by him in that now overthrown Republic, are by right of no value to our movement ... It is a great pity that so great an artist as Dr. Wilhelm Furtwaengler entered personally into this controversy and chose to identify himself with Hindemith's cause ... Herr Furtwaengler lingers in his nineteenth-century ideas and has manifestly lost all sense of the national struggle of our times.[12]

Of course, it was Rosenberg's *Myth of the Twentieth Century* that was hopelessly mired in the backwaters of nineteenth-century Romanticism. Then, too, if the tenuous situation of a purified German culture without Jews was not to deteriorate altogether, certain practical accommodations were clearly called for on all sides. Thus in October 1934 Furtwängler warned his good friend Ludwig Curtius not to engage in unnecessary provocations of the new regime, such as the hiring of a Jewish governess: 'to be guided by feelings of humanity and decency in this situation is pure Romanticism.' Any German wishing to retain his position '*must* arrive at practical compromises with the ruling party ... if not, if he *wants* to leave, then it's another matter'. He, Furtwängler, was not really tied to his positions, hence could 'act as a free man' in the matter of his faithful secretary, Berta Geissmar, whose Jewish descent was a thorn in the flesh of his superiors. At any rate, 'it won't be long before I know whether I shall be able to remain in Germany'.[13] In April 1935, having rejected the option of leaving his native country, Furtwängler swallowed his pride and humbly resumed his post as director of the Berlin Philharmonic, though not that of vice-president of the Reich Music Chamber.

Up to a point the cases of Schünemann, the musicologist-educator, of Paul Hindemith, the composer, and of Furtwängler, the conductor, proved a boon to minor figures in German music whose talents were quite disproportionate to their exaggerated ambitions and who had every reason to believe that their patriotic zeal in ferreting out 'unreliable elements' would be duly rewarded. And as a rule the removal of an established artist did permit some deserving party loyalist to step into a

[12] Transl. in Nicolas Slonimsky, *Music Since 1900* (New York, 1949), 386–7.
[13] Wilhelm Furtwängler, *Briefe*, ed. Frank Thiess (Wiesbaden, 1964), 77.

position which in open competition would have been well beyond his reach. Opportunism certainly rode high in those early years—the violinist Gustav Havemann comes immediately to mind as one whose vitriolic attacks on Jewish and other 'system' colleagues were in no way ideologically motivated. But the musical *Gleichschaltung* of 'the new Germany' proceeded by and large along practical political and predetermined aesthetic lines. As for the former, an artist's potential usefulness was measured in terms of three basic factors: race, ideology, and political adaptability. Those whose credentials met every test with respect to all three could count on success, whether or not their talents justified their newly acquired importance. Those racially tainted, on the other hand, were automatically out of the running, irrespective of their ideological orientation or of their ability to play the political game judiciously. An uncertain future awaited primarily those who were racially pure but failed to satisfy one or both of the remaining criteria—unless their worldwide reputations justified the exception, as was clearly the case with Furtwängler.

During the initial stages a musical scholar of the second rank like Josef Müller-Blattau managed to profit handsomely from his impressive triple qualifications, not to speak of an ambitious young man like Wolfgang Boetticher, who ascended to a key position in Alfred Rosenberg's office. Others, including Hans-Joachim Moser, though armed with impeccable racial and ideological credentials, repeatedly suffered the consequences of their manifest lack of political instincts, which no measure of naked ambition could outweigh. This was certainly why Hans Pfitzner, the veteran composer and principal flag-carrier for the cause of aesthetic 'purity' throughout the years of 'struggle', never found his proper place among the cultural leaders of the Thousand Year Reich, even though the recurring attacks of nationalistic paranoia from which Pfitzner suffered with increasing frequency and vehemence had endeared him greatly to Hitler's more romantically inclined early followers. His scurrilous assault on what he called 'The New Aesthetic of Musical Impotence', published shortly after the First World War, had in fact made an invaluable contribution to the *Dolchstoßlegende*, which held that Germany had not been defeated on the battlefield but by alien forces who were said to have fostered moral decay from within. Typically, however, the same Pfitzner who held Jewish 'aberrations' responsible for virtually everything that made the new music anathema to him and to others hopelessly stuck in a post-Wagnerian aesthetic that was more politically than artistically inspired, had long sought and enjoyed the invaluable support of both

Jewish musicians and patrons. Gustav Mahler for one, who married a student of Pfitzner's, regularly performed his works, despite an instinctive initial reluctance. Later, during the so-called *System* days, the Mahler disciple Bruno Walter promoted his cause in opera-houses all over the world.

When the Nazis came to power, such unconscionable former affiliations inevitably raised questions as to Pfitzner's loyalty. But if Party purists had little use for a doubtful cultural asset like Pfitzner, others impressed with his relentless condemnations of the 'Jewish element' valued him as a 'spiritual path-breaker for the National Socialist idea', antedating the party itself and hence amply deserving of a place of honour in the forefront of Germany's new intellectual and artistic leadership.[14] Soon, however, the Pfitzner controversy took a totally unexpected turn when his many enemies began to insinuate that Mrs Pfitzner was anything but a pure Aryan. The fact is that Pfitzner's often scurrilous prejudices against Jews in general had not prevented him from marrying the granddaughter of Ferdinand Hiller, the composer and pianist of Jewish descent who had played such a significant role in the musical life of nineteenth-century Cologne and who, while strongly identified with the Mendelssohn–Schumann circle, had also been a close friend of the young Richard Wagner. Those who had promoted their idol as eminently worthy of emulation by the Third Reich's aspiring young composers now found themselves in considerable disarray. And even after the official Pfitzner biographer, Walter Abendroth, restored the family's racial credibility to the party inquisitors' nominal satisfaction, the composer never fully regained the broad footing that had virtually assured his national fame when the Nazis first seized power.

Abendroth's documentary proof to the effect that Hiller's wife was of Polish-Christian descent and not, as Wagner had intimated, a Jewess, calmed the storm for a while. Before long, of course, the Nazis were to rank Poles only slightly above Jews in their novel ethnic hierarchy. In the meantime, it was quite within the bounds of Nazi logic for Abendroth to declare that, if the Hillers' daughter, Antonie, was only one-half Jewish and married to the full-blooded Dutchman James Kwast, her daughter Frau Mimi Pfitzner, 'the daughter of a pure German and a half-Jew, cannot under any circumstances be regarded as "Jewish"'.[15]

Exonerated of all violations of the racial code, the composer of *Von*

---

[14] 'Fanfare für Hans Pfitzner', *Die Musik*, 26/3 (Dec. 1933), 193. Cited in Wulf, 339.
[15] Ibid., 339.

deutscher Seele seemed at last eligible for honours due to the man chosen by 'destiny' to replace his erstwhile benefactor Gustav Mahler. Even so, suspicion lingered on, the more so as his frequently irrational behaviour was hopelessly at odds with the party goose-step mentality. As late as February 1940, an urgent investigation was ordered as to why Hans Pfitzner had never become a member of the party and had shunned its affiliated organizations as well. While the National Socialist youth movement claimed virtually every German youngster, Pfitzner had even succeeded in keeping his two step-children out. How this happened— and indeed why it happened—was never firmly established. The investigative report remains inconclusive regarding the motivation of this 'difficult' individual, 'a grouchy man prone to deal harshly with his employees and musicians'. Still, there could be no question but that he had always taken 'an affirmative position with respect to National Socialism'.[16]

Unlike Pfitzner, whose unappealing personality was matched by a genuine disdain for the 'better things in life', his rival Richard Strauss, an elegant man of the world, was ever ready to take advantage of material opportunities. Thus Strauss had been quick to accept the presidency of the newly created Reich Music Chamber, which was charged with the reorganization and oversight of German musical life in the spirit of the racial and aesthetic doctrines of the Third Reich. Jewish family connections were hardly an issue in his case, a non-Aryan daughter-in-law notwithstanding. Instead, the most successful opera-composer of the twentieth century, who owed so much to his erstwhile librettist of Jewish descent, Hugo von Hofmannsthal, seemed unable to comprehend why his continued collaboration with the Jewish novelist Stefan Zweig was not only undesirable but totally unacceptable. Their latest joint effort, *Die Schweigsame Frau*, was actually staged at the Dresden State Opera as late as 24 July 1935, with Zweig's name, at Strauss's insistence, prominently displayed on the programme. Outraged Gestapo officials, however, had intercepted a letter from Strauss to Zweig in Switzerland, in which the politically unsophisticated composer had not only berated Zweig for his 'Jewish obstinacy' but had also declared bluntly, though with the qualification 'perhaps—*qui le sait*', that his own work had never been 'guided by the thought that I am "German" . . . I know only two types of people, those with and those without talent'. As for his public, Strauss went on to explain that he couldn't care less whether they were

Chinese, Bavarians, New Zealanders, or Berliners: 'what matters is that they pay full price for admission.'[17] It was solely 'for the orchestra's sake' that he had unhesitatingly taken the place of Bruno Walter, after the great conductor, who had contributed so decisively to his world-wide success, had been summarily dismissed. If he had gladly replaced Toscanini in Bayreuth, that had 'nothing to do with politics'; it was 'for the sake of Bayreuth'. And 'only for good purposes and to prevent greater disasters', had he consented to 'ape the president of the Reich Music Chamber'.

Even for Strauss, whose single-minded pursuit of personal goals, artistic as well as material, at the expense, if need be, of accepted moral standards, was no secret among the initiated, this was an exceptionally strong and in a sense quite disarmingly written confession. Unable to ignore it once it had fallen into their hands, the Nazis requested his immediate resignation 'on health grounds' from the presidency of the Reich Music Chamber. His status as Germany's composer laureate remained unaffected. Indeed, the ink on the document relieving him of his administrative duties had barely dried when he received the commission to compose the official hymn for the 1936 Olympic Games in Berlin.

The fact that Strauss, unlike Pfitzner, had never been in any way ideologically committed hardly assured him of a clean political bill of health. On the contrary, it clearly counted against him in the eyes of those who demanded undivided fealty to the Führer and who, therefore, openly favoured Paul Graener, now serving as vice president of the Reich Music Chamber. In contrast to Strauss, Graener obviously savoured the petty politics of everyday Nazi life and hence met the requisite criteria in every way. That he too had to live down prior Jewish associations was amply outweighed by his oft-avowed post-Romantic academicism and pious stance in favour of 'purity in tonal art', that early Romantic legacy which a national priesthood of musicians was expected to defend against all alien intrusions. The Nazi regime, catering to racial myths and socio-economic illusions, appreciated such psychological and artistic naïveté even more than Graener's immaculate pre-1933 party-membership.

Carried to victory on waves of politicized Wagnerianism, Hitler and his associates envisaged Bayreuth as a national shrine, the spiritual centre of a reborn Teutonic realm of pagan gods and heroes. In such a false world the incorruptible commitment to truth on the part of composers endowed with the mantle of prophecy, like Mahler and Schoenberg, who

[17] *A Confidential Matter: The Letters of Richard Strauss and Stefan Zweig 1931–1935*, transl. Max Knight (Berkeley, 1977), 99–100.

had produced such trenchant stylistic changes in twentieth-century music, inevitably evoked fearful images of *Entartung*, 'Jewish aberrations'. Nor were the Germans alone in their desire for 'escape into beauty' and the refusal to face an often ugly truth. The vast majority of music-lovers everywhere favoured, as it still does, the lyrical effusions of nineteenth-century Romanticism. The modest talents of a Paul Graener were, at any rate, perfectly in tune with the parochialism of a party bureaucracy promoting 'Strength through Joy'. His lament over the fate of Germany's musical patrimony at the hands of a generation 'which for the most part had lost all respect for the severity and purity of German art as created by the masters, a generation which, as in daily life, all too often confused freedom with anarchy, which placed the brain above the heart, which preferred to promote everything foreign, international rather than the home-grown',[18] makes him seem like a latter-day Hans Sachs pleading on behalf of 'German masters'. However, his own music leaves little doubt that it was rather Beckmesser, the reactionary, who spoke through him, not Sachs, the progressive conservative committed to a vibrant tradition thriving on 'what sounded so new, yet was so old'.

Well before the turn of the century Leo Tolstoy predicted that 'the ideal of excellence in the future will not be the exclusiveness of feeling, accessible only to some but, on the contrary, its universality, and not bulkiness, obscurity, and complexity of form, as is now esteemed, but, on the contrary, brevity, clearness, and simplicity of expression. Only when art has attained to that, will art neither divert nor deprave man as it does now ... '[19] Similar sentiments had been expressed throughout the ages, though primarily in ecclesiastical circles and with respect to the past rather than the future. And these sentiments were always predicated on the conviction that art in general, and music in particular, has unique moral powers and, therefore, unsurpassed responsibilities as well. In the nineteenth century, when art encroached more and more upon the traditional prerogatives of religion, a Mazzini would call Meyerbeer 'the prophet of the music to come, of that music whose high and holy mission will place it but one step below religion itself'.[20] In the National Socialist scheme of things, inspired as it was by so much misguided Wagnerianism, music occupied a central position as an effective means of ideological conditioning, especially in the context of mass rallies and

---

[18] Quoted in Wulf, *Musik im Dritten Reich*, 126.

[19] Leo Tolstoy, *What is Art?*, as transl. in Julius Portnoy, *The Philosopher and Music* (New York, 1954), 201.

[20] Cf. Jacques Barzun, *The Pleasures of Music* (New York, 1961), 304–5.

related public Party rituals. Far from wishing to confront the individual
with his inner self, Nazi culture consisted of an array of propagandistic
tools designed to conjure up an heroic collective reality and to dissimu-
late, in so doing, the true state of human affairs. Musical experiences
were not supposed to jar the mind or tear at the heart but to soothe and,
at the same time, project images of a glorious future in a world of racial
harmony and contingent moral purity.

Under these circumstances, and given the persistence of the Romantic
concept of music as a language of feeling, it is hardly surprising that the
party leadership of the Third Reich should have been particularly
anxious to subject the young to the most intensive and extensive musical
conditioning. When, in May 1938, the Hitler Youth organized a week-
long Beethoven Festival under the personal chairmanship of *Obergebiets-
führer* Cerff, the chief for cultural and broadcasting activities in the Reich
Youth leadership, Germany's foremost Aryan artists, including conductor Eugen Jochum and violinist Georg Kulenkampf, lent their services,
and the famous pianist Elly Ney could not resist the opportunity to vent
her dedication to the New Order in the following terms:

> Beethoven for the Hitler Youth!
> Living German Youth, you who are sustained by the fire of enthusiasm.
> A longing for beauty has come alive in you, for truth and for heroism
> straining for action . . .
> Beethoven's musical language conceals a profound certainty.
> It suggests no hesitation, no indecision, no ambivalence.
> It is truth, justice, and innocence, and it radiates the healthy humour of
> a powerful yearning for life . . .
> Heroism is the essence of all Nordic music. Here it lives in every tone.
> Indeed, the human essence of our master was simple and heroic!
> Unyieldingly he shapes the law of nature, the truth, often to the point
> of rawness.
> And this sacred fire shall ignite the hearts of youth, arouse its sense of
> responsibility, render it strong in struggle, console and restore in
> suffering.
> Come then, O German youth! Leave all work-a-day cares behind you.
> In these days and hours let us together open ourselves to the streams of
> our people's spiritual powers.
> And may thus be generated great and luminous deeds on behalf of our
> Führer.[21]

[21] 'Geleitsätze zum Beethovenfest der Hitler-Jugend', *Zeitschrift für Musik*, 105/7 (July
1938), 732.

On the very day the Beethoven Festival ended in Bad Wildbad (May 22), the 1938 Reich Music Days opened in Düsseldorf, where the visitors brought in by the bus- and train-load from all over Germany were offered a very special treat, the exhibit *Entartete Musik* (deviate music), devoted to that disgraceful *System* era of the 1920s and 1930s, when innocent German audiences reeled under the brazen advances of 'Jewish-Bolshevist' composers 'alien to the race'. Quite a few of the thousands who came to see and hear the evidence savoured the nostalgic moment of refreshment at the once bubbling springs of musical change; others merely enjoyed the taste of officially forbidden fruit. Thus in some respects this clumsy effort at aesthetic indoctrination backfired. The powers that be hardly cared, however, since their target was clearly not the old concert and opera public at all but the largely uninitiated new audiences formed by such party-sponsored organizations as *Kraft durch Freude* (Strength through Joy) and, above all, the young, who were told throughout the exhibit that the Weimar Republic, 'so rich in disintegrative forces', had produced virtually nothing but 'musical one-day flies . . . Today things are different; once again we may look back upon our great musical past with pride, precisely because the present can boast of achievements of the greatest variety, because that present has itself become creative.'[22]

Notions such as these were not, nor have they been since, limited to Nazi Germany. Quite to the contrary—they typify the totalitarian aesthetic in all its manifold guises. In Fascist Italy Alfredo Casella recanted his early enthusiasm for Arnold Schoenberg, on aesthetic rather than racial grounds. And three months before Hitler became Chancellor of Germany, Ottorino Respighi, Ildebrando Pizzetti, and Riccardo Zandonai, co-signed a manifesto against 'the Biblical confusion of Babel' caused by 'a continual revolution in music'. The time had come, they declared in the name of all genuinely creative musicians, to acknowledge the 'logical chain' that 'binds the past and the future' and to see to it that 'the romanticism of yesterday will again be the romanticism of tomorrow'.[23] When, in 1935, Zandonai received the Mussolini Prize for his services to Italian opera, Respighi, his fellow fighter for 'musical sanity', praised him as the one who had uniquely managed to preserve that 'sacred tradition' unsullied 'in its modern guise'.[24]

[22] Cf. Horst Büttner, "Reichsmusiktage in Düsseldorf', *Zeitschrift für Musik*, 105/7 (July 1938), 737.

[23] Cf. Slonimsky, *Music since 1900*, 358.

[24] Ibid., 605.

Much like Italy's veteran composers in Mussolini's quasi-operatic version of ancient Rome 'in modern guise', the Soviet Communist-Party paper *Pravda* in January 1936 denounced Dimitri Shostakovitch's new opera, *Lady Macbeth of the Mzensk District*, as a 'leftist mess instead of human music'.[25] It did so on grounds quite indistinguishable from those which little less than a year earlier had caused Propaganda Minister Goebbels to utter his contempt for 'atonal musicians who in order to make sensation, exhibit on the stage nude women in the bath-tub in the most disgusting and obscene situations, and further befoul these scenes with the most atrocious dissonance of musical impotence'.[26] In matters of public morality, whether musically induced or otherwise, totalitarians of all countries seemed singularly united.

Viewed in this—admittedly disconcerting—light, socialist realism, which created such an 'uproar in Moscow' in the wake of the Second World War, loses much of its puzzling obscurity. For there too, as in the Fascist and Nazi contexts, 'the Romanticism of yesterday' was supposed to set the pattern for the 'Romanticism of tomorrow'. As Zhdanov put it at the 1948 Conference of Musicians organized by the Central Committee of the All-Union Communist Party:

There is a struggle going on, though an outwardly hidden struggle, between two schools. One stands for the healthy and progressive things in Soviet music, for the full recognition of the importance of our classical heritage, particularly of the Russian classical school; it stands for a high ideological level, truthfulness and realism, and a deep organic connection with the People and its folk songs—the whole combined with a high degree of craftsmanship. The other school stands for formalism, which is alien to Soviet art, a renunciation of classical traditions. It is anti-People, and prefers to cater for the individualistic experiences of a clique of aesthetes.[27]

The parallels with Alfred Rosenberg's postscript to the Hindemith affair are so obvious they hardly deserve comment. Suffice it to say that in Russia, at least during the years immediately following the Second World

[25] Cf. Slonimsky, *Music since 1900*, 403.

[26] Ibid., 387.

[27] As translated in Alexander Werth, *Musical Uproar in Moscow* (London, 1948), 80. The seemingly universal disinclination of the lowest strata of society towards sophisticated, let alone disturbing, experiences had not eluded the more observant and objective among the radical Left. Thus Gustav Landauer in Weimar Germany concluded well before the advent of Hitlerism and Stalinism that the proletariat had a deep and powerful inclination toward philistinism, *Spießertum*. Cf. Walter Laqueur, *Weimar: A Cultural History* (New York, 1974), 48.

War, anti-Semitism was not a matter of systematic concern, even though formalism in music was generally associated with the corrupting influence of Arnold Schoenberg and his school. It would seem that in official circles good music was simply that which the Soviet bureaucracy was able to follow and enjoy. In fact, Zhdanov confessed as much when he said: 'to be quite candid and to express what the Soviet listener really feels, it would not be bad at all if we produced a lot of works which *were* like the works of the Russian Classics, in content, form, elegance, and musical beauty.'[28] As one plotting the future of Russian society, more-over, he wondered whether 'disharmonious music' did not have 'a bad effect on the psycho-physiological activities of man'.[29] Surely, if music was to edify the new Communist man and suggest to him untold glories yet to come, brilliantly orchestrated, fundamentally consonant music suggested itself as a patriotic duty.

That such music was not necessarily at its best when inspired by folk-music was a dilemma with which all totalitarian policy-makers had to contend. In Central Europe neither Wagner's nor Bruckner's works could be said to reflect much dedication to folk-song. Yet it was Mahler who was condemned for his racially engendered inability to 'attain the heights of German symphonic art as a binding expression of the German cultural will as well as the nuclear power of all such music, German folk-song'.[30] In Soviet Russia both genuine folk-music research and the dissemination of its results suffered for a long time from the official passion for simple tunes in symphonic guises or, at the very least, overblown choral arrangements. In Nazi Germany the emphasis was on the 'new' German folk-song embodied in the party's battle-hymns. As Professor Müller-Blattau explained, 'the longing of the best' had 'found the right expression' long since 'in Leibl's Song of Dedication set to Hensel's sturdy old tune: we lift our hands from the depths of bitter suffering; Lord send us the Führer ... Fulfilment came—the National Socialist revolution brought about the new era of folk-song. The Third Reich has not only been fought but sung into existence.'[31]

The irony of it all finally broke through the charred surface of the German Democratic Republic when, in the wake of the Nazi defeat, once fanatic Nazis and opportunistic fellow travellers scrambled to offer themselves to their new rulers. Perhaps the most unsavoury case in point

[28] Alexander Werth, *Musical Uproar in Moscow* (London, 1948), 82.

[29] Ibid., 83.

[30] Josef Müller-Blattau, *Geschichte der deutschen Musik* (Berlin, 1938), 302.

[31] Ibid., 307.

is that of Gustav Havemann, the erstwhile prize pupil of Joseph Joachim, the great Hungarian Jewish violinist and close friend of Johannes Brahms. Havemann had a brilliant career as soloist, concert-master, and leader of the well-known Havemann Quartet, which in the 1920s promoted the music of Schoenberg, Hindemith, and other 'moderns'. But that was before Professor Havemann jumped on the Nazi bandwagon and became one of the worst of the Jew-baiters, backbiters, and blacklisters among musicians. What has been published of his correspondence with Nazi officialdom makes clear that the 'purification' of German music could simply not move fast enough for him.[32] And even though his previous associations with Jews, social democrats (including Professor Schünemann), and others who were anathema to the Nazis counted against him in some party circles, his zealous, missionary approach to *Gleichschaltung* in music quickly earned him leading administrative positions, as behoved one characterized officially as 'the remorseless fighter for the ideals of his Führer, the great musician and the modest, humble, always helpful human being'.[33] In early 1933 Havemann created the *Kampfbundorchester*, a select party orchestra. Now a conductor as well, he greeted the 'New Order' with a much reported performance of Beethoven's Ninth Symphony. Twelve years later, in Soviet-occupied East Germany, he returned to teaching at the German Academy for Music and soon assumed the direction of one of its major departments. Upon his death in early 1960 he was eulogized in the official music journal of the German Democratic Republic by a younger colleague who merely regretted that the deceased had recognized rather late the fateful road upon which Germany embarked in 1933.[34]

By then, to be sure, much water had gone down the Elbe, the Volga, and, indeed, the Potomac. The musical uproar in Stalin's Moscow found almost immediate echoes in Washington, where the House Committee on Un-American Activities precipitated the departure of Hanns Eisler on the eve of his scheduled deportation from the United States, and subjected an American composer of Aaron Copland's stature to its histrionic machinations. Typically, though, the American inquisition limited its loaded questions almost exclusively to political views and affiliations. Intrinsically musical matters were avoided by the elected representatives of a society that has traditionally looked upon music as 'a

[32] Wulf, *Musik im Dritten Reich*, 106–15, devotes an entire section to this unsavoury figure.

[33] *Männer im dritten Reich* (Bremen, 1934), 97.

[34] Fred K. Prieberg, *Musik im andern Deutschland* (Cologne, 1968), 137.

form of decoration' rather than 'a system of thought'.[35] Still, as the Cold War heated up and irrational apprehensions spread terror through the land, musical careers were broken, friends betrayed, and creative impulses stifled. When the 'thaw' finally set in, not only in post-Stalin Russia and eastern Europe but also in post-McCarthy America, the 'Prague Spring', its most dramatic cultural symbol, signalled vigorous fresh musical growths nearly everywhere, not only in the Soviet orbit but in the United States as well.

Thanks mainly to the efforts of Hanns Eisler, Arnold Schoenberg's one-time pupil and, later, fellow refugee in California, even the German Democratic Republic, the last country to pursue a policy of musical puritanism, came to recognize that dodecaphonic music and socialism were not necessarily incompatible. On the tenth anniversary of Schoenberg's death, Eisler, about to conclude his own life's work, argued as follows with those who persisted in regarding his revered teacher as the symbol of 'decadence' in modern music:

He is just as decadent (or similarly decadent) as Marcel Proust, James Joyce, or like certain periods of our magnificent Pablo Picasso or the Austrian writer Musil and others. But we must beware not to dismiss with a simple slogan a complicated personality like Schoenberg. We want to obtain a museum for the working class, the German working class, that is rich and varied. We don't want to proceed dogmatically. We don't want to withhold anything valuable from the new youth. To be sure, we will deal with this 'museum of music' critically; thus we won't recommend everything at random. But we will insist on the variety and wealth of the heritage—that is our duty and our responsibility.[36]

Thirteen years later the musical world remembered the hundredth anniversary of Arnold Schoenberg's birth, and the German Democratic Republic outdid itself with a splendid exhibition organized by Luigi Nono, the composer's son-in-law. During the intervening period Nono, an ardent socialist himself, had joined forces with Eisler in uncovering 'the variety and wealth of the heritage' that had remained buried for more than a generation under the icy crust of the corporate state. And as the 'decadent' artists displayed in Eisler's imaginary museum rose one by one from the tombs of totalitarian history, they were greeted with a veritable avalanche of creative responses everywhere on the part of scores of talented yet spiritually starved young people for whom devotion to good causes was to become a way of life.

[35] Paul Bowles, 'Film Music', New York Times, 19 Jan. 1943.
[36] Günther Mayer, 'Arnold Schönberg im Urteil Hanns Eislers', Beiträge zur Musikwissenschaft, 18 (1976), 209.

APPENDIX A

ALFRED HEUSS

'Arnold Schönberg—
Prussian Teacher of Composition'

THE appointment of Arnold Schönberg as director of one of the three master-classes for composition at the Prussian Academy of the Arts in Berlin strikes a blow against the cause of German music that is so provocative in nature it would be difficult to imagine anything worse in the present situation. As little as two or three years ago, when broader circles nurtured high hopes for the 'new' music, the matter might have been susceptible to discussion, one might have argued that the music of the later Schönberg and his musical aesthetic in general, with its conscious rejection of tradition, must be regarded as an aberration and that, therefore, placing this man in an exposed position as an official educator in German music would be an act of artistic malfeasance of the worst kind. Today there is no longer any need for discussion, for in the meantime the facts have forcefully spoken for themselves; anyone familiar with the situation, whether from the right or the left, knows that the time of the Schönbergian attacks of hysteria and sudden high fever in music has passed and that music is steering and must be steered in quite different directions, because in the long run the embodiment of the unnatural cannot possibly be elevated to a principle. And yet, just now, at a time when German music is beginning to recover slowly, one dares to accord this man and his mad theories the highest sanction of the state, publicizes him prominently, and, in so doing, makes clear that one cares neither for progress as such nor, above all, for the welfare of German music. And that amounts to a provocation, is intended as a contest of strength between German-dom and—and now we must also be quite frank—the specifically Jewish spirit in music. For one thing is clear to anyone with any insight into racial differences, and that is that Schönberg's fanaticism, which speaks from his ruthless tendency to draw the very last consequences from a narrow premise, has nothing in common with German attitudes, which preclude any nihilistic fanaticism even where petty narrowness may tend to prevail. Surely, such fundamental issues must be raised without inhibitions, on behalf not only of what is truly German but also of what is specifically Jewish, which, after all, is in danger of losing itself in Schönbergian fanaticisms, if it can't form ties to indigenous cultures. Only thus could Mendelssohn, Heine, Liszt, Meyerbeer, etc., gain their importance; they dug in and, as a result, developed their powers fully for all to see. If Schönberg were only some twenty years older and had grown up when Wagnerianism was freshly flourishing instead of beginning to decline, it might have caused him to develop in a normal Jewish way, as after all his first works suggest. But around 1900 the foundations of German music were already permeated with decay, and none was more acutely aware of this state of affairs than Schönberg, who, because he had no strong sense of a German past, had little choice but to rely increasingly upon himself and, in so doing, to turn his ever more evident rootlessness into a principle upon which he drew abundantly and with fanatic zeal. His subsequent development has been predicated on both his personality and his race. Schönberg was and is honest in the manner of any true fanatic, and there is in fact nothing objectionable in his person. But his evolution, his fate, have not the least to do with German music, which has always found ways and means of moving in new directions naturally, that is to say, without having to force the issues violently. That would have been the case this time as well, had it not been thrown off the track and into confusion, pushed close to the abyss, and primarily so by that fanatic Schönberg. The by now unavoidable test of its existence will cost German music at least several decades. Its source will remain muddy for a long time to come, because, for the first time in its history, specifically Jewish elements have taken its development in hand, at a moment when it is lacking in inner strength. The Jew who relies only on himself, is no longer rooted in any soil, and consciously defies tradition—that kind of Jew as fanatic leader means nothing else than the road to perdition, and I think that if we have experienced anything it is precisely this, and none agrees more readily than those genuine Jews who have made themselves truly at home in a culture and are in their way capable of contributions of great importance, and have actually done so. *Rooted and rootless Jews*, that is the principal issue in this matter. What sort of Judaism Schönberg belongs to and wishes to be part of he has not only demonstrated with great clarity but also stated in so many words.

His appointment, however, amounts in the present circumstances not merely to a provocation; it represents—about this, too, we want to speak openly—a stupidity of the first order, and that is the redeeming aspect of this affair. The reasons are obvious in view of what has already been said. If anybody, then precisely that those Jews who have not been blinded have known for a while that Schönberg has finished himself off and, even though there is still forced talk of him as a 'leader'—a leader without troops—, there is a vital desire for sounds quite different from those produced by Schönberg. Significantly, the Jewish part of the Berlin press sang no Hosannas on the occasion of the Schönberg's nomination; it all sounded rather muffled. Charming, for example, the voice of B. Kastner in the *Morgenpost*, who not so long ago spoke of *Pierrot Lunaire* in terms of highest revelations and now places the emphasis on Schönberg's theory of harmony. What a manifestation of Berlin humour! As if the later Schönberg had not long since 'passed by' his theory of harmony, i.e. has completely done away with it! By thinking up continuously new cerebral tone-systems! And so, in short, we interpret Schönberg's appointment as follows: Those who have this on their conscience, by going characteristically over the heads of the Academy, those were struck by their *LORD*—who, after all, must know—with both blindness and by now convulsive, provocative arrogance.

Hence, there can be no question about one thing: the days of the current musical regime in Prussia are counted. Thus, one way or another, Schönberg, the musician and the teacher, can no longer do damage to German music but at most to a Jewish music without roots in the above-mentioned sense. And if so, why shouldn't we intone a Handelian Halleluja!

APPENDIX B

Der biblische Weg, Conclusion of Act I

THE speech of Max Aruns before the youthful pioneers gathered for a festive day of athletic competition in celebration of their completed training for settlement in New Palestine (conclusion of Act I of *Der biblische Weg*).

What is this festival?
Is it a sports event? A parade? A party convention? A people's assembly?
Is not this day like all others?
No, it is not; it is one that will be commemorated for all time among Jews.
Just like that day on which the youngest male asks:
'Why today do we sit reclining?'
But here you will have to ask instead:
'Why today do we all stand up?
Why did we rise? Why don't we remain seated on the floor, low, like in all those days past?'
We got up, we rose and rose to a size that nobody could have foreseen.

We straightened our round backs, bent because they had to be ready to receive every blow that others deserved. We stand erect again like that old, tough, defiant, obstinate people of the Bible; but unlike them we are no longer obstinately *against* our God but *for* Him, who designated us as His people.

Brothers! Do you still know those inconspicuous, battered, weak little Jews 'Hep-Hep'* who gazed timidly about them whenever they faced others than our own people; but who were none the less accused of arrogance, and maligned as 'impudent Jews' as soon as they dared to make a move, let alone refuse to take every offence lying down; who represented an inferior race in the imagination of the least of the other races; who were despised and mocked by all the peoples, most of all those who could not arrive at their own spiritual concepts without the help of ours?

Brothers! Do you still remember those humiliated, denigrated, persecuted little Jews who, despised though they were, had enough courage nevertheless, one against ten, not to let their race perish, too proud to intermix with those who regarded them as unworthy aliens.

These cowardly Jews, who had the courage to be called cowards, if only they were allowed to remain Jews, made every sacrifice, endured every persecution and every insult and every blow to their pride, because they never ceased, even for a moment, to feel that we were chosen for such suffering; that from it would

---

* The dreaded cry of the mob about to kill and burn Jews in their homes and synagogues down the centuries.

issue our future blessings; that only in pain is birth given; that we must suffer, because we were chosen to sustain the Messianic idea across the ages. [Interpolation in Schoenberg's own hand: the severe, pure, immortal idea that there is only one unique, eternal, invisible, and unimaginable God.]

We are an old people.

What would a God mean to us whom we could understand, of whom we could form an image, on whom we might prevail?

We don't need miracles: persecution and contempt have made us strong, have multiplied our tenacity and resilience, generated and improved organs that enhance our ability to resist.

We are an old people.

True, not every one of us is yet capable of grasping fully our God-idea: to be content that all that happens depends on the highest Being, whose laws we sense and recognize without being permitted to question their meaning.

But as soon as every last one can do this: that is when the Messiah will have come.

The Messiah of inner equilibrium!

Dear young friends! Your teachers and leaders have implanted this faith in you, have developed your minds and trained your bodies.

Since you have realized that the recognition of the true essence of God exceeds all knowledge and all other aspirations of the mind; and since you have learned to value your physical strength and turn it into a source of joy, you were able in a short time to demonstrate your capacity for achievements and the ability to manage efforts that would have caused your physically destitute fathers to fail. Today you rank in no way behind the peoples among whom we live. You possess the strength which, within a few generations, will be common to all our people. Your strength and health will renew all that is old and brittle in the trunk of Israel: you alone are capable of reshaping our people, of transforming a people of scholars, artists, merchants, and money-changers into a healthy and forceful people suited for a life worthy of a people who received their homeland as a gift from God.

Thus you are now able to complete the great task!

You have the elasticity, impetus, enthusiasm, flexibility, and readiness for sacrifice.

Upon you has fallen the most difficult task.

For whatever we attempt is done for the sake of youth.

Theirs is the future; they will enjoy it at a time when no Jew will have to wonder any longer about the respect or disrespect of those of different races.

That is why the decisive part of our work must be theirs: you young people shall be the pioneers in our new land; you shall prepare the soil, lay the foundation on which the proud structure of our state will arise.

This is the deeper meaning of our festive day and that is why it will remain a day of commemoration for all time:

Today you bring your people the sacrifice of all your former striving after those intellectual goods that served the Diaspora. And today you affirm with all your strength that you are ready to serve a knowledge higher than all human wisdom:

That you want to make it possible for your people to live out its God-idea, to dream it to the very end.

APPENDIX C*

ARNOLD SCHOENBERG

A Four-Point Program for Jewry

I. THE FIGHT AGAINST ANTI-SEMITISM MUST BE STOPPED.

II. A UNITED JEWISH PARTY MUST BE CREATED.

III. UNANIMITY IN JEWRY MUST BE ENFORCED WITH ALL MEANS.

IV. WAYS MUST BE PREPARED TO OBTAIN A PLACE TO ERECT AN INDEPEN-
DENT JEWISH STATE.

I

500,000 Jews from Germany, 300,000 from Austria, 400,000 from Czechoslovakia, 500,000 from Hungary, 60,000 from Italy—more than one million and
eight hundred thousand Jews will have to migrate in how short a time, one does
not know. May God provide there will not be an additional 3,500,000 from
Poland, 900,000 from Rumania, 240,000 from Lithuania and 160,000 from
Latvia—almost 5,000,000; and Yugoslavia with 64,000, Bulgaria with 40,000 and
Greece with 80,000 might follow at once, not to speak of other countries, which
are at present less active.

Is there room in the world for almost 7,000,000 people?

Are they condemned to doom? Will they become extinct? Famished?
Butchered?

Every keen and realistic observer should have known this beforehand, as I
knew it almost twenty years ago. Even one who does not overrate Jewish
intelligence in political affairs will admit that every Jew should have known at
least that the fate of the Austrian and Hungarian Jews was sealed years ago. And
can a man with foresight deny that the Jews of Rumania and Poland are in danger
of a similar fate.

What have our Jewish leaders, our Jewish men with foresight, done to avert
this disaster? What have they done to alleviate the sufferings of the people already
stricken by this mishap? What have they done to find a place for the first 500,000
people who must migrate or die?

Let us forget that at the time when the waves of turmoil and pity went high,
1933, one could hear remarks of satisfaction about the punishment inflicted upon
Western Jews. Let us forget that it was much due to selfishness that no efficient
plans were laid. Let us judge what our leaders did, proposed, promoted; let us
judge these only from the results they achieved.

They, the leaders, proclaimed the war on anti-semitism and started a boycott;
they proposed to transfer a certain percentage of the unfortunates; they promoted

* This Appendix is given in Schoenberg's original English.

the emigration to Palestine. Every keen and realistic observer could have realized the inadequacy and danger of these actions.

In Paris, in 1933, I had arranged my personal affairs in such a manner that I could earn my living and settle down in one of the democratic countries. In the meantime I had contacted prominent Jewish people intending to move them to start the right action. Among them were many Americans whom I considered the most useful, because America was and is in many respects the promised land, especially in what concerns the hopes of Jewry. It was my desire to come to America and start here that movement which in my belief offers the only way out of our problems. Therefore, when suddenly I was offered a position, although it was neither financially nor artistically commensurate with my reputation, I accepted at once, sacrificed my European chances and went over to do what I considered my duty as a Jew.

In Paris I had already fought this unfortunate idea of the boycott. In New York I talked to many prominent Jews against it and had always the satisfaction that my argument was never refuted. However, American Jewry was hypnotized by the boycott, and I found no opportunity to express my views in a magazine or newspaper.

Let me quote what I said and wrote at that time, because it shows that my judgment was correct and it might help to add weight to what I am going to say today.

1. 'The interest of the liberals and democrats of all countries in the fight against Germany is at least as great as that of Jewry; but the interest of the internationalists, socialists, communists, catholics and protestants is certainly greater than ours. Why, therefore, should the Jews make this a Jewish boycott, when it could be an international boycott serving the interests of the liberals, democrats, socialists, communists, catholics and protestants. Why should the Jew offer himself as scapegoat; was he not often enough made scapegoat in similar affairs—without having participated?

2. 'Does not the example of Russia, during her revolution, prove the ineffectiveness of a boycott?

3. 'Accordingly, the boycott might damage Germany but will bring no advantage to the Jews. We have no interest in damage to Germany. Our only interest is to save the Jews. We have not to fight against anti-semitism or nazism, but *for* something; for the existence of a Jewish nation.

4. 'I would have called the boycott a waste, but it was only a waste of time, not of money. And I suspected correctly that it was used only because it required no money, because it was the cheapest way to give the impression that something was being done.'

Today it is unimportant whether or not my prediction was correct. But it is very important to state that the predictions of our leaders were wrong, entirely wrong. And it must be stated that persons who were guilty of such fatal error have lost the right to speak in the name of their people.

The boycott was a failure and the fight against anti-semitism was and is another.

What makes us a nation is not so much our race, as our religion. That we are God's chosen people is a part of his religious belief that no Jew has yet abandoned. Accordingly, we belong together on account of our religion. Races have become extinct through wars, annihilation, biological processes; races have been absorbed by other peoples, have disappeared thus in a new, mixed race. This is a natural process from which we are excepted because we are chosen to survive, to endure through the centuries, to refute the laws of nature. This imposes upon us the duty of self-preservation. Larger minorities than ours among dominating people have been absorbed. Assimilation was never successful with us, and when many of us were ready to assimilate, persecution arose to preserve the nation, as if it were a tool of God to stimulate us when we were in danger of forgetting our inherited belief.

On the other hand, there is no conceivable reason why people should hate us. We know we are not as our enemies describe us. On the contrary, if it were for our qualities we should be liked and admired. We are generous, good-natured, faithful, honest at least in the same degree as other people. In our minds is anchored the obligation to help the poor, which has been an especial part of our religious law for five thousand years. But we possess one quality which seems remarkable if not unique—whilst other peoples have been converted, it has been impossible to convert Israel. It is our devotion to an idea, to an ideal, and it springs from our deep devotion to our inherited faith. Once convinced by an ideal the Jew is willing to suffer or die for it; trained in martyrdom, the Jew is a ready martyr on every mental front.

What Jews have achieved for the advantage of peoples among which they lived asks for thankful recognition. Called to establish trade in different countries they invariably succeeded in making those countries wealthy and sometimes world-dominating. They brought science, medicine, culture, music and literature to barbarian countries; and let us not forget that the Bible in its legal and moral viewpoints is the backbone of the civilization of almost half the people of the world. It might be human that those whom we benefited should want to be rid of us as soon as we had given them all we had. But it seems it is not we who should be ashamed of that.

There is, however, a basic reason: the arrogant Jews. Many will admit they do not know why we were marked in this way. Considered a minor kind of human being, suppressed, outlawed, suspected, shown ill-will and hostility, we scarcely dared ask to be treated lawfully and avoided as much as possible the irritation of our enemies so as not to become exposed to their anger. How could it happen that men who even did not ask for equality could be called arrogant?

Nevertheless, the arrogance of Jews is the very cause of anti-semitism. Only this term does not refer to the behavior or attitude of the single person, but to the whole of us, to the entire Jewry. Every non-Jew believes, consciously or subconsciously, that in every Jew is alive the feeling that he is different from all other peoples by his belonging to God's elected people. This is what they antagonizingly call great presumption, and to that they react with contempt and hatred.

Thus, if Jewry is a religion, if our nationality is based on the belief that we are God's chosen people, anti-semitism would seem inescapable and the fight against it nonsense. Try to fight against rain and snow, against lightning and blizzard, against hurricane and earthquake; try to fight against death and destiny.

This final conclusion must be convincing even to those unfortunate persons who have lost their religious faith, because it is proved by our history. Where is the country where we have not been persecuted, the century in which we have not been hated? Is it perhaps better to believe that we deserve contempt for the defects of character which are falsely ascribed to our race? Does not courage ask us to face the full truth and acknowledge that, enjoying the glory of God's favour, we must endure the consequences, suffer for this privilege as the genius must suffer? One must abandon false hopes. Anti-semitism is natural and cannot be fought. Never has this fight achieved more than a mere postponement, a breathing pause, and the final outburst of anger was the stronger the longer it was kept latent.

Once the fiend has stormed, entered the fortress and started to plunder, there is no chance of negotiation and offer to surrender. There remains either to abandon resistance in despair or to fight the fiend to the bitter end. The decision will not be sought any more in discussing right or wrong. His right is force, the other's wrong is weakness.

Fortunately the fiend has not yet laid hold on the whole fortress, though he possesses a considerable number of forts. Protesting anti-semitism has been proved inadequate and futile. It has brought us rather close to doom. It has lulled into sleep every manly attitude, every energetic and intelligent action. And it has hindered us in doing what intelligence and honour ask us to do. The fight against anti-semitism is not only stupid, immoral, cowardly, undignified, but it is—and this makes it decisive—a waste, a fatal waste of energy. It gives rise to deceptive hopes and directs vital powers in false directions.

There is now no time for idealistic conversations, for sentimental speeches, no time to mention our merits, our good will, to dispute our defects; there is only time to take a different position and do what still might help.

But for this purpose, the fight against anti-semitism must at once be stopped.

II

A UNITED JEWISH PARTY MUST BE CREATED

Does there exist one man who knows the number of parties into which Jews are divided? America has only three or four principal parties. In France they might be mixed, subdivided and shaded off to amount to perhaps more than ten. But the

Jewish body is divided in a very complex way. Primarily, the whole body is divided into three principal sections, hostile to each other, according to religion: orthodox, reformist, atheist; then each of these groups is broken according to socio-political principles into conservatives, liberals, socialists. Further, the origin of the Jews, as Western, Eastern, Oriental, again subdivides every group. And finally, each one of these geographic groups includes 'nationalities' eager to preserve their respective peculiarities, proud of them, hostile toward all the others, and increasing the tendency to splinter into an almost unlimited number of 'isms'. This is bad enough, but in fact it is still worse. Jews are individualists. Educated during thousands of years by their teachers in exegesis of the secrets of the Bible, they are accustomed to finding individual resolutions of their problems. They are now applying the same individualism in the field of politics. Probably every Jew will apply his own way of thinking, a home-made theory, a personal attitude to every problem he faces.

Nothing could be more disastrous to a people than that.

The recent history of Jewry shows the effects. One will read for example the reports on the Zionist Central Council and find that a man in a leading position resigned because his ideas had failed of the necessary support. This seems inconceivable to me. How is it possible for a man who believes in his idea and in the necessity and usefulness of the organization in which he plays a leading role, how is it possible for him to abandon both? Because his vanity has been offended? If at a fire one group of the men who came to fight it thought that it should be fought from the right side and another group contended it could only be extinguished from the left side—what would one think of that group who left the other in the lurch, knowing that everyone would be necessary for the work? Is there not a moral duty to cooperate for the common purpose notwithstanding one's own viewpoint?

A body of heterogeneous concepts is indomitably inclined to refuse all things which do not conform to the idea of each man. The aversion of every single member to agreement makes it hopeless to find a majority for an idea, but provides always majorities against it. When Theodore Herzl, recognizing his error, decided to abandon for a time the idea of Palestine and accepted the offer of England (Uganda as a Jewish colony), he was exposed to such tremendous opposition that the excitement and fear of failure of the whole enterprise probably caused his death. He displayed an excellent grasp of realistic policy in correcting an error instead of continuing with it. Thus, as after Herzl's death the Congress voted against the Uganda Project, one might even doubt whether they were for the Palestine Project, or merely against something, against a person, against a shade of the idea, against the behaviour of a group or of a single person, or really against the whole of the Uganda Project. I assume it had become of secondary importance to the majority of the members, who perhaps were dominated only by their aim for opposition and infuriated by the 'unreasonable' demand to vote in favor of an idea which was not exactly their own.

The consequences of such an attitude are shown by the later development. The friends and followers of Herzl, staying faithfully with his idea when outvoted by the majority, found no better way of administering the inheritance than to step out of the party and erect a new one. This is very honourable, but it is not practical politics.

On, of course, a lesser scale, I acted differently. I was a kind of dictator, 1920, in a musical society, erected by myself in my ideas and on the whole very successful. Suddenly there arose a strong opposition to my plans, instigated by some political extremists. Fruitlessly I tried to convince them, fruitlessly I showed that the idea would break down if they continued with their opposition, but fast arose the danger that they could gain a majority against my principles. I did not resign. On the contrary, I did something which under other circumstances could be called illegal: I dissolved the whole society, built a new one, accepted only such members who were in perfect agreement with my artistic principles and excluded the entire opposition. There were some sentimentalists who considered it wrong, but it was the only healthful means of avoiding the encroachment of non-artistic principles upon artistic ones. Right or wrong—these principles were my country.

Had the followers and friends of Herzl possessed the power to act similarly, many disastrous steps might have been avoided. They should have remained within the party and within it continued the fight for their ideas; they should not have given up, but should have tried to convince the outsiders. New members should have been acquired, the old ones conquered with all means until their majority were annihilated; with all means, had they only been fit to do the work: He who wants to work for his nation cannot be a sentimentalist, but must be—if necessary—unscrupulous, faithful only to his goal. These honourable citizens who acted really like gentlemen, but not like statesmen, had no right to meddle with the affairs of a nation, to try to decide the fate of a people.

When I said that it was doubtful that the Congress wanted to vote for Palestine, I did not intend to make this really doubtful. To every Jew the idea of Palestine is self-evident, without any question, a matter of fact, which needs no special mention and is not dependent on voting. Every Jew feels, knows and can never forget that Palestine is ours and that we have been deprived of it by mere force; that we will never consent to the claim of another nation upon our promised land. This conviction dominates emotionally our political standpoints, but a statesman must suppress sentimentalities. When Herzl realized that at that time a 'Judenstaat' could not be erected in Palestine, there should have been nothing to hinder his accepting and carrying out the Uganda Project.

How different would be today's Jewish situation were there now an independent state in Uganda, founded in about 1905, counting perhaps a population of five to ten million, able to provide homes for ten to twenty millions in addition, independent economically, perhaps also provided with a modern armament and even perhaps not without political and diplomatic influence. It might be that this state could not offer protection from the persecutions of anti-semitic powers, nor offer anything of value in negotiations. But certainly it could offer a land, a home, a place where refugees were safe. Do all of those men who voted against the Uganda Project realize what they did? Do they know that it was their damned individualism, their insane stubbornness, their fanciless dogmaticalness, their political shortsightedness, their arrogant incompetence in world and state affairs, their vanity, their pride, their thoughtlessness, levity and frivolity, which has brought upon us this situation, which has made us powerless in the face of disaster? Do they know that their names should be registered in the history of our people as the names of those men on whom will be laid the blame for this enormous mishap?

I do not want to be cruel and therefore I will admit that there were men among them who had great merits in other fields of the organization, men who had conviction, men who were prepared to suffer for their ideas, who were ready to sacrifice all their possessions and capacities for the final success of their ideal. I will admit that their error was not exclusively one of their own, but one which was caused by circumstances beyond their control. Freedom of thought, action and life had been given to Jewry through the victory of democracy. No wonder they believed in democracy, no wonder they applied democracy in their own realm, no wonder they watched with jealousy their right to decide what they believed to be their own affair, no wonder they believed in voting, in the better understanding of a majority, in the capacity of a majority to do not only what everybody wanted, but what was the best for everybody, including opponents. They doubted the capacity of a single man or a small group who could not convince their opponents, though history had always shown that the great men, standing alone, persecuted, unsupported, eventually achieved victory and were proved right. This has a repulsing effect on the average Jewish intellectualist: an individualist, in spite of his professed democracy, he will never acknowledge it voluntarily.

The decision over the fate of a nation seems to be much too important a question to submit to a majority, even were the majority overwhelming. This decision in an organization like the Zionist Congress could well depend on a majority of one voice, the voice of one man who might have slept while the importance of the matter was being discussed. How would an army act if the commanding general were obliged to find a majority among his colonels, after they, on their part, had got the decision of the captains who depended on what the sergeants believed or what was agreed by the last private; should one attack on the left or on the right flank, or frontal, should one attack at all or perhaps retreat. The majority might have found a correct decision, but in all probability it will have come too late. Speeches, explanations, discussions, controversy must precede the voting in every group, some might adjourn their vote and ask for more information and when finally the subordinates of the man in command can vote, they have no opportunity, because the enemy has already taken position and the army is in flight.

Did not this happen to the Zionist Congress? Have they not been voting since 1904 to resolve the problem of a Jewish state? Had Herzl alone at that time possessed the right to decide, Uganda would be ours, and we would now know where to place Jewish refugees. It has taken more than thirty years to make the leaders of the Jewry conscious of their mistake, and it is problematical whether even now they are conscious of it.

A United Jewish Party must be created and organized in such a manner that these evils may be avoided as far a human foresight can avail.

It should not be necessary to explain what this little word 'united' means. It should be obvious to everybody. But one knows from experience that people find in every concept a left and a right side, a before and a behind, a when and an if, a but and an in spite of.

This unity does not mean a union of the different Jewish organizations in which the respective ideas of all these organizations will be represented. It does not mean that there will be elected a president, a number of vice-presidents, a board of directors into which all the organizations delegate their representatives; there will not be appointed a number of prominent men of each country as honorary members or honorary presidents or honorary whatnots. There will not be more social affairs, dinners, receptions, meetings, to satisfy ambitions, vanities and desires for publicity.

A United Party should be like an ideal matrimony: A man and a woman joined to the purpose of producing children of whom this man is the father and this woman is the mother. Everything which contradicts this only purpose must be avoided, no other inclination can be admitted, no other contact allowed. Everything which promotes this common purpose is duty, is moral, is law.

Accordingly a United Party cannot possess an opposition, there can be no majority which does not include all the members, there can never be admitted one thought connected by inclination to the principles of other parties; every contact which may interfere with the unanimity of the United Party must be broken. It will be duty and moral of the members to do everything which promotes the unanimity of this party. With, of course, one exception: as no husband and no wife may do anything which is against the law, so, in every country, every member will have to avoid conflict with the laws of the respective countries. This limitation cannot hinder the unanimity of the party. It might sometimes limit its activities, and the fact that Jews, in case of war, in obedience and devotion to the laws of the countries, might have to kill each other, will not interfere with the principles of the party. Life and death of the individual are without influence on historic processes, and while a Jew within the party will be only a Jew and nothing else, as a citizen he will fulfil all duties to which the other citizens of his country are commanded.

The inclination of people to join this party who are followers of other ideas or who belong to political parties of contradictory principles, might not be very strong. Let them remain where they wish. The time will come when they feel and realize where they belong.

III

UNANIMITY IN JEWRY MUST BE ENFORCED WITH ALL MEANS

Unanimity is very seldom a thing in the life of a nation at which a people arrive voluntarily. Consider that there are men with a real conviction, men dominated by vanity and believing they alone know the right way, men burning with ambition to play a role, indifferent men who do not understand at all, men who are inconstant, fickle, wavering and who can always be caught by the last idea to impress them, and you will agree that it is a miracle that unanimity occurs at all.

'Doubt is the beginning of philosophy' and, may I add, skepticism is its shabby, misshapen, vulgar little brother. Skepticism can kill everything: religion, science, art, ideas, facts, and even miracles. Skepticism is a subconsciously hidden hope in wonders—in which it does not believe; in facts, which it denies; in actions, which it belittles. Credulity is a close relative of optimism. But skepticism has done more harm to the world than optimism, which is also a killer, but one of another kind. 'What will you do if that happens?' and you will be answered 'But it will not happen, because ...' 'But if it happens nevertheless?' Optimism pretends: 'But it cannot happen!' and then it happens nevertheless and optimism has deprived you of the opportunity of guarding in time against the worst. One might summarize this: The skeptic is optimistically anticipating the failure of favourable matters while the optimist is skeptically anticipating the failure of unfavourable matters. Thus placed on a common formula, one sees that both live not on recognition, but on anticipations. They are gamblers and would better decide their stand by dice than by reasoning.

Another obstacle to unity is the Jewish sort of intelligence: they are masters and champions of discussion. Never enter into discussion, because every Jew is superior to every other Jew, and will apply logic better than every other Jew, and he will win or at least the other will lose. At least, time will be lost. Victory does not seem to be the aim of the disputation, but, varying 'l'art pour l'art' (art for art's sake) one could say, discussion for discussion's sake only.

Never enter into discussion!

One who fights for unanimity would be in danger of becoming bewitched with admiration of this mental power, or of becoming confused through the contradictory results of perfect logics, or of becoming sentimental over so much and sincere conviction. Yes, conviction; conviction is certainly the motivating force behind the bad habits of these skeptics, optimists and debaters. The fighter for unanimity would best ignore them. But if contempt were an implement against them one should consider its use.

If used ruthlessly, contempt might really serve as an efficient weapon but it would fail to achieve the main purpose of unanimity, which is not to make every Jew a powerless yet resisting slave, but an active and convinced fighter for the common purpose. Of course, every experienced businessman knows how to conquer resisting competitors. And recent history has also taught us how to produce, if not real and voluntary unity, at least something which has the same effect. It would not be unwise for us to learn from others, even if we did not agree with them, and were hostile to their aims.

But the goal of Jewish unanimity is based on reconciliation. And, in addition, we must consider our mentality from a different angle. In spite of its antagonism to unanimity, one will understand that it is not by accident that we are thus constituted.

It is my belief that this astonishing mentality is a divine gift, destined to protect us, to enable us to outlast the diaspora with its persecutions and its dangers to personal life and to the existence of our people. Our religion bases its convincing power in a smaller degree on miracles but asks for mental penetration. Discussion of its concepts is not restricted to the priests, but recommended for all men. Every learned man can be a rabbi if only his zeal, his studies, his apperception and the dignity of his conduct mark him as a man who lives with God in the ideas of the faith. To read the Bible and to understand it was the foremost purpose of teaching in the 'Schul', and one might doubt that even 'Am Horez' (which means in Hebrew an ignorant person) signified an alphabet. This constant occupation with the word of God kept alive our religion: our national fundament. Every animal has a way to protect itself and its race. Its defense might be based on power, teeth, speed, poison, mimicry, fertility, etc. Among mankind, facing every kind of persecution, we Jews were deprived of the use of all such weapons. No wonder we developed the only tool of which we were not deprived: our intelligence. Overwhelming power makes the tiger a bloodthirsty killer who runs amuck without being hungry; the possession of poison makes snakes dangerous even to harmless creatures; the tremendous swiftness of the greyhound might have made the use of brain superfluous to it; and thus very often overdevelopment of one capacity can produce undesirable counter-effects. It seems one could not call the overdevelopment of Jewish intelligence a defect were it not the cause of our disunion. But it was necessary, it was our only way to cope with the weapons of others, it was our only way to protect ourselves and our race. We had always to stand one against from ten to a hundred enemies, and it was of course not cowardice that made the one recognize that resistance is nonsense. Intelligence sometimes helped—if it could be applied. From this viewpoint it would be unjust and ungrateful to regard this divine gift with contempt, even if it were overdeveloped and in spite of its hindrance to unanimity. One must, on the contrary, respect it highly, and find out how to redirect it so as to promote the understanding of the necessity of unity.

No doubt, this will not be an easy task and one will have to discover how it can be done. There is certainly even among Jews a certain percentage which can be won by persuasion. In spite of the natural tendency toward skepticism, the participation of a great number of Jews in diverse radical parties can be explained only on the basis of real idealism, conviction and enthusiasm. These driving forces could be directed the right way. It should be possible to convince them that he who wants to reform the world should at first reform his own house. The same idealism, devotion, self-sacrificing spirit, courage, intelligence, force of will and persistency applied to what is really our own matter as Jews must work wonders. And if it was possible to make a Jew a follower of those parties, it must also be possible to convert him to devotion to his own affairs. This begs also a discussion of so-called Jewish Internationalism, a very confused concept. Suspicion is justified as to whether it is not intentionally ambiguous, because it can thus easily be applied to manifold political purposes. Fascism, which at the beginning was called 'no article of exportation,' is today an international movement, as a form of government and as an international defense against communism. National Socialism is today also not restricted to the nation which originated it. If one considers today's alliances, one will have difficulty in discovering principal differences between fascist aims for international alliances to conquer communism, and communist aims for international alliances to conquer capitalism — and, recently added, fascism. But let us mention that 'internationalism' is not exclusively ignominious. There are too many human activities based on internationality that are not ignominious: trade, navigation, aviation, mail, telegraphy, etc.; also peace-movements, Red Cross and, last but not least, the Catholic church. But the slogan 'Jewish Internationalism' refers to socialism on the one hand and capitalism on the other. Neither is exclusively Jewish, each is opposed to the other, both are firstly national and they are international only so far as their interests may require. There is no general Jewish interest in communism or in capitalism, but only mutual international antipathy. Jewish internationalism should be for Jewish interests exclusively, and if it existed as such, the Jewish situation today would be quite different.

This is not the place to decide whether or not Jewish internationalism should degenerate into non-participation in the civic life of the respective nations among which we live. Nor could it be decided at this hour. That is a question of practical policies and such problems are not decided by principles but by necessities. At first there is no indication that such an attitude is desirable. Concentration on affairs of our own does not ask for it and it is mentioned because it might be considered a logical consequence of the principles developed here. For example, among the leaders of a United Jewish Party might be extreme-conservatives and also extreme-radicals, who at the same time might be important in their respective civic activities. The hostility between extreme rightists and leftists is so strong that they could not act impartially in the Jewish body. Such problems one must anticipate and they must be resolved without sentimentality.

There will arise more problems, predictable and unpredictable. There will be difficulties constantly, difficulties in such number and of such measure that despair might reign among the members and the leaders, and it will very often appear as if everything were lost and as if the whole movement were to break down. And perhaps a temporary breakdown might occur; this will be a strong moral strain and heavy burden on the leaders and will cause dangerous discouragement among the members.

For all these reasons I think the party should avoid growing too fast. It must not be an overnight mass-party. This would be dangerous as long as there have not arisen numerous leaders, carefully selected, manifoldly tested, chosen not only for their intelligence (super-intelligence would endanger unanimity), but for their character, steadiness, faithfulness, directness, courage and devotion. With some exaggeration one could say the party should at first consist of not much more than the future leaders. If they can preserve unanimity among themselves, they will succeed in unifying the members they have won. Anticipating the difficulty of producing incontestable unity among the leaders, one will agree that this is the first test to which these leaders must be submitted. Are they capable of unanimity among themselves? Then, and only then, will they be capable of enforcing unanimity among the members: One who cannot obey, cannot command—an ancient military axiom.

IV

WAYS MUST BE PREPARED TO OBTAIN A PLACE TO ERECT AN INDEPENDENT JEWISH STATE

If it was difficult to discuss the first three points of this program, it is much more difficult to treat this fourth point publicly. It asks for an almost unreasonable amount of tact and discretion, and if in the preceding many points could not be expressed directly, then here much more cannot be said—but only hinted at. One will begin to understand why diplomats use that peculiar sort of speech which sounds to the average citizen as he himself might·have said it but which to the experienced connoisseur means something very different.

During more than three centuries after Columbus discovered America it would have been somewhat easier to find a country for an independent Jewish state. Considering the expulsion of the Jews by the Spaniards and Portuguese, or a number of major and minor persecutions and expulsions in other countries, there was reason enough to try it—had there only existed a little intelligent political understanding. Why, if Puritans could find the means to migrate, could not Jews? It is an historical fact that at this time Jews were soldiers, some of high rank, seamen and adventurers of all kinds, merchants who rigged out ships bound for the east or West Indies. Jews were active in the East India Company and potent in the Hanseatic League and its enterprises; there were present all the conditions to invite venturesome people to participate when the earth was being shared. And there were also venturesome Jews: in England, in Holland, in the Hanseatic League and elsewhere.

But for two thousand years Jews had been longing for their sacred promised land, for their old Jerusalem. And this unquenchable desire for Zion, this very pathetic idea was decisive. It excluded every other idea, excluded any desire for an independent state other than in Palestine.

As our destiny differs from that of all other people, so does our feeling. Where is a second people who during two thousand years has not lost its desire for a native land, of which scarcely one out of a thousand knows much more than a few dry facts—some names and some photographic pictures.

It would be a mistake to believe that it is only on account of our history that we feel this way. Of course, this land our forefathers conquered by the sword; there we developed our religious and social culture; there our heroes fought against overwhelming enemies and against paganism and its idols; there we were beaten by the one but won against the others; this is history, but it does not mean so much to us as the other inextinguishable fact; this is the land which our God has given us.

That this sentiment is stronger than our intelligence is a very regrettable circumstance. Save for it, there must have been a number of men throughout the diaspora who reflected thus: The Holy Land was promised to our people, but we did not get it for nothing. A people who insists on calling land its own must take it with the same means with which it wants to keep it. Our forefathers had to remain for forty years in the desert in order to become strong. One must be strong to take what one wants and to protect what one has.

If one considers the political, geographic and strategic position of Palestine, one will doubt whether ever the opportunity can arise which will allow us to take possession of it. The other religions to whom Zion has become a sacred place would not cease to dispute our right. And surrounded by Mohammedans, Palestine will be in the worst strategical situation. Only a ruler of the world like England could undertake to protect us, and even she will do it only so far as her interests allow and require it. Jewish leaders should understand that world politics is dominated largely by economic questions. If they have neglected to take this into account, here at least it shall be discussed: Is it not evident that Palestine is desirable to the great powers for other than idealistic and religious reasons? Suppose Jewry did possess Palestine under the best possible conditions. Let us say, for example, that instead of building a Jewish university and a Jewish orchestra, we had built an army there of a hundred thousand men and were ready to spend our total funds for reinforcements; suppose we were strong enough to conquer the Arabs; suppose we were supported by treaties and had alliances with powerful nations. One must still understand that the relative independence of the Arabs under English protectorate is only admitted by England because the Arabs are not powerful. No first rate power would allow a powerful nation to remain in possession of this country because it opens the way to India. We Jews did not lose this land because other people did not like us, but only because other people liked our land—for their trade. Only a powerless nation can possess it, one which cannot deny others the right to cross through it.

To know history is one thing and to understand it is another thing. But it seems that politicians neither know nor understand. And it seems that they become leaders only by 'virtue' of a lack of understanding of historical processes. And one could almost believe that a man with a de facto insight into the driving forces of human activities could scarcely become a leader unless he were able to carefully hide his superiority.

I do not want to say this, but I must. All these facts and conclusions seem to me so self-evident, so simple, so clear, that I cannot understand how these pseudo-leaders could misinterpret them. But there is something else in it and this seems almost an enigma to me. It appears that these leaders have even now not acknowledged the responsibility a man takes upon himself who interferes with the destiny of a people. There were a number of leaders of other parties in a number of nations who suddenly awoke to reality and had to face a very old idea: that the life of a man is at stake who mixes in politics; that only such men who are ready to die for their ideas should attempt to play a role in the fate of their people; that a leader cannot simply withdraw, in case of failure, but must suffer to the bitter end. They act often, however, like gamblers, who simply disappear instead of paying for their losses. They stay stubbornly with their idea, thinking they can leave the party, if they lose. Why did Brutus and Varus kill themselves when they had lost? Justice asks the life of a man whose fault it is that people suffer or die who trusted him—he cannot simply withdraw and become a private person.

Theodore Herzl died when the Uganda Project was rejected by the Zionist Congress: his heart committed harakiri. But those men who led Jewry into the useless boycott, into the useless fight against anti-semitism, encouraged people to go to Palestine, who have started the meaningless fight against Italian fascism, who have only provoked Mussolini and given him good excuse for his anti-Jewish policies—have those men realized what they did to our people? Do they understand that they ought not further to open their mouths in Jewish affairs?

Do they realise that fascism or democracy, feudalism or communism, monarchism or republicanism are no questions of the Jewry as such, of the Jewry as a nation, but are merely different forms of government, matters of internal policy. Our attitude toward them must be subject to change in accordance with the question of our freedom. In one country fascism might be more favorable, democracy in another; in another state feudalism might offer better protection than communism. The fight for social or governmental theories should have no influence on Jewish national policies. Probably within a Jewish state the same contest between opposing political theories will occur.

Do all those leaders know how superficially they acted when they based their policies on the differences in internal affairs; on their like or dislike of monarchism, republicanism, feudalism, democracy, fascism, socialism, communism?

Will they start again their useless struggles with words, with speeches, with discussion, and waste the short space of time which is now left for action? They should not dare it; the time for words is over and if action does not start at once, it may be too late.

There is only one way to save Jewry: to obtain a land to which the Jewish people can migrate. Whether this land will be given to us as a colony, or as an independent state, under a protectorate or under any other conditions, will not matter. Whether we buy this land or get it free should not worry us. Whether this land offers good or bad climatic, geographical or commercial conditions is also unimportant; one knows that present technic makes life possible anywhere: in the jungle, in the desert or at the poles. It need only be a land. We must accommodate ourselves.

There is still land enough which is not inhabited by other peoples. And there are a number of states which need money. And as long as Jews possess money, they will be able to buy a land and perhaps even one which provides the best conditions for a modern state. Is it necessary to mention that one can buy everything on installments today? Such contracts are sometimes agreed over a period of '99' years. But it seems that Jews could remove their debts in thirty or forty years. If there were loans, our commercial, industrial and inventive capacities would certainly enable us to pay interests and amortize the capital.

Can there be a doubt that it will be of the greatest interest to world bankers to finance such a program once they recognize it is sound? Can there be a doubt that such a program is promising which plans to provide a country with all the necessities, facilities, machines and raw materials for building roads, and to create agriculture, industry and all things which represent a state? Is there a doubt that it would produce a boom in all those countries which participated in business with the new state? Can there be a doubt that unemployment in those countries would disappear when they undertook to furnish all the things our state needs? How many ships will be needed to bring twelve to fifteen millions of men to the new country and how many ships will be needed to transport the goods?

Might not such an enterprise perhaps solve, at least for a time, the problems of the present crisis in production and trade? Has one ever considered such an enterprise from the standpoint of the great business it is?

If the Jews would not undertake it, it seems that the great financial non-Jewish powers should interest themselves in it. There is only one question:

Will the Jews be able to repay the loans?

It seems not too daring to me to answer this question emphatically in the affirmative.

At present it is not wise to go into details. All depends on the readiness of the Jewry to undertake decisive steps in this direction, and much depends on the willingness of non-Jews to resolve these problems in a humane, a lawful and dignified way.

But first:

1. THE FIGHT AGAINST ANTI-SEMITISM MUST BE STOPPED.
2. A UNITED JEWISH PARTY MUST BE CREATED.
3. UNANIMITY IN JEWRY MUST BE ENFORCED WITH ALL MEANS.
4. WAYS MUST BE PREPARED TO OBTAIN A PLACE TO ERECT AN INDEPENDENT JEWISH STATE.

APPENDIX D

Arnold Schoenberg on the Sacredness of Art
Letter to Oedon Partosh, Jerusalem

To Mr Frank Pelleg   Los Angeles, 26.4.1951
Director of the Music Section
in the Ministry for Education and Culture
for his kind attention,
official action and transmission to the
Director of the Israel Academy of Music in Jerusalem.

Mr O. Partosh.

I accept my appointment as Honorary President of the Israel Academy of Music with pride and satisfaction but feel, by the same token, that I should explain why I consider it so important that you chose me in particular for that distinction.

I told your friends, who visited me recently here in Los Angeles, as I told you, esteemed Director Partosh, how for over four decades it was my most ardent wish to witness the creation of an independent Israeli state. And more than that: to become a resident citizen of that state.

Whether my health will grant me fulfillment of this second wish, I cannot say at the moment. I do hope to be able, at any rate, to arrange it so that the greatest possible number of my many compositions, literary works and articles, which I produced with an eye on the artistic propagation of my plans, will get into your hands for the Israel National Library. How much I would like to contribute personally to the institution's direction and instruction I cannot express in words. I was always an impassioned teacher. I have always felt the urge to find out what is most helpful to beginners, how to imbue them with a sense of the technical, intellectual and ethical prerequisites of our art; how to convey to them that there is such a thing as artistic morality and why one must never cease to cultivate it and, conversely, to oppose as forcefully as possible anyone who commits an offense against it.

Unfortunately, I must give up any further thought of such wishes. But it seems to me that the half century by which my experience antedates that of many of my colleagues authorizes me to explain what I would have attempted to make of this institution, had I the good fortune and the strength as yet to do something along these lines.

And here I address myself with my warmest good wishes to the Director, Mr O. Partosh.

I would have tried to give this Academy universal significance so as to place it in a position to serve as an alternative for a mankind that caters in so many ways to an amoral, business-inspired materialism. A materialism behind which any ethical assumptions of our art are rapidly disappearing. A universal model cannot condone half-knowledge. It cannot train instrumentalists whose greatest skill is their ability to comply to perfection with the universal demand for entertainment.

From such an institution must go forth true priests of art who confront art with the same sense of consecration that the priest brings to God's altar. For, just as God chose Israel whose task it is to preserve, in spite of all suffering, the pure, true, mosaic monotheism, so it behooves Israeli musicians to offer the world a model possessed of the unique capacity to make our souls function once more in ways apt to further the development of humanity toward ever higher goals.

These are my wishes, and if I should be able to serve you with additional comments or explanations regarding certain details, I can only hope that you'll call on me.

                                                          Arnold Schoenberg

REFERENCES CITED

ADLER, O., *Das Testament der Astrologie, i. Die allgemeine Grundlegung der Astrologie, Tierkreis und Mensch* (Vienna, 1950).

ADORNO, T. W., *Philosophie der neuen Musik* (Frankfurt am Main, 1949).

AVINERI, S., *Moses Hess: Prophet of Communism and Zionism* (New York and London, 1985).

BARZUN, J., *The Pleasures of Music* (New York, 1961).

BECK, C. H., *Geschichte der Juden* (Munich, 1983).

BEHR, H., *Die goldenen zwanziger Jahre* (Hamburg, 1964).

BEIN, A., *Die Judenfrage* (Stuttgart, 1980).

BEN-AMI, Y., *Years of Wrath, Days of Glory* (New York, 1982).

BENZ, E., *Emanuel Swedenborg* (Munich, 1948).

BERG, A., 'Die musikalischen Formen in meiner Oper "Wozzeck"', *Die Musik*, 16 (1928), 587–9.

—— 'Das "Opernproblem"', in W. Reich (ed.), *Alban Berg* (Vienna, 1937), 174–7.

BERL, H., 'Die Juden in der bildenden Kunst', *Der Jude*, 8 (1924), 323–38.

—— *Das Judentum in der Musik* (Stuttgart, Berlin, and Leipzig, 1926).

—— 'Musik: Bearbeitungen jüdischer Melodien', *Der Jude*, 8 (1924), 618–24.

BERTALOT, J., 'Number Symbolism in Bach: Pt. 1', *Musical Opinion*, 1246 (Aug. 1981), 413–15.

BLITZSTEIN, M., 'Theater-Music in Paris', *Modern Music*, 12 (1935), 132–3.

BLOCH, E., 'Lied der Seeräuber-Jenny in der "Dreigroschenoper"', *Anbruch*, 11 (1929), 125–7.

BOHLMANN, P. V., 'The Archives of the World Centre for Jewish Music in Palestine 1936–1940', *Yuval*, 5 (1986), 238–64.

BOWLES, P., 'Film Music', *New York Times*, 19 Jan. 1943.

BROD, M., *Heidentum, Christentum, Judentum* (2 vols.; Munich, 1921).

BRONSEN, D., 'Austrian versus Jew: The Torn Identity of Joseph Roth', *Leo Baeck Institute Yearbook*, 18 (1973), 220–31.

BUBER, M., *Vom Geist des Judentums* (Munich, 1916).

—— 'Geleitwort', in R. Beer-Hoffmann, Gesammelte Werke (Frankfurt, 1963).

—— *On Judaism*, ed. N. N. Glatzer (New York, 1967).

BÜTTNER, H., 'Reichsmusiktage in Düsseldorf', *Zeitschrift für Musik*, 105 (1938), 736–43.

COHEN, H., *Reason and Hope*, ed. E. Jospe (New York, 1971).

DAVIDOWICZ, L., *The Jewish Presence* (New York, 1978).

DIBELIUS, U. (ed.), *Herausforderung Schönberg* (Munich, 1974).

DIEKREITER, M., *Der Musiktheoretiker Johannes Kepler* (Berne, 1973).

DREW, D., 'To the Editor', *Kurt Weill Newsletter*, 5/2 (1987), 3–4.

DÜMLING, A., *Die fremden Klänge der hängenden Gärten* (Munich, 1981).

ERMAN, H., *Berliner Geschichten, Geschichte Berlins* (Herrenalb, 1966).

ERWIN, C. E., and SIMMS, B. R., 'Schoenberg's Correspondence with Heinrich Schenker', *JASI*, 5 (1981), 23–43.

FEDERHOFER, H., *Heinrich Schenker* (Hildesheim, Zurich, and New York, 1985).

FIELD, G. G., 'Antisemitism and Weltpolitik', *Leo Baeck Institute Yearbook*, 18 (1973), 65–91.

Die Frechheit, 4 (Sept., 1928).

FREITAG, E., *Schönberg* (Hamburg, 1973).

FURTWÄNGLER, W., *Briefe*, ed. F. Thiess (Wiesbaden, 1964).

GAY, P., and WEBB, R., *Modern Europe*, ii (New York, 1973).

GEISSMAR, B., *Two Worlds of Music* (New York, 1946).

'Geleitsätze zum Beethovenfest der Hitler-Jugend', *Zeitschrift für Musik*, 105 (1938), 732–3.

GOEHR, A., 'Schoenberg's "Gedanke" Manuscript', *JASI*, 2/1 (Oct. 1977), 4–25.

GOLDMAN, A., and SPRINCHORN, E. (eds.), *Wagner on Music and Drama* (New York, 1965).

GRADENWITZ, P., 'Gustav Mahler and Arnold Schoenberg', *Leo Baeck Institute Yearbook*, 5 (1960), 262–84.

—— 'The Religious Works of Arnold Schoenberg', *The Music Review*, 21/1 (1960), 19–29.

GRUNFELD, F. V., *Prophets without Honor* (New York, 1979).

GUTTMANN, A., 'Jewish Radicals, Jewish Writers', *American Scholar*, 32/4 (1963), 563–75.

HANSLICK, E., *Vienna's Golden Years of Music 1850–1900*), (transl. Henry Pleasants III) (New York, 1950).

HEUSS, A., 'Arnold Schönberg, Preußischer Kompositionslehrer', *Neue Zeitschrift für Musik*, 92/10 (1925), 583–5.

HILMAR, E. (ed.), *Arnold Schönberg Gedenkausstellung* (Vienna, 1974).

HINDEMITH, P., *Paul Hindemith: Zeugnis in Bildern*, with an introduction by Heinrich Strobel (Mainz, 1955).

IDELSOHN, A. Z., 'My Life', *Yuval*, 5 (*The Abraham Zvi Idelsohn Memorial Volume*, ed. I. Adler, B. Bayer, and E. Schleifer; 1986), 18–23.

ISAAC, E., and ISAAC, R., 'The Impact of Jabotinsky on Likud's Politics', *Middle East Review*, 10/1 (autumn, 1977), 33.

JANIK, A., and TOULMIN, S. *Wittgenstein's Vienna* (New York, 1973).

KALLEN, H. M., 'Jewish Unity', in A. Hertzberg (ed.), *The Zionist Idea* (New York, 1966), 531–5.

KANDINSKY, W., and MARC, F., *The Blaue Reiter Almanac* (New York, 1974).

KAUFMANN, W., *Nietzsche* (New York, 1956).

—— *The Faith of a Heretic* (New York, 1963).

KEPLER, J. *Die Zusammenklänge der Welt*, ed. and transl. Otto J. Birk (Jena, 1918), 99.

KESTENBERG, L., *Bewegte Zeiten* (Wolfenbüttel and Zurich, 1961).

KIMMEN, J., (ed.), *The Arnold Schoenberg–Hans Nachod Collection* (Detroit, 1979).

KISCH, G., *Judentaufen* (Berlin, 1913).

KLATZKIN, J., *Probleme des modernen Judentums*, 3rd rev. edn. (Berlin, 1930).

KNÜLTER, H. H., *Die Juden und die deutsche Linke in der Weimarer Republik 1918–1933* (Düsseldorf, 1971).

KNUST, H., 'Grosz' contribution to the Berlin Schwejk Performance of 1928', *Theatrical Drawings and Watercolors by Georg Grosz* (Cambridge, Mass., 1973).

KOHN, H., *Karl Kraus, Arthur Schnitzler, Otto Weininger: Aus dem jüdischen Wien der Jahrhundertwende* (Tübingen, 1962).

LAQUEUR, W., *Weimar: A Cultural History* (New York, 1974).

LEWIS, R., *In Praise of Music* (New York, 1963).

McGRATH, W., *Dionysian Art and Populist Politics in Austria* (New Haven, 1974).

MÄCKELMANN, M., *Arnold Schönberg und das Judentum* (Hamburger Beiträge zur Musikwissenschaft, 28; Hamburg, 1984).

Männer im Dritten Reich (Bremen, 1934).

MANN, K., *Mephisto* (Amsterdam, 1936).

MARC, F., *Schriften*, ed. K. Lankheit (Cologne, 1978).

MASUR, G., *Imperial Berlin* (New York, 1971).

MAYER, G., 'Arnold Schönberg im Urteil Hanns Eislers', *Beiträge zur Musikwissenschaft*, 18 (1976), 195–214.

MAYER, S., *Die Wiener Juden, 1700–1900* (Vienna and Berlin, 1917).

MEYER, H., *Die Zahlenallegorese im Mittelatter* (Munich, 1975).

MIESEL, V., *Voices of German Expressionism* (Englewood Cliffs, 1970).

MORGENSTERN, S., *Composers on Music* (New York, 1956).

MOSSE, G., *The Culture of Western Europe: The Nineteenth and Twentieth Centuries, An Introduction* (Chicago, 1961).

—— *Deutsches Judentum in Krieg und Revolution, 1916–1923* (Tübingen, 1971).

MÜLLER-BLATTAU, J., *Geschichte der deutschen Musik* (Berlin, 1938).

NADEL, A., 'Jüdische Musik', *Der Jude*, 7 (1923), 227–36.

NÉHER, A., *David Gans: Disciple du Maharal de Prague* (Paris, 1974).

—— *Faust et le Maharal de Prague* (Paris, 1987).

NETTL, P., *Alte jüdische Spielleute und Musiker* (Prague, 1923).

—— *Forgotten Musicians* (New York, 1951).

NEWLIN, D., 'Self Revelation and the Law: Arnold Schoenberg and His Religious Works', *Yuval*, 1 (1968), 204–20.

NORMAN, G., and SCHRIFTE, M. L., *Letters of Composers* (New York, 1946).

OBRECHT, J., *Opera Omnia: Missa VI, 'Sub Tuum Presidium'*, ed. M. van Crevel (Amsterdam, 1959).

PAWEL, E., *The Nightmare of Reason: A Life of Franz Kafka* (New York, 1985).

PENKOWER, M. N., *The Jews Were Expendable* (Urbana and Chicago, 1983).

PFITZNER, H., *Gesammelte Schriften*, i (Augsburg, 1926).

PORTNOY, J., *The Philosopher and Music* (New York, 1954).

PRIEBERG, F. K., *Musik im andern Deutschland* (Cologne, 1968).

—— *Musik im NS-Staat* (Frankfurt am Main, 1982).

READ, R., *The Meaning of Art* (Baltimore, 1961).

REICH, W., *Alban Berg* (Vienna, 1937).

—— *Schoenberg: A Critical Biography* (New York, 1971).

RINGER, A. L., 'Europäische Musik im Banne der Exotik', *Forum Musicologicum*, 4 (1984), 77–98.

—— 'Schoenbergiana in Jerusalem', *Musical Quarterly*, 59/1 (1973), 1–14.

—— 'Dance on a Volcano: Notes on Musical Satire and Parody in Weimar Germany', *Comparative Literature Studies*, 13/3 (1975), 248–59.

—— 'Arnold Schoenberg and the Prophetic Image in Music', *Journal of the Arnold Schoenberg Institute*, 1/1 (1976), 26–38.

—— 'Arnold Schoenberg and the Concept of Law', in R. Stephan (ed.), *Bericht über den 1. Kongress der Internationalen Schönberg-Gesellschaft* (Vienna, 1978), 165–72.

—— 'Arnold Schoenberg and the Politics of Jewish Survival', *Journal of the Arnold Schoenberg Institute*, 3/1 (1979), 11–48.

—— 'Schoenberg, Weill and Epic Theater', *Journal of the Arnold Schoenberg Institute*, 4/1 (1980), 77–98.

—— 'Faith and Symbol: On Arnold Schoenberg's Last Musical Utterance', *Journal of the Arnold Schoenberg Institute*, 6/1 (1982), 80–95.

—— 'Jewish Music: Old Problems, New Dilemmas', in J. Cohen (ed.), *Proceedings of the World Congress on Jewish Music, Jerusalem 1978* (Tel Aviv, 1982), 251–64.

—— 'Of Music, Myth and the Corporate State', *Israel Studies in Musicology*, 3 (1983), 70–95.

—— 'Joachim Stutschewsky und das Wiener Streichquartett', *OMZ*, 39/6 (June 1984), 306–11.

—— 'Die Parthey des vernünftigen Fortschritts—Max Bruch und Friedrich Gernsheim', *Die Musikforschung*, 25 (1972), 17–27.

—— 'Salomon Sulzer, Joseph Mainzer and the Romantic a cappella Movement', *Studia Musicologica*, 11 (1969), 355–70.

ROLLER, A. (ed.), *Die Bildnisse von Gustav Mahler* (Leipzig and Vienna, 1922).

ROSENBLÜTH, P. E., 'Die geistigen und religiösen Strömungen in der deutschen Judenheit', in W. E. Mosse (ed.), *Juden im Wilhelminischen Deutschland 1890–1914* (Tübingen, 1979).

ROSENSAFT, M. Z., 'Jews and Antisemites in Austria at the End of the Nineteenth century', *Leo Baeck Institute Yearbook*, 21 (1976), 57–86.

RUBSAMEN, W., 'Schoenberg in America', *Musical Quarterly*, 37/4 (1951), 469–89.

RUFER, J., *The Works of Arnold Schoenberg* (London, 1962).

SACHAR, H. M., *The Course of Modern Jewish History* (Cleveland, 1958).

SALMEN, W., 'Social Obligations of the Emancipated Musician in the Nineteenth Century' in W. Salmon (ed.), *The Social Status of the Professional Musician from the Middle Ages to the Nineteenth Century* (New York, 1983), 1–29.

SCHAYA, L., *The Universal Meaning of the Kabbalah* (Seacaucus, NJ, 1971).

SCHMIDT, C. M., 'Uber Schönbergs Geschichtsbewußtsein', in R. Stephan (ed.), *Zwischen Tradition und Fortschritt* (Mainz, 1973), 85–95.

SCHNITZLER, A., *My Youth in Vienna* (New York, Chicago, and San Francisco, 1970).

SCHOENBERG, A., *Briefe*, ed. E. Stein (Mainz, 1958).

—— *Gesammelte Schriften*, ed. I. Vojtech (Frankfurt am Main, 1976).

—— *Arnold Schoenberg Letters*, ed. E. Stein (London, 1964).

—— *Moderne Psalmen*, ed. R. Kolisch (Mainz, 1956).

—— *Schöpferische Konfessionen*, ed. W. Reich (Zurich, 1964).

—— *Style and Idea*, ed. L. Stein (New York, 1975).

—— *Texte* (Vienna, 1926).

—— *Theory of Harmony*, trans. R. E. Carter (Berkeley and Los Angeles, 1978).

SCHOENBERG, E. R., 'Arnold Schoenberg and Albert Einstein', *JASI*, 10 (1987), 134–87.

SCHOLEM, G. G., *Major Trends in Jewish Mysticism* (London, 1955).

SEIDEN, R. (ed.), *Pro Zion* (Vienna, 1924).

SHILOAH, A., 'The Symbolism of Music in the Kabbalistic Tradition', *The World of Music*, 20/3 (1978), 56–67.

SIMMS, B. R., 'The Society for Private Musical Performances', *JASI*, 3/2 (1979), 127–49.

SLONIMSKY, N., *Music Since 1900* (New York, 1949).

STEFAN, P., *Der Tod in Wien* (Vienna, 1912).

STEIN, E., 'Das gedankliche Prinzip in Beethovens Musik und seine Auswirkung bei Schönberg', *Anbruch*, 9 (1927), 117–21.

STEINER, E., 'Schoenberg on Holiday', *Musical Quarterly* 72/1 (1986), 48.

STEINER, G., 'Some "Meta-Rabbis" ', in D. Villiers (ed.), *Next Year in Jerusalem* (New York, 1976), 64–76.

STEPHAN, R., 'Der musikalische Gedanke bei Schönberg', *OMZ*, 37/10 (1982), 530–40.

STRAUSS, R., *A Confidential Matter: The Letters of Richard Strauss and Stefan Zweig 1931–1935*, trans. M. Knight (Berkeley, 1977).

STRAVINSKY, I., and CRAFT, R., *Dialogs and a Diary* (London, 1968).

STRUNK, O. (ed.), *Source Readings in Music History* (New York, 1950).

STUCKENSCHMIDT, H. H., *Schönberg* (Zurich and Freiburg im Breisgau, 1974).

—— *Schoenberg: His Life, World and Work* (London, 1977).

SULLIVAN, J. W. N., *Beethoven: His Spiritual Development* (New York, 1949).

SWEDENBORG, E., *The Heavenly Arcana* (New York, 1873).

TALDOR, M., 'A Shortened and Falsified Schoenberg, *Tatzlil*, 2 (1962), 62–3.

TRAMER, H., 'Der Beitrag der Juden zu Geist und Kultur', in W. E. Mosse (ed.), in *Deutsches Judentum in Krieg und Revolution 1916–1923* (Tübingen, 1971).

VALENTIN, V., *The German People: Their History and Civilization from the Holy Roman Empire to the Third Reich* (New York, 1949).

VALLAS, L., *Achille-Claude Debussy* (Paris, 1944).

VINAVER, C. (ed.), *Anthology of Jewish Music* (New York, 1953).

VOGEL, M., *Die Zahl Sieben in der spekulativen Musiktheorie* (Bonn, 1955).

VON RAUCHHAUPT, U. (ed.), Schoenberg, Berg, Webern: *The String Quartets, A Documentary Study* (Hamburg, 1971).

WAGNER, R., *Sämtliche Briefe*, ed. G. Strobel and W. Wolf (Leipzig, 1980).

WASSERMANN, J., *Mein Weg als Deutscher und Jude* (Berlin, 1921).

WEBER, L., 'Musik und Volksgemeinschaft', *Die Musik*, 27 (1934), 81–7.

WEILL, K. 'Bekenntnis zur Oper', in H. Heinsheimer and P. Stefan (eds.), *25 Jahre Neue Musik: Jahrbuch der Universal-Edition* (Vienna, Leipzig, and New York, 1926), 226–38.

—— 'Gestus in Music', trans. E. Albrecht, *Tulane Drama Review*, 6 (1961), 28–32.

—— 'Über den gestischen Charkter der Musik', *Die Musik*, 21 (1929), 419–23.

—— 'Korrespondenz über Dreigroschenoper', *Anbruch*, 11 (1929), 24–5.

—— 'Busonis "Faust" und die Erneuerung der Opernform', *Anbruch*, 60 (1927), 53–6.

—— 'Aktuelles Theater', reprinted from *Melos*, 8 (1924) in *Melos*, 37 (1970), 277.

—— *Ausgewählte Schriften*, ed. D. Drew (Frankfurt am Main, 1975).

WEISGAL, M., . . . *So Far* (London, 1971).

WEISSTEIN, U. (ed.), *The Essence of Opera* (New York, 1969).

WELLESZ, E., *Arnold Schönberg* (London, n.d.).

—— 'Reminiscences of Mahler', *The Score*, 28 (1961), 52–7.

—— 'Erinnerungen an Gustav Mahler und Arnold Schönberg', *Orbis Musicae*, 1 (summer 1971), 72–82.

WERTH, A., *Musical Uproar in Moscow* (London, 1948).

WHITE, P. C., *Schoenberg and the God-Idea* (Ann Arbor, 1985).

WISE, S. S., *Challenging Years: An Autobiography* (New York, 1949).

—— *Servant of the People: Selected Letters*, ed. C. H. Voss (Philadelphia, 1970).

WOLFSON, H., *Philo* (Cambridge, Mass., 1947).

WÖRNER, K., *Schoenbergs 'Moses und Aron'* (London, 1963).

WULF, J., *Musik im Dritten Reich* (Gütersloh, 1966).

ZILLIG, W., 'Notes on Arnold Schoenberg's Unfinished Oratorio "Die Jakobsleiter"', *The Score*, 25 (1959), 7–16.

ZWEIG, A., *Juden auf der deutschen Bühne* (Berlin, 1928).

ZWEIG, S., *The World of Yesterday* (New York, 1943).

—— *Zeit und Welt* (Berlin and Frankfurt am Main, 1946).

INDEX